BREAKFAST AT THE EXIT CAFE

Travels
Through America

Wayne Grady/Merilyn Simonds

BREAKFAST
AT THE
EXIT
CAFE

GREYSTONE BOOKS

D&M PUBLISHERS INC.

Vancouver/Toronto/Berkeley

Greystone Books
An imprint of D&M Publishers Inc.
2323 Quebec Street, Suite 201
Vancouver BC Canada V5T 4S7
www.greystonebooks.com

Cataloguing data available from Library and Archives Canada
ISBN 978-1-55365-522-0 (cloth)
ISBN 978-1-55365-826-9 (pbk.)
ISBN 978-155365-656-2 (ebook)

Editing by Nancy Flight
Cover and text design by Naomi MacDougall
Cover photograph by Micheal McLaughlin/Gallery Stock
Map by Eric Leinberger
Printed and bound in Canada by Friesens
Text printed on acid-free, 100% post-consumer paper
Distributed in the U.S. by Publishers Group West

We gratefully acknowledge the financial support of
the Canada Council for the Arts, the British Columbia Arts
Council, the Province of British Columbia through the
Book Publishing Tax Credit, and the Government of Canada
through the Canada Book Fund for our publishing activities.

Contents

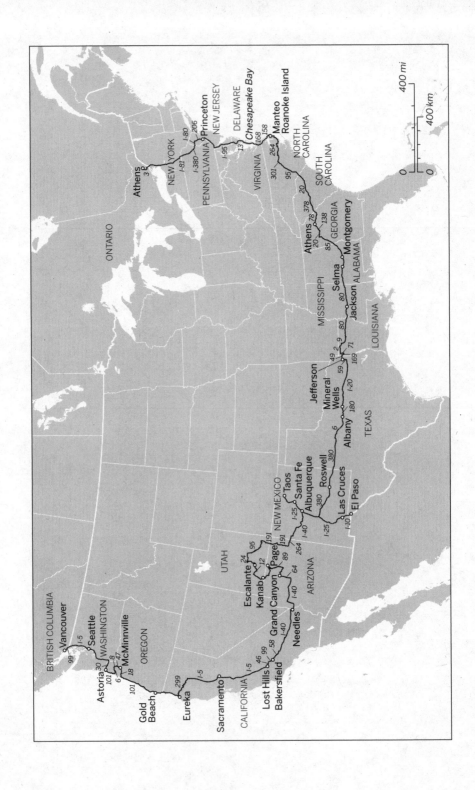

400 mi
400 km

Vancouver
BRITISH COLUMBIA
Seattle   WASHINGTON
I-5
McMinnville
Astoria   OREGON
Gold
Beach
Eureka
Sacramento
CALIFORNIA
Lost Hills
Bakersfield
I-5
299
99
46
58   Grand Canyon
Needles   I-40
I-40
64
I-40   ARIZONA
89   264
Page   191
Kanab   12
Escalante   24   191
UTAH   95
NEW MEXICO
Taos
Santa Fe
I-25
Albuquerque
I-40
Roswell   380
Las Cruces
El Paso   I-10
I-25
Albany   180   TEXAS
6
Mineral   I-20
Wells
Jefferson   59
49   9   169
2   71
80
Jackson   ALABAMA
80
Selma   LOUISIANA
Montgomery
Athens   85
20   MISSISSIPPI
138   GEORGIA
78
378
20   SOUTH
95   CAROLINA
301   NORTH
264   CAROLINA
168   Manteo
158   Roanoke Island
VIRGINIA   Chesapeake Bay
I-95   13   DELAWARE
PENNSYLVANIA   NEW JERSEY
I-380   Princeton
I-81   206
I-80
NEW YORK
Athens
3

ONTARIO

WE didn't set out to write a book. We were in Vancouver, intending to drive back to Ontario in our green Toyota Echo, and we decided to take the long way home, down along the Pacific coast, across the southern states, then up the Atlantic seaboard. It was to be a holiday, an excursion. It was just before Christmas 2006, and we were keen to avoid driving across the Prairies in winter. We were naive. We were curious. We wanted to see the mountains of Washington and the forests of Oregon, the deserts of California and Arizona and New Mexico, the canyonlands of Utah, the arid farmlands of Texas, the troubled cities of Mississippi and Alabama, the exhausted plantations of Georgia and Virginia, the great, wind-beaten banks of the Carolinas. We thought this would be relaxing, a break from our writing lives.

We should have known better. Put two writers together in a car and keep them there for a couple of months, and it's more than likely you'll get a book. But what kind of book would it be? Both of us grew up, for the most part, in southern Ontario, close to the American border, although neither of us had travelled much in the United States. What we knew of America had come *from* America, not from our own experience of that country. We knew what Americans looked like and sounded like; we knew how they acted and sang and wrote. What we didn't know was what they were like at home.

We had no itinerary, no agenda. We didn't stick to the interstates, as Larry McMurtry did when he wrote *Roads;* we didn't drive only on smaller highways, as William Least Heat-Moon did in *Blue Highways*. The routes we travelled were blue and red and white and yellow on the maps, solid lines and dotted lines and sometimes no lines at all. We didn't tell anyone we were coming: we were neighbours who were dropping in unexpectedly, wanting only a cup of coffee and some conversation.

By the time we got home, we had driven more than fifteen thousand kilometres; travelled through twenty-two states; put on twenty pounds each; replaced half the car; slept in mom-and-pop motels, boutique hotels, dreary motor inns, the car; eaten in diners, cafes, bistros, five-star restaurants, chain eateries, food courts, the car. Our favourite meal of the day was breakfast, because eating breakfast every day in a restaurant is one kind of proof that you're on the road. And everyone else in there is travelling, too. Part of the reason we chose the title of our book is that the places we had breakfast took on for us a kind of iconic status. Like America itself, they became, for a time, our home.

John Steinbeck, in *Travels with Charley,* his book about driving the rim of America, wrote that "people don't take trips, trips take people." He was right. This trip not only took us into America, into the heart of the neighbour we thought we knew, but also took us into ourselves. Throughout the book, Wayne speaks in his voice—his sections begin with *W*—and Merilyn speaks in hers—*M*. The result is a conversation and a twinned meditation, too, as we each engage with the landscape we're travelling through as well as our own interior geography.

We discovered that a marriage between two people is not unlike the sometimes uneasy truce that exists between two countries that have lain beside each other for a long time. We each came to that in our own way, and that, too, was part of the journey.

1 / **MEGALOPOLIS, USA**

*W*ASHINGTON looms across the border from British Columbia at the end of a long line of cars and buses. As we await our turn at customs, we watch a man playing with his young son on the wide stretch of grass between two parallel roads, the one we are on leading into the United States and the other disappearing behind us into Canada. The man is tossing his son into the air and catching him on the way down, and the child is laughing hysterically, obviously frightened out of his wits. The man keeps throwing him higher into the air and catching him at the last minute, the boy's head swinging closer and closer to the ground each time. We watch with resigned fascination until we arrive at a stop sign a few metres from the border, beside a placard that reads *Canada This Way*, with an arrow pointing behind us.

We are driving into America.

Border crossings always unnerve me, which, as Merilyn says, is an odd and tiresome thing, because I have crossed this and many other borders in my life and ought to know what to expect. I have no particular reason to expect to be unnerved. But to me, crossing a border is a harrowing experience, perhaps because I grew up in a border city—Windsor, Ontario, just across the river from Detroit, Michigan.

The saying in Windsor was that the light at the end of the tunnel was downtown Detroit, and it was meant as a positive thing.

Every year before school started, my parents would whisk my younger brother and me through the tunnel to the United States because everything was so much cheaper on the other side. They'd drag us up and down Woodward Avenue, into all the really cheap department stores, with their dark, uneven hardwood floors and sticky, glass-fronted cases, buying us cheap shirts and sweaters and pants and socks and windbreakers. At a designated spot between Woodward Avenue and the Detroit Tunnel, my father would pull the car over and my mother would frantically cut the price tags off all the pants with a pair of nail scissors, pull all the cardboard stiffeners out of the shirts, stuff all the bags and tags and cardboard and tissue paper and shoeboxes into one of the shopping bags, and toss the whole thing into a garbage pail practically within hearing distance of the customs shed. Then she would make us put on all the clothes we'd just bought, to hide them from the customs official, who, if he spied an overlooked price tag or caught the whiff of new denim, would yank us from the car and make us take off all our clothes and then arrest my parents. In my family, "duty" was something one paid if one were caught wearing two pairs of pants.

Now I watch nervously as the guard comes out of his tiny kiosk, pistol jutting from a little holster that looks like a miniature leather jockstrap, and leans over to ask what the hell I think I'm doing, trying to get into the United States. What business do I have going into his country? Because things are cheaper there, is that it? Well, buddy, things aren't cheap in America so that foreigners like me can come in and buy everything up. Do I imagine that Americans work as hard as they do at keeping prices down for the benefit of non-Americans? I can think of no answer to such a question. In fact, it seems like sound economic theory to me. All of us in this line—they should turn us back, close the border. We'll ruin America. Besides, the mouthy literalist in me wants to add, I don't like your country. I think your country is too big and plays too rough, like a sulking adolescent with divorcing parents, and I am certain my thoughts are written all over my face, like price tags sticking out from the collar of a brand-new flannelette shirt.

"Where are you coming from?" the guard asks politely, taking our passports.

"Ontario," I say.

"Vancouver," Merilyn says, simultaneously.

"Oh," I say, "you mean today? Yes, Vancouver."

"And where are you going?"

"Ontario," I say, stupidly.

"Seattle," says Merilyn.

The guard looks at me. "I mean we're taking the long way home. Down the coast, and"—I feel Merilyn's elbow jabbing me in the ribs; she has warned me about saying too much at borders, it's the first thing they look for—"through Seattle," I add lamely.

The guard smiles and hands me our passports. "Welcome to America," he says.

IT'S THE twentieth of December. Merilyn has spent the past three months as writer-in-residence at the University of British Columbia while I stayed home in Ontario looking after, in reverse order, the gardens, the house, the cat, and myself. We've both had time to get used to being alone, a rarity for a couple who usually eat, sleep, and write in the same house. We've probably become rugged individualists, more American than Canadian. I flew to British Columbia so that we could drive home together, thinking the trip home would give us time to rediscover our communal selves before settling in for the winter.

We could head back straight across Canada, but the weather is making us cautious. High winds have been buffeting Vancouver, with heavy snow causing power outages and trees falling like drunks in Stanley Park and across the city's streets. Climate change is making

Vancouverites freeze in the dark. No snow on the Prairies yet, but Saskatchewan and Alberta are known for sudden changes in weather. And everyone expects a white Christmas in Ontario. Even if it doesn't snow, the Trans-Canada will be cold, icy, and treacherous. Driving home through the southern reaches of America seems to us a better bet.

The terrors of the border are balanced, too, by the appealing thought that we'll be able to just get lost for a few weeks. Not lost in the literal sense of not knowing where we are, for we are travellers in an age of cellular phones and wireless Internet access. No, I mean lost in a more ancient sense, the way Thoreau meant lost when he advised packing a few vittles in a sack and disappearing into the woods for a few weeks, "absolutely free from all worldly engagements." Or in Paul Theroux's sense: after a trip to Africa, he wrote, "The word 'safari' in Swahili means journey—it has nothing to do with animals. Someone 'on safari' is just away and unobtainable and out of touch." For the next month or two, we would be on safari.

In *A Field Guide to Getting Lost,* Rebecca Solnit asks an important question: "Love, wisdom, grace, inspiration—how do you go about finding these things that are in some ways about extending the boundaries of the self into unknown territory, about becoming someone else?"

Well, one way is to take the old self into unknown territory and see what happens. To lose ourselves in America.

★　★　★

*M*ADLY, without forethought or direction, we are speeding into America. It's the week before Christmas, the day before the winter solstice. Any other year, the children, and their children, would be getting ready to come home. I would be baking shortbread and unpacking ornaments. Instead, I'm sitting in this little green Toyota, feeling restless. Restless for stasis.

We left Vancouver in a rush, anxious to be on the road, deciding at the last minute to head south, away from the snow, instead of east.

The back seat is piled with coats and bags of shoes and what I could salvage of my office. "How will we convince customs that we didn't buy all that stuff in the States?" Wayne moaned, already anticipating crossing back into Canada. So I packed up most of my things and shipped them home, but I refused to be parted with the manuscript I've been working on for months. "Come on, who's going to think I bought that?"

I reach back and jostle the bags and the box that holds the novel. Establishing a little order, is what I tell Wayne, but really, I just want to touch my things. I set a small jar of hand cream, a handkerchief, and my asthma puffer in the handhold of the passenger door. I open the glove compartment, which Wayne oddly insists on calling a glove box, and straighten the emergency manual, the car registration, our passports. I add the mileage book, the small pad I bought to keep track of our expenses, a new Sudoku, my Palm. The novel I'm reading and my notebook go into the door pocket.

I gather the various state maps and brochures that arrived just as we were leaving, and arrange them under my seat. I dig a highlighter and a Sharpie out of my purse and clip them to the MapArt book that condenses the continent of North America to a series of neat, brightly coloured squares. Across the first few pages, a yellow line rises up out of Ontario to flatten across the Prairies, the Rockies, and British Columbia, coming to a stop at Vancouver—a record of our drive west in September, 5,001 kilometres, door to door.

I rest my hand flat on the open map and look out the window, suffering a moment of horizontal vertigo, the kind of dislocation that comes in a moving vehicle when you take your eyes from the landscape, then look up, miles later, uncertain where you are. The last thing I saw was the low grey obelisk jutting out of the grass beside the car as we inched toward customs. It looked like one of the posts that surround the old prison quarry back home where convicts once did hard time. In the grassy stretch between the twin roads moving into and out of the two countries stood an oddly Grecian monument, *Brethren Dwelling Together in Unity* carved on the side facing us as we headed to the United States. I turned and craned my neck to see what drivers heading into Canada would see: *Children of a Common Mother*. How strange, I thought. Canadians were brethren as they entered the United States, kids when they returned. What kind of Faustian bargain were we making, crossing this border?

"There's a plaque, too. I'm going to go read it," I said, jumping out of the car as Wayne looked on, aghast. "Don't worry, I'll be back before we move another inch."

The brass plate was framed by two women, each extending her country's coat of arms to meet in the middle. An eagle and a rampant lion: a scavenger and a predator. The scavenger I understood, but Canada, predatory? Not exactly how I think of my country. Where was the beaver, that amiable, trepidatious rodent that warns his fellows, then dives for cover at the faintest threat?

The words flanked by the women were optimistic: *More than a century old friendship between these countries, a lesson of peace to all nations.*

I peered at the two women. They were hardly more than girls. The American was fine-boned and pretty. In one hand, she cradled a cornucopia overflowing with vegetables and fruit. The Canadian girl was muscled, as if the sculptor intended to carve a man, then thought better of it and added breasts. She was lugging a huge sheaf of wheat, her arm clearly broken in some agricultural mishap and poorly set.

None of it fit. Our two countries were brethren, or children, or women: which was it? And what kind of friends are we? Squabbling kids who trade loyalties like baseball cards? Men who, like Wayne, play hockey together for years without ever knowing the names of each other's wives?

No, I thought, as I headed back to the car. The plaque had it right. It's a women's friendship. Never an easy thing, especially if one of them is outgoing and pretty.

We've left the monuments behind and are zipping over the tidal flats where the United States and Britain drew their final line in the sand. Here, the distinction between one country and another seems arbitrary, inconsequential. The landscape refuses nationality. The same sandy loam sifts on either side of the border; the same clouds scuttle overhead. The birds, looking down, recognize no boundaries. Even I, staring out at the low bungalows along the roadside, at the cars that pass by—the usual mix of American cars and imports, as many BC plates as Washington State—have trouble discerning any difference.

Yet there *is* a difference. Not out there, beyond the windshield, where a steady drizzle is fingering horizontal lines across the glass, but in here, inside me.

"What do you love about the States?" I ask Wayne.

"The *New Yorker,* baseball, *Star Trek,* bourbon, L.L. Bean, John McPhee, Amazon."

I rhyme off my list: The *New Yorker. Sex and the City.* The Coen brothers. Richard Ford. Martin Luther King, Jr. Sweet potato pie. *Oprah.* "And what do you hate?"

"Reality TV, Coca-Cola, Homeland Security, the Ku Klux Klan, the National Rifle Association. And you?"

"The CIA, the bomb, aerial spraying, Tommy Hilfiger, Ugly Americans, the fact that they think they own the world. Oh, and *Oprah.*"

How on earth will we ever see past all that?

"Good travel is like good reading," Wayne says. "It sucks you into a world and holds you there."

"Long enough for us to really see?"

He shrugs. "That's the idea."

I uncap the highlighter and set the point on the map, on the city of Vancouver, then drag it half an inch south, past the border, the first indication that this line might, at some point, become a unifying circle.

* * *

*W*E stop for a late breakfast in Fairhaven, a settlement on the shore of Bellingham Bay that was once a village in its own right but has been swept into the greater urban embrace of the city of Bellingham. It is a quaint little place, its brick buildings recently sandblasted, its pitted woodwork filled and repainted. It has a persistent, nineteenth-century look about it. Rather than allow box-store malls to suck the life out of its core, Bellingham passed a municipal design bylaw requiring new buildings to be constructed to look old. The instant nostalgia seems to be working; even in late December, in the rain, Fairhaven's quaint streets are swarming with shoppers. The storefronts along the main street are filled with Christmas goodies: gingerbread men, old-fashioned sleds tied in red ribbon. A recipe for mulled wine is posted on the window of the wine shop in front of which we park the car.

We ignore the seasonal frippery and head for Village Books. We've been here before: it's an establishment worth whipping down from Vancouver for, its shelves burdened with books, both new and used. On either side of the door, plaques embedded in the red brick advise: *A Room Without Books is Like a Body Without a Soul* (Cicero) and *Some Books Leave us Free and Some Books Make us Free* (Ralph Waldo Emerson).

"What does that mean?" Merilyn says, puzzled before the Emerson quote.

"Damned if I know."

Heading for the nature section, I buy Ellen Meloy's *Eating Stone* and Ann Zwinger's *Wind in the Rock,* both about the American desert, which I am looking forward to seeing. In the mystery corner, I pick out Michael Collins's *Death of a Writer.*

"Do you carry Canadian books?" I ask the man behind the order desk on the second floor, a pleasant-looking bookman with short, greying hair and studious glasses. His card says he is the Consignment Coordinator.

"A few," he says. "Lots of Canadians come through here, and we go up there, too, of course. But fiction, nature, books about Canada—there's not much interest. Not really. A few break though the barrier, the Margaret Atwoods, the Alice Munros, but not many. I don't think Americans are very interested in other countries."

Looking through the shelves, though, I notice several books by Canadian writers: Ron Wright's *A Short History of Progress,* Bill Deverell's *April Fool,* Karen Connelly's *The Lizard Cage,* and *Tree,* the book I co-wrote with David Suzuki. We are not identified as Canadians; it seems Americans are consuming foreign culture without knowing it. As they say in the ads, Don't tell them it's good for them.

Merilyn and I take our loot next door to the Colophon Cafe, which looks like a 1950s diner. There is a framed citation on the wall above our heads: *Best Use of Poultry, 1998.*

"I think I'll have the chicken," I say.

"Nineteen ninety-eight was a long time ago," Merilyn warns. "Besides, this is breakfast, remember?"

She's right. And I love diner breakfasts. Merilyn orders the quiche "made nightly by our own bakers." I scan the menu for bacon and eggs and order the closest thing to it: the Truly Decadent California Croissant, which consists of scrambled eggs, Swiss cheese, avocado, and tomato on a flaky French pastry. Merilyn looks at me askance.

"Why not?" I say defensively. "We're headed for California."

At the table across the aisle, a woman and a much younger man are sharing a bottle of wine. Suddenly, I'm a censorious moralist. What's an older woman doing having a bottle of wine with a young man at twelve-thirty in the afternoon? A Wednesday afternoon? Maybe it's her son; the boy has that surly, I-wish-I-were-anywhere-else-on-the-planet look about him, and he clearly isn't used to drinking wine. He holds his glass with his long fingers curled around the bulb and his thumb hooked over the rim.

"No, no, I don't think that's why she did it," the woman is saying animatedly. "I can't see her thinking that."

For a moment I think she must be his literature tutor; they are discussing motivation in *Madame Bovary* or *Anna Karenina.* Then the boy says, "I need to walk around a bit, stretch my legs," and he gets up and goes into the bookstore, where I can see him pacing back and forth with his hands thrust in his pockets. As soon as he leaves, the woman's jaw sags, her eyes look nervously about her, and she sets down her wine. She seems to have aged in an instant. When the waitress passes her table, the woman plucks at her, like a troll from under a bridge, and asks for the check.

By the time our own check comes, I have constructed an entire story around the couple. Several stories, actually. She's his mother and he's depressed, which I call the Canadian version. She's his high school English teacher, trying to seduce him or, having already seduced him, trying to hang on to him (the British version). Or she's his father's new wife, wanting to win him over (the wine) and yet smart enough to know not to say anything against his mother ("She'd never do anything to hurt you"). This sparse scenario seems quintessentially American to me, a little mini-drama about the breakdown of the nuclear family. It reminds me of Gary Snyder's remark, in his essay "White Indians," that "the modern American family is the smallest and most barren family that has ever existed." I'd like to see how it turns out, but as with the tossing of the child into the air at the border, the finale remains a mystery as we climb the stairs from the cafe and make our way back to the street.

★ ★ ★

*M*EGALOPOLIS. That's what demographers call this part of the Pacific Northwest. After we leave Fairhaven, signs along the I-5 point to a succession of towns—Mt. Vernon, Arlington, Marysville—but the urban sprawl is more or less continuous. A conurbation. A megacity.

Most of the population of the Pacific Northwest is concentrated here, clustered like crystals in a supersaturated solution on this thread of an interstate that dangles south from Vancouver through

Seattle to Portland. Nine million Americans, almost a third as many people as live in the entire country of Canada, occupy the thin strip of land between the coastal mountains and the sea, as if those who surged west across the United States during the last century were suddenly stopped in their tracks by the ocean, piling up on one another, nowhere else to go.

A trip never really begins until you put some distance between yourself and home, so we are speeding through the landscape at sixty miles an hour, which is the speed we usually drive at home, though it's legal here. I take note of these subtle differences, trying to feel like an explorer in a strange land.

"Do you suppose there is some international agreement that regulates the colour of highway signs?" I muse, as we whip past blue Adopt-a-Highway signs, green exit signs, exactly what we would see at home.

"Canadians probably order their signs from American companies," Wayne says. "Just like our computers, which keep telling us we're spelling 'colour' wrong." He's still tense from the border crossing, though it was the driver ahead of us who was handed the orange card and directed to the covered bays, where cars and trucks and RVs had their doors flung wide, like prisoners being strip-searched, and men with knee pads crouched, strafing the undercarriages with beams of light.

"Adrenalin can take up to seventy-two hours to dissipate," I say, patting his knee.

We're crossing a long bridge over yet another river. The body of a dead deer is slung over the railing. Wayne looks at it bleakly and mutters, "Compared to him, I'm fine."

On the political map of the United States, this part of the country is painted Democrat blue, which I always find confusing, since we Canadians paint our Liberal ridings red. Abortion, gay marriage, women's rights: all the items on the left-wing agenda have been taken up with enthusiasm here in the Pacific Northwest, even the right to die by your own hand. It's always had a reputation as the home of radicals. At the turn of the last century, this part of the world was a stronghold of the Wobblies, the International Workers of the World. Anarchists set up communes all along this coast. One of the longest-lasting was Home, started by three men who, in the summer of 1895, rowed into Puget Sound in a boat they'd built themselves and bought some land around an isolated bay, and within a few years dozens of anarchists, communists, food faddists, and freethinkers were living there.

These humid, forested slopes tucked up into the far corner of the country seem to attract people of an independent mind, or maybe people are transformed once they get here. It's true that humans have an impact on a landscape, but it works the other way, too. We are like Darwin's finches, whose beaks change shape almost annually depending on the food supply: there's no reason to expect humans to be any less susceptible to the place in which they find themselves.

I think of something Byron wrote in *Don Juan:* "As the soil is, so the heart of man." It's a Romantic notion, I suppose, that landscape can influence character, but observation makes me think it's true. When driving through Europe one autumn, I noticed how differently farmers in each country cured their hay: in bales, in stooks or stacks like enormous hives, layered on wooden ricks. John Ruskin tried to prove the principle in *The Poetry of Architecture,* using variations in cottage design to illustrate the effect of landscape, which he called a "gigantic instrument of soul culture."

The people who settled this landscape sit between a metaphorical rock and a hard place—between the turbulent ocean and the Cascades, which are part of the volcanic Pacific Rim of Fire. Easterners who ended up here from their cozy New England villages and sprawling Great Plains farms had a choice: tough it out, or leave. It's a form of natural selection. The stubborn and the single-minded stayed, reproduced, and proliferated.

Wayne and I are birdwatchers, observers of nature. We're inclined to think of humans not as civilized beings but as just another species.

When we travel, we look at all the populations—feathered, furred, clothed—with a curious eye.

So, thinking about the kind of people who ended up here, I expect them to be self-reliant and freethinking, something Americans claim as a national birthright. Historically, Americans seem always to be running from home, whether from England or New England, resolutely heading into the setting sun, away from family and tradition, looking for places to survive on their own. But once they arrived here in the Northwest, they became social-minded. Not only did they elect the first woman mayor and erect the first Hispanic college, but this is the home of consumers' co-ops, mutual aid societies, and publicly owned utilities. Internet cafes, emblems of both real and virtual connectivity, were spawned here. They may have the lowest rate of church attendance and the highest percentage of atheism in the country, but social conscience runs high: three of the ten greenest communities in the United States are part of this I-5 megacity. And the two biggest online magazines devoted to environmental sustainability are produced out of Seattle. Maybe that's because they still have an environment to save—over half of the land mass of Washington, the Evergreen State, is still covered with forest.

At least, that's the way it looks on the map. From where I sit, though, gridlocked in traffic in the endless urban sprawl that is Seattle, this could just as easily be Mississauga or Washington, D.C. Fifty years ago, when John Steinbeck approached Seattle after decades living away from the Pacific, which he called his home ocean, he wrote that he "remembered Seattle as a town sitting on hills beside a matchless harborage—a little city of space and trees and gardens, its houses matched to such a background. It is no longer so. The tops of hills are shaved off to make level warrens for the rabbits of the present. The highways eight lanes wide cut like glaciers through the uneasy land."

The highway is twelve lanes wide now, and we can hardly see the earth for houses. We certainly can't see the matchless harborage: skyscrapers block the view. Wayne counts twelve building cranes rising above the downtown high-rises. The rain pours down. The traffic is going nowhere. Clouds settle like tired Sasquatches onto office tower roofs.

"Let's just drive on," Wayne says. He would rather be moving. Something about sitting behind the wheel of a car sucks the curiosity out of him. He's not venturing through new territory, he's locked in a video game, earning points for every car he passes. Sitting still is not sitting well with him.

"How about going into Fremont?"

"What's that?"

"The Artists' Republic of Fremont. It's the old hippie part of Seattle."

"An artists' republic?" he says, lighting up. "I thought Plato kicked artists *out* of the republic."

We ease off the interstate and down past small, cottage-like houses pressed into the hillsides. I watch for the sign that says *Entering the Republic of Fremont, the Center of the Universe, Set Your Watch Back Five Minutes.* Or the one that advises *Entering the Republic of Fremont, the Center of the Universe, Set Your Watch Forward Five Minutes.*

"Maybe somebody stole them," Wayne suggests. He seems to like the idea. "Or maybe they disappeared into the temporal shift when everyone changed their watches." He likes that idea even better.

We do find a pole stuck with arrows painted in Neapolitan-ice-cream shades. They point every which way: *Timbuktu 10,029 mi. Bermuda Triangle 3.75. Xanadu, East of the Sun. Dinosaurs 3 Blocks. Troll 2 Blocks.* The pole itself is striped with an arrow that points straight down: *Center of the Universe.*

We get out to stretch our legs and stroll past a sixteen-foot bronze statue of Lenin; a rocket mounted on the side of a building, blowing smoke as if trying to blast off; a corral of life-size dinosaurs shaped from living hedges. Tucked under the highway overpass, someone has shaped a giant troll in ferro-cement, a real v w Beetle crushed under the weight of its left hand. A block away, three billy goats gambol across a yard, cut-outs in rusting steel. But these are relics of a quirky past. The stores that line the short main street sell souvenirs made in China, bins of organic vegetables, and vintage clothing arranged by colour on chrome racks.

."Do artists still live here?" I ask a young woman wearing a heavy brown khaki jacket and pants and a Peruvian woollen cap. In one hand she holds a bouquet of brushes and balances a palette; with the other, she dabs at the painting on her easel. It's a reasonable likeness of the troll.

"No way, it's too expensive. There's lofts in old warehouses south of the piers," she adds after some thought. "Some artists live there."

"Is that where you live?"

She hesitates. If I'd brought a pair of gloves, I'd give them to her; her fingers are blanched from the cold.

"No," she says. "I live with my parents."

Fremont's motto may still be "De Libertas Quirkas," but clearly, the freedom to be peculiar is not what it once was. The artists have crept back into Seattle, leaving painters to paint each other's art. And the hippies are history, just another part of the Fremont brand.

History, it seems, is malleable. Fremont, indeed all of Seattle, is in King County, which was named in 1852 in honour of a plantation owner from Selma, Alabama, a certain William Rufus DeVane King, who was a United States senator, a supporter of the Fugitive Slave Act and the Compromise of 1850, which extended slavery into new states and territories. At the time, William Rufus King was vice-president-elect of the United States. A hundred and thirty-four years later, in 1986, the county councillors decided they were no longer comfortable living in a place named for a slave owner, so they passed a resolution denouncing Rufus King and replacing him with Martin Luther King, Jr., "renaming" the county for this other King, who embodied "the attributes for which the citizens of King County can be proud, and claim as their own."

"The King is dead," Wayne says, as he manoeuvres out of the parking space. "Long live the King."

I read the story of the Kings in a brochure I picked up in a coffee shop, where Wayne bought a T-shirt: *Entering the Republic of Fremont, the Center of the Universe: throw away your watch.* We ask store clerks and waiters and the concierge of the downtown hotel where we take a room for the night; they've all heard of the Fremont signs, but no one has ever seen one, which strikes me, in an odd way, as perfect.

Chatting with the concierge, I have a hard time remembering we're in a foreign country. The hotel is a chain: we've stayed in dozens exactly like it back home. The Stars and Stripes is nowhere in evidence. The people we meet speak in the same flat tones as we do, they dress like us, drive the same cars, buy the same snacks in convenience stores, drink our favourite coffee. It may be that we all watch the same TV shows and buy goods from the same manufacturers, or maybe it's because for seventy years after the American War of Independence, Washington, like Canada, was still part of British North America.

And then we see the sign on a post going into the hotel bar: *No knives. No guns.*

We *have* entered a different country, after all.

* * *

"*W*HAT's that yummy smell?"

After checking into our hotel, Merilyn and I have gone for a walk—our favourite urban pastime—and now find ourselves outside the Pike Place Fish Market, on the corner of Pike and Post Alley, in downtown Seattle. The marketplace is crowded, people milling about, bent over tables of produce, pinching lettuce leaves, peering into the eyes of fish. Fresh Pacific salmon bask on crushed ice, hosed-down organic greenery drips from every stall. An Asian woman smiles at us from behind a counter covered with wooden dinosaurs; another sells woollen baby bonnets knitted to look like strawberries. I inhale.

"Caramel," I say.

"Caramel popcorn," corrects Merilyn, sniffing suspiciously as we carry on past the meats and cheeses, the chili peppers, and the apples. "It's everywhere. They must pipe it in."

Merilyn and I are a lot less naive than Orhan Pamuk, the Turkish novelist who visited New York in 1986. Like most outsiders, he wandered among the towers of Manhattan expecting to be overwhelmed by meaning and significance. Instead, he was overwhelmed by absurdity and fakery. His disillusionment reached its peak when he complained to the workers in a bakery that the cinnamon rolls he'd bought there the day before had lost their flavour by the time he got them home. The bakery workers laughed at him. "They explained that the heavenly cinnamon smell that made you long for the sweet rolls the moment you walked into the bakery was actually an artificial fragrance they pumped into the store."

The "bakery," it turned out, did not even have an oven on the premises. The rolls hadn't lost their flavour; they hadn't had any flavour to begin with. It was fake-'n'-bake. Like this aroma of caramel popcorn, although here there is not a kernel of popcorn to be seen. At least the bakery sold cinnamon rolls.

What astounded Pamuk was not that so much of America was fake but that everyone knew that everything was fake and they loved it anyway. It was like Dorothy finding out at the *beginning* of the movie that the Wizard of Oz was a little old man behind a screen and going along with the gag for the fun of it. Americans, Pamuk suspected, may even love things *because* they are fake. The fake Gothicism in New York's architecture, the fake ice cream in the ads, the fake smiles on the faces of the people in the elevators and on the streets—nobody believed in any of it, but they still wanted it. Why? "Why do they keep smiling at me, why are they always apologizing, why are they so solicitous?"

Pamuk found the whole experience Orwellian. Americans behaved the way they did not because they were happy or sorry or cared about

Turkish politics and customs, he said, but because they had collectively agreed to forget "the old philosophical distinction between appearance and reality." They didn't want buildings that were featureless and functional—the Soviets had those—or bakeries that smelled of diazinon and blocked drains. Or, apparently, vegetable stalls that smelled like vegetables and fish markets that reeked of fish. They wanted the appearance of civility, of artistry, of benevolence, solicitude, whimsy. For if they had the appearance of them, and if they didn't make fine distinctions between appearance and reality, then they would have the reality of them, too.

Jonathan Raban found the same thing when he visited New York a year later. In the first part of his book about America, *Hunting Mister Heartbreak,* he spends considerable time trying to deconstruct Macy's department store. When it was just a department store, it was going broke, like Gimbels, which finally crumbled during the Reagan years. But when Ed Finkelstein took over its management in 1974 and turned it into a glittering showcase of designer clothing and high-end consumer goods, when Macy's started marketing fashion and home furnishings instead of clothing and pots and pans, people flocked to see its "emptily fantastic" displays, to marvel at its "elaborate cunning." Finkelstein, Raban writes, turned Macy's into a place where "customers were now spectators of an unrolling fantasy about the goings-on of an imaginary *haute bourgeoisie.*" And they believed in the fantasy. Watching Macy's Thanksgiving Day Parade, with its giant Snoopy and Garfield balloons, Raban comments drily: "Here was America going by."

Not that Canada is unaffected by the hype. There's a Macy's in downtown Seattle, and when Merilyn and I walked through it, expecting to be dazzled by the Christmas displays, what struck us most was that it was exactly like any big department store in Toronto or Vancouver. Ralph Lauren perfume and polo shirts, Jones New York dresses and suitcases, Louis Vuitton, Calvin Klein, saleswomen made up like supermodels, looking less alive than the mannequins. Raban could have gone into any outlet of the Bay or Holt Renfrew in Canada and said with equal accuracy: "Here was America going by." We have a prime minister, after all, who does not believe there is any such thing as Canadian culture, that there is only some amorphous, conglomerate thing he calls "North American culture."

But Canada doesn't seem to have embraced the fakery as thoroughly, as desperately, as the United States. We have retained an attitude of bemusement toward it. If appearance and reality are two sides of the same flipped coin, in Canada we most often call reality. I see this in our respective film industries. Canada makes documentaries—in fact, the word "documentary" was coined by a Canadian filmmaker, John Grierson, ten years before he was hired to start up the National Film Board in 1939. He was writing in the *New York Sun,* praising the "documentary value" of Robert Flaherty's 1926 film *Moana.* Documentary, as he defined it, was the creative interpretation of reality. America had already opted for Hollywood, the Disneyland of the film world. I think the difference between documentaries and feature films goes a long way toward defining the difference between the two cultures. Recently, America has become infatuated with what it calls "reality TV," but of course there's nothing real about reality TV: it offers only the appearance of reality. Coke may be the Real Thing, but nobody ever asks what, exactly, is "real" about it.

America's is essentially an entrepreneurial culture: the sizzle *is* the steak, because, after all, if you buy the sizzle, the steak comes with it. Canada's, in contrast, is a primary-producing culture: we'll buy the steak and hope to get a little sizzle with it. But we know we can't eat sizzle.

AS MERILYN and I leave the market and walk along 1st Avenue toward our hotel, we pass six Starbucks locations, including the first one, opened thirty years ago—Ground Zero of the North American coffee explosion. I don't think there is a spot in Seattle where you can't see at least one Starbucks, often two or three. Even the coffee packets in our hotel room are from Starbucks. Eventually, we come to an interesting-looking restaurant; through the mullioned windows we can see dark wooden booths and mirrors and small rooms with white tablecloths, heavy silver, and art deco lamps. The kind of place that looks like an old Seattle landmark. At last, I think. The real thing.

"Let's stop for dinner," Merilyn says, and in we go.

When Merilyn enters a restaurant, it is never a simple matter of being shown to a table. First she asks to see the menu, which she reads with the concentration of a medieval prioress checking a hand-copied manuscript for signs of satanic influences. Then she goes on an exhaustive tour of the establishment; she wants to see all the rooms, scrutinize the staff, possibly look into the kitchen, inquire about the ingredients in the sauces. Finally, she selects a table. I follow her around, and the little maître d' trundles behind, holding the menus against her chest defensively. When we're seated, Merilyn asks her about the specials of the day.

"Your server will be with you shortly," the maître d' says, smiling, and then vanishes.

"This is a great place," I say, looking around. A long mahogany bar runs down one side of the room, with stools and place settings. Behind it scurry waiters in white shirts and ankle-length aprons tied at the waist, very Cafe-du-Nouveau-Monde. "I'll bet it's been here for years." I can already imagine myself telling friends back home and hearing them say, Oh, you went *there!*

Meanwhile, Merilyn has found the brochure propped between the salt and pepper shakers. "It's a chain," she says despondently. "There are eighty of them, all across the States."

"No."

"Yup. Started in Portland in 1977."

"Eighty? But it looks so authentic!"

"It isn't," Merilyn says. "It's all fake."

But it's not like Orhan Pamuk's fake bakery, I tell myself, wanting to believe. Look at the wait staff: they're really bustling, they care. Our waitress is very pleasant. The food isn't bad. And, I remind myself, I've never minded eating in a British pub back home in Ontario.

It's no use. The lustre is gone. The portions are too large, the sauces thickened with cornstarch, the waitress too pointedly chipper as she asks, "And how are your first bites?" then scurries off before we have time to answer. Now I hear our friends when we get home saying: Oh, you went *there?*

* * *

MORE than anything, almost, Wayne and I like books, so it's no surprise that we end our first day on the road in another bookstore. Elliott Bay Book Company anchors a corner of Seattle's Pioneer Square, down by the water. It is a sprawl of wooden shelves, bins, and passageways lined floor to ceiling with enough books to last a lifetime.

Wayne heads for the travel section. I look around at the other book lovers. Bespectacled, lean for the most part, mostly female, but not all middle-aged, people with backpacks and cloth shopping bags, sensible lace-up shoes, most of them quietly peering at titles, a few of them chatting, some exclaiming, but no one is pushy, no one is what my mother would have called "loud," which implied much more than the volume of their voice. If I were teleported into this room, would I know I was in the United States? I don't think so. I used to say to Wayne that I could tell a Frenchman or a German before they spoke by the shape of their mouths, but these people speak English, with pretty much the same accent as me.

I try to remember my first American. I was born in Winnipeg, just across the border from North Dakota. I grew up in southwestern Ontario, scarcely an hour's drive from Buffalo. My mind reels back, before school bus trips to Niagara Falls, back before *Seventeen* magazine and *Father Knows Best*, before television came to our house, back to when there was only radio and Canada's Happy Gang, and I realize with a start: until the age of five, I had not seen a single American, not heard an American voice.

The fall I turned five, my father took me by train to Detroit. I don't remember much about the trip except the train's diesel snout pointing west, snorting like a beast with a scent. Then me smiling on the steps of my Aunt Mabel's house. There is a photograph of the two of us standing there, in some Detroit suburb, so maybe it's not a memory at all, though I do remember her kitchen, the white oak cupboard she called a Hoosier.

"What's a Hoosier?" I asked.

"A cupboard," she laughed.

"Why don't you call it a cupboard?"

"Because here it's a Hoosier."

This was my introduction to the foreign language of America and that American specialty, branding. Aunt Mabel's pantry cupboard— described as "the woman's workbench" in the Eaton's catalogue—was about four feet wide and six feet tall, with cupboards above and below an enamelled counter. The largest manufacturer of these efficient baking stations was the Hoosier Manufacturing Company of New Castle, Indiana, which is why such cupboards are Hoosiers to Americans (Indiana being the Hoosier State), just as tissues are Kleenex and all colas, Coke. This is the reward the United States offers for entrepreneurial success: linguistic immortality.

But still no bona fide Americans. My aunt was Canadian. She moved to Detroit to marry her cousin Wheeler, who was dead by the time I went to visit her. Her story strikes an iconic note for Canadians, one that the director Sandy Wilson explores in her poignant coming-of-age film, *My American Cousin*. There is something seductive and faintly sinful about those people to the south who look like us, talk almost like us, seem to come from the same places, from common mother countries, and yet we desire them, and despise them, too,

because after all, they're family and that's what we do in families, love
and hate in extreme.

Then suddenly I was seven, and Americans were everywhere. I
was in New York City, at Radio City Music Hall, in the front row of a
balcony overlooking the stage of *The Garry Moore Show,* where commercials for soap flakes and vacuum cleaners were acted out live on
either side of the main action at middle stage so you could see all
the parts of the show at once, something that ruined me forever for
television.

"The little girl in the green dress in the balcony." Garry Moore was
pointing up at me, at the hand I'd thrust in the air. "What's the matter,
cat got your tongue?"

I said something in the end, I have no idea what, and sat down
amid a hot rush of laughter. I was alone at the edge of the balcony: my
family was leaning back and away, as if I'd brought them shame by
pushing myself forward. Just like an American, my mother said.

It was my father who loved Americans. The American multina-
tional that bought the factory in our small Canadian town regularly
summoned my father to its headquarters in Niagara Falls, New York
(properly pronounced as one long, important word), trips from which
he would return to us boasting about the computer that filled a whole
room, drinks that no one in Canada had heard of yet, hotels that really
knew how to make a man feel at home.

When we moved to Brazil, where my father was to start another
factory for the American company, his love affair with the United
States intensified. As our ship sailed past Cuba, where Che and Castro
were waging war on Batista from their caves in the Sierra Maestra, my
father drank Cuba Libres, but it was Americans he raised his glass to,
saviours of the world.

In Brazil, I went to American schools, learned the states of the
Union and their capitals before I knew the names of the provinces of
Canada. I pledged allegiance to the flag of America every morning and

sang, "Oh say, can you see . . ." I wish I could say that, like Jimmy Carter, I lusted only in my heart, that I never actually mouthed the words, but I did. I belted out "Yankee Doodle Dandy" and "America the Beautiful" at the Fourth of July picnics where all the ex-pats brought their apple pies and baked beans and fried chicken and corn on the cob—food I grew up thinking of as American, though it is the gastronomic heritage of my birth country, too. Everyone at those picnics wore red, white, and blue (also the patriotic colours of Canada's flag of the time). They talked about how wonderful life was stateside, where roads were smoothly paved (not a string of dusty potholes) and where you could count on your workers to show up on time (not like these lazy South Americans). This is ex-pat patter, I know that now. Americans don't have a corner on it. I've heard Germans in Canada and Canadians in France and Swiss in Italy go through the same loving litany of home disguised as a whiner's rant.

The Brazilians mistook my family for Americans. The Americans knew better—I entered the schoolyard each morning to taunts of "Canadian bacon"—though the distinction was lost on the coffee-skinned boy who opened his pants and peed on my feet, cursing me as I stood there astonished, stuttering, "Mas no estou Americana!"

I worried my family had become American by association, which, given my dampened shoes, did not seem like such a good thing. Didn't we beg our friends to send us sticks of Juicy Fruit chewing gum and Hershey chocolate bars in their letters? Wasn't it Pat Boone and Elvis Presley my sisters shimmied to on their beds?

I realized we'd escaped with our identity intact when we boarded the Air Canada flight for home. I was a teenager by then, but I felt what a baby must feel when, after being handed around, it finds itself safe in its mother's arms. The stewardesses cut their vowels short and round, the way we did. They were reserved and polite and seemed pleased that we were, too. They didn't gush, which was a relief. No one talked too loud. Everyone said "Excuse me" and "Sorry," even when they hadn't done anything wrong.

There were Americans after that, but they were on my turf, which made it easier to look down my nose. My father still adored everything stamped Made in America—*I Love Lucy, Gilligan's Island,* the Rose Bowl Parade—but when I looked south, I saw only racists, warmongers, and assassins. The Americans I admired—John F. Kennedy, Robert Kennedy, Martin Luther King, Jr.—seemed not to rise from that country's soil so much as hover above it, where they were blown to smithereens. On a cold October day in 1969, I stood on the Ambassador Bridge, which spans the river between Windsor and Detroit, the busiest border crossing on the continent, and pounded my fists on the hoods of cars lined up to enter the United States, denouncing the war in Vietnam, the treatment of blacks in the South. I was in a permanent rage.

Now, thirty-five years later, I'm cruising the shelves of a bookstore in one of America's biggest cities. I feel oddly at home, bending sideways to squint at the titles, moving through fiction to biography, past the children's section.

That's where it comes to me. My first Americans were two kids: a blonde girl in a pink dress and a brown-haired boy in shorts. They had a dog, Spot, and a kitten, Puff, and a baby sister, Sally. I loved them with all my heart. They ran through the pages of the first book I ever read, exuberant, laughing. I admired them even when they wept, for they weren't afraid to cry. Maybe they knew, as Americans seem to, that things will work out for them in the end.

"*Fun with Dick and Jane!*" I exclaim. Wayne looks at me over the shelf, as if unsure whether to acknowledge me. But it's too late to sidle away. I'm pulling at his sleeve. "I figured it out, and wouldn't you know it? My first Americans were characters in a book."

2 / **ASTORIA**

*W*E continue south the next morning on Interstate 5, a fine drizzle making itself noticeable on the windshield, the wipers giving a cozy kind of syncopated rhythm to the passing parade. Merilyn is in the co-pilot's seat, navigating with the aid of two maps spread out on her lap, one American Automobile Association map of the entire United States as it appeared fifteen years ago and a smaller, more recent MapArt book open to the state of Washington. Various brochures and booklets are also arranged about her half of the car, but neatly, like the cymbals on a set of drums. She is marking our actual route on the larger map with a yellow highlighter and various alternative routes on the smaller map. Merilyn is both a dedicated planner and a Libran, which means that (a) there must be a plan and (b) every plan must be balanced by an alternative plan. Three alternative plans are better than two, but since that would upset the balance, a fourth plan is required. The small map soon becomes cross-veined with yellow marker lines. In my view, if you aren't going anywhere in particular, it doesn't much matter how you get there. To which she replies that if the destination isn't important, then the route to it must be.

"We could stay on the I-5 to Portland," she says, "and from there cut over to Highway 101 and go down the coast to San Francisco. I've never been to San Francisco."

"That sounds good," I say. "In Portland, we could visit Powell's City of Books. It's supposed to be the biggest bookstore in the world—a whole city block of books." I mentally calculate how much room we have in the trunk. Not enough.

"Or we could turn east here and go down the 82 and the 395, which would eventually take us into Yosemite."

"I've never been to Yosemite," I say. In this state, all the minor route numbers are printed on a portrait of George Washington's head. The I-5 is lined with the first president's head on a stick.

"Neither have I," she says, "but we can also get there from San Francisco. Or we could get off the I-5 and drive over to the coast. Find a romantic little motel somewhere overlooking the Pacific Ocean."

"Let's do that."

As Merilyn returns to her maps, my mind drifts off into something I read in the *New Yorker* about the differences between what men and women expect when they're on holiday. According to the article, men want sex, while women want mostly "an interlude of near-monastic solitude." I'm sure that is a gross oversimplification. Men don't want just sex. They also want to be left alone. Or maybe they want sex and then to be left alone, whereas women apparently just want to be left alone. But men, I contend, also want other things when travelling: alcohol, a good book, a quiet room, Internet access, great food, courteous and prompt service, other people's kids kept at a discreet distance, clean water in the pool, the sand raked at night, something interesting to walk to around the point, like a bar. In other words, the same things women want.

"Or we could stay on the I-5 all the way down to San Francisco. That would save us some time. Or we could turn east at Eugene, cross the mountains, and hit the 395 at Burns. What do you think?"

"Fine by me. But wouldn't that mean missing San Francisco?"

The word on the street used to be that men think about sex every twenty seconds, whereas women think about it once a week or so. This had a scientific ring to it, as though someone had actually timed it. Actually, somebody had: Alfred Kinsey, whose *Sexual Behavior in the Human Male* made all kinds of claims about what men do and think about based, as far as I can remember, on studies conducted with a group of college students in Florida in the 1950s. What the Kinsey Institute's report actually stated, however, is that, on average, 54 per cent of men think about sex once or twice a day, 43 per cent think about it once a week to once a month, and 3 per cent think about it less than once a month, if at all. And that women think about sex approximately half as often as men do. The difference doesn't seem to be enough on which to base an entire philosophy of the fundamental incompatibility of men and women. Besides, the whole Kinsey Report has been debunked. More recent studies show that women think about sex even more often than men do, they just don't talk about it as much, at least not to men.

"We can see San Francisco anytime," Merilyn says. "I think I'd rather avoid big cities."

"Me, too."

* * *

"MAYBE we should eat soon," Wayne says before we've driven very far. "I'm so hungry my stomach thinks my throat's been cut." It was one of his father's favourite phrases.

The morning broke with strong winds and rain that seemed pitched in great fistfuls from the hands of the gods. We ignored it, pulling the blankets over our heads. We are habitually early risers, but not this morning. We eased into the day, sitting up in bed with our books and mugs of Starbucks coffee we made ourselves, Wayne spiking his with cream he pilfered from the restaurant the night before. The room was small but cozy, strewn with our things, the air scented with the flowers I lifted from the waste bins behind the Pike Market.

We left with reluctance, pulling out of Seattle close to noon. We weren't quite in travel mode yet, that frame of mind that makes the car, and the road, the best place in the world to be.

"We'll eat at one of those great little diners," I say vaguely.

Breakfast is our favourite meal on the road, the one that proves we're not home. We often eat lunch at a restaurant, and dinner, too, but the first meal of the day is not normally taken with strangers. At home we cook our porridge with cranberries in the microwave, or grab pieces of fruit and go off to our respective desks. On the road, our appetites become gargantuan and we sit in diners before platters of food heaped with enough calories to last a lumberjack all day. It must be the ancient nomad in us coming out. Stock up while you can, our reptilian brain insists; you never know when you'll eat again.

We pull off the interstate at an exit to nowhere that we can see, lured by a low wooden building with a huge sign tacked to the roof: *All-Day Breakfast*. Not a diner, but close enough. Everyone in the place but us seems to be a regular. We stand at the door as the waitress moves among the tables, calling everyone by name.

"Hey there, Bob, how's it shakin'? Want some more coffee, just a splash? Sure thing, Jake. I'll be with ya in a minute. And what's a nice girl like you doing out on a day like this, Sue? Great earrings. It's set to snow something awful, I hear. Pancakes, the usual? Yeah, I'm here right through Christmas."

The place is draped with tinsel garlands; Christmasy cut-outs of Santa Claus, Rudolph, and Frosty are stuck to the walls. Elves dangle from the ceiling on red ribbons. A necklace of Christmas lights flashes at our waitress's throat as she leads us to a table topped with a silver-dusted red plastic poinsettia.

"What can I bring you this morning?"

"I think it's already afternoon."

"Honey, here it's morning all day long. Coffee?"

"Do you have decaf?"

"I'll have to make some fresh."

Breakfast is a plate of grease. That's how the gumshoe would have described it in *The Bookman's Promise,* the audiobook we've been listening to for the past hour. I order bacon and hash browns with a single poached egg, no toast. Wayne orders eggs and links with biscuits and gravy.

"You ever had biscuits and gravy?" I ask him.

"No."

"You sure you want that?" I used to work in a short-order kitchen. I know where gravy like that comes from.

"Sure I'm sure," he says defensively. "Who doesn't like gravy?"

A few years ago, we took a road trip through Quebec that turned into a search for the perfect *confit de canard*—duck leg simmered to a tender crisp in its own lard. Before that, a trip to France became a quest for the perfect crème caramel. When my breakfast arrives, I decide that on this drive through America, I'll be on the lookout for the perfect hash browns. The ones on the plate before me are grated and browned on the grill to the consistency of fibreboard. The yolk of my egg, which should be absorbed by the potato, runs in thin, pale rivulets across the plate. The bacon is deep mahogany and tastes of salt, not pork. Wayne's biscuits are buried in a grey lava flow.

"How we doin' so far?" the waitress says brightly, refilling our cups and moving on while we are still deciding whether to be honest or polite. By the time we smile and nod, Wayne's mouth full of dry biscuit, she is long gone.

But really, I love the place, weak coffee, burnt bacon, greasy potatoes, grey gravy, and all. The morning smell of it. The fuggy warmth. The way everyone calls out, "Bye, Dorothy, Merry Christmas!" as they push through the door into the driving, sleeting rain, saying it the way you'd say, "Bye, Mom." As if you know you'll be back soon.

"What's the best way to get to the Pacific coast?" we ask Dorothy when she brings our bill.

That stops her. She sets her coffee pot down on the table and looks up past the garlands, as if the answer is written on the ceiling tiles.

We've seen this look before, on the face of a matron on a sidewalk in Pittenweem, Scotland. We'd asked her where to find the Harbour Guest House, the only bayside hotel in a village of not much more than a thousand souls. She'd looked at us blankly. "I don't know," she said, "I've only lived here these nine years." Wayne was gobsmacked. "Never ask a local," I'd said.

"I wouldn't know," Dorothy says finally with a laugh. "The Sound is right here, but the coast? I've never been."

* ★ ★

*W*E turn off the I-5 onto Highway 30 just south of Kelso, Washington, and cross the Columbia Gorge. The Columbia River is the dividing line between Washington State and Oregon. Highway 30, as we call it (we still aren't used to saying "route" instead of "highway"), looks deceptively tame on the map. In reality, it hugs the high land above the Columbia Valley on the Oregon side, twisting and turning like an asphalt snake that is losing its grip on the slippery granite cliffs. The Columbia gleams occasionally far below. There is a logging truck behind us, more impatient to get to the coast than—in its estimation—we are. On the few straight stretches of highway, it comes so close to our tail that the word "Freightliner," read backwards, fills the rear-view mirror and seems to be snapping at us to get out of its way. On the curves, which arc out over the sheer drop to the river below, it shrinks back as though momentarily looking for a weak spot on our unguarded flank.

"How far to the coast?" I ask Merilyn.

She looks at the map and counts. "About sixty kilometres," she says.

"Kilometres?" I ask.

"All right, miles," she says, as though the difference isn't worth quibbling over.

Finally a road appears on our left, rising away from the river, and I turn abruptly onto it. The truck roars by behind a wall of water, sounding disappointed, like a tomcat whose catnip mouse has fallen down a furnace vent. I turn the car around, and we sit at the intersection for a while looking out across the valley. The rain is still coming down hard and a strong wind is bending some fairly substantial trees above our heads. Before us, far below, we can make out the edge of the river on the Washington side, a fishing village, perhaps, or a farm. Maybe a winery. It looks calm down there.

"There's a nice-looking hotel in Astoria," Merilyn says. She spent much of last night surfing the Internet for likely lodgings. "Maybe we should stay there tonight."

"Sounds good," I say half-heartedly. We are vagabonds in America, dogged by rain. But Astoria seems too close to Seattle. Shouldn't we try to make it farther down the coast?

"We have lots of time," Merilyn says, as if reading my mind. "We're on holiday."

PERHAPS IT was our close encounter with the transport truck, or my post-border jitters, but I am still nervous about our trip. I have always had rather ambivalent feelings about America or, at least, America as seen from afar. It speaks a version of our language, but with its own idiosyncratic touches: chinos, sneakers, zee. Maybe that's why America makes me uneasy: it's eerily familiar, like a song I don't remember hearing yet somehow know the words to. Being in America is like walking around in someone else's dream.

Here is what I have come to believe about America, based, I admit, largely on circumstantial and even hearsay evidence: America is an annoying and dangerous mixture of arrogance and ignorance. Its citizens barge around foreign countries looking for hamburgers and pizza and fried chicken, unaware of, or unconcerned about, or impatient with the possibility that the country they are in might have its own cuisine, customs, economy, political system, and religion with which it is quite happy, thank you very much. It holds that "different" is a synonym for "inferior." In an Irish pub in Buenos Aires I met an American who told me his hotel was better than mine because his was closer to a Wendy's.

The dream we're walking around in is "the American Dream," which seems to involve having a chicken in every pot, a new Detroit car in every garage, 2.86 television sets in every home, and broadband Internet access on every street. It's the dream of fame and fortune, of success measured in material wealth. This is a newish version; the original American Dream, as defined in 1931 by James Truslow Adams in *The Epic of America,* had more substance. It was of "a land in which life should be better and richer and fuller for everyone, with opportunity to each according to his ability or achievement." Nothing would be handed to you on a silver platter: you had to earn it: "It is not a dream of motor cars and high wages merely, but a dream of social order in which each man and each woman shall be able to attain to the fullest stature of which they are innately capable." This is a dream I could live in.

But the dream has changed. In *What Is America?* Canadian writer Ronald Wright charts how far the American Dream has sunk: "Here are the ingredients of the American Dream: love of the new and dismissal of the old; invaders presented as 'pilgrims'; hard work both rewarded and required; and selfishness as natural law."

There is an appalling arrogance and a pitiable naïveté in America, which assumes that the winner of four out of seven baseball games between teams from, let us say, St. Louis and Detroit is by definition the best team in the world. The same attitude caused Oliver Wendell Holmes, Sr., in 1860, to declare Boston "the thinking center of the continent, and therefore of the planet," and causes a place like Utah to advertise itself as having "the best snow in the world."

"America shapes the way non-Americans live and think," wrote Ian Jack, then editor of *Granta,* in his introduction to a 2002 issue entitled "What We Think of America." "What do we think of when we think of America?" Jack asked. "Fear, resentment, envy, anger, wonder, hope?"

All of those things, I would say, and almost in that order. I am in the "fear" stage at the moment, moving into "resentment." The very thought of Homeland Security rattles me: it's as if the whole country were a border. It makes the United States a nation of 300 million border guards.

These thoughts are not unique to me: according to recent polls, 37 per cent of Canadians dislike the United States. In fact, it is almost a national pastime, identifying ourselves by what we are not: that is, American.

Nor are the sentiments new. The word "anti-American" appeared in Noah Webster's first dictionary in 1828 and was defined pretty much as it is today: "Opposed to America, or to the true interests or government of the United States." It's hard to imagine being opposed to an entire nation, but consider the remark of an earlier prime minister, Sir Wilfrid Laurier, in the House of Commons in 1903: "We are living beside a great neighbour who . . . are very grasping in their national acts, and who are determined upon every occasion to get the best in any agreement which they make." Pierre Trudeau said something similar when addressing the National Press Club in Washington, D.C., in 1969: "Living next to you is in some ways like sleeping with an elephant. No matter how friendly or even-tempered the beast . . . one is affected by every twitch and grunt." People are always saying things like that about Americans, which may be why only 26 per cent of them think they are liked by other countries, and much fewer than that give a damn. But most Canadians agreed with Trudeau when he said, "We are a different people from you and a different people partly because of you."

When asked to think about America, some *Granta* contributors thought of things that had arrived in their countries from the United States. The Lebanese writer Hanan al-Shaykh, for example, remembered a gift sent by a cousin who had immigrated to the United States to study aeronautical engineering—a red satin pillow with a picture of the Statue of Liberty, "a good-hearted woman wearing a crown on her head and holding a lamp, a torch." It is a torch, but I like Franz Kafka's version better. In his novel *Amerika*, published in 1927, his hero, Karl Rossmann, looks at the Statue of Liberty as his ship edges into the New York harbour: as Kafka describes it, the woman is "holding aloft a sword," one of those Freudian slips that no one seems to have caught. But of course it's a sword—how appropriate! With what else would the United States bring democracy and freedom to, for example, the Middle East? A lamp?

Having grown up sharing a river with America, it is difficult for me to pinpoint any one thing that came to me from across the border. Everything did. In few other places on the continent do Canadian cheeks live in such close proximity to American jowls. Almost everything in the room, including the air, would have been from the States. The dance music my father played, the books my mother read voraciously, all American. The Pablum I ate, although invented in Canada, was produced and marketed in Chicago. During the day, my father worked at Chrysler's and my mother shopped at Woolworth's. At school, we played baseball—hardball, not softball, and not hockey. When we got our first television set, I watched Soupy Sales and Bugs Bunny and Popeye, all of whom I thought lived in Detroit. It never occurred to us to be anti-American; it would have been like being against life itself, and not even the good life, just life. Canada was a long way from Windsor; America was just down the street.

That was in the mid-1950s, when the American Dream was already beginning to morph into the American Disturbed Sleep Pattern. I was too young to know about McCarthyism and was blind to racism, but they were as present in our home as Frank Sinatra and Roy Rogers. They "came with," as the waitresses in Woolworth's would say to my mother about the Jell-O. My father joined the Royal Canadian Air Force in 1957, and we left Windsor to live on remote radar bases in the north, DEW Line stations (for Distant Early Warning—distant from whom?) that were built in Canada by Americans during the Cold War so that

Canadians could stand on guard for missiles coming across the Arctic Ocean aimed at Washington, D.C. We imbibed the fear of creeping Communism with our Sergeant Rock comic books, soaked in racism with every episode of *Amos 'n' Andy*, and loved every minute of it.

Only later did I resent living the American Dream in Canada. I wonder how I'll feel about travelling through it in the United States.

"The Cannery Pier Hotel," Merilyn reads from the brochure, placing special emphasis on its strangely Germanic sprinkling of capital letters, "is a luxury boutique hotel built on the former site of a historic cannery six hundred feet out into the Mighty Columbia River in Astoria, Oregon. The Hotel offers..."

"How do we get to it?" I ask. "By boat?"

"... the Hotel offers guests an unparalleled experience in a real working river. Private river-view balconies in all rooms. Fireplace. High-Speed Internet in room. Clawfoot tubs with views. Terry robes."

I am still feeling anxious.

"Who," I ask, "is Terry Robes?"

* * *

*M*Y estimates are wildly out of whack. Clearly, I have forgotten how long a mile can be. It is late in the afternoon by the time we turn west off the I-5, toward the Pacific. The direction seems all wrong. Aren't we supposed to be heading home?

US Route 30, the highway we're on, ends just a few miles down the road, in Astoria. If we turned the other way, we'd be in Atlantic City in just over forty-eight hours. We'd head east through Bliss (Bliss!) and Twin Falls, Idaho, across the Missouri and the Mississippi Rivers, skim the southern edge of Chicago, then cut straight through Indiana, Ohio, Pennsylvania, New Jersey, until we hit Virginia Avenue, a few blocks up from the boardwalk in Atlantic City.

Route 30 is the main east-west highway in the United States. It's not an interstate; it's a highway. A main cross-country road, like

Route 66, except that long stretches of that iconic cross-country road have been replaced by multi-lane throughways that stop for nothing, not a crossroad, not a town, not a megacity. "Life doesn't happen along the interstates," William Least Heat-Moon notes laconically in *Blue Highways*. "It's against the law."

This narrow road taking us west to the sea is the only red highway that still runs uninterrupted across the continental United States. Even Route 66 went only to Chicago. Not only is Route 30 the last of its kind, it was the first of its kind in North America. In 1912, Carl Fisher, the man who built the Indianapolis Motor Speedway and turned a Florida swamp into Miami Beach, proposed what he called the Coast-to-Coast Rock Highway. There were already some 2.5 million miles of roads in the United States, but they weren't connected. Dirt tracks radiated from settlements to farms, logging camps, and mines, petering out at the last signs of human habitation. Fisher's idea was to connect all those communities with a gravelled road that would run from Times Square in New York City through thirteen states to Lincoln Park in San Francisco, the first transcontinental road built for the automobile instead of oxen, horses, or mules. A Main Street across America—which is how it came to be known.

The road would cost $10 million, with each community along the way pitching in to do the work. To pay the bills, Fisher asked automobile manufacturers and accessory companies to contribute 1 per cent of their revenues to the project. Packard and Goodyear agreed; Ford refused. The public would never learn to pay for their roads if industry built them, Henry said.

Fisher went ahead anyway. To whip up public enthusiasm, he renamed his new road the Lincoln Highway (after the president, not the car, which was later manufactured by Ford). The idea caught on, and so within a few years, highways with names like the Dixie Highway, Jefferson Davis Highway, the Atlantic Highway, and the Old Spanish Trail criss-crossed the country. There was no system of road signs, just painted bands on telephone poles at important intersections, something like the pointing markers on Fremont's Center-of-the-Universe post.

The Lincoln Highway opened in 1915 in time for the Panama-Pacific International Exposition in San Francisco. Most of it was graded and oiled, but parts never evolved beyond muddy tracks; it all depended on the locals in charge.

By the time the idea for Route 30 came along in 1925, government was taking over road building. With bureaucracy came a federal highway system determined to make sense of the myriad quaintly named thoroughfares. To a foreigner like me, the United States National Highway System illustrates the remarkable pragmatism of the American character. Look at a road sign and just by the number, you can pinpoint where in the country you are. Major east-west routes are numbered in multiples of ten, from US 10 across the north to US 90 across the south. Major north-south routes end in 1 or 5, with the numbers starting at 1 in the east and increasing as they move west. The US Route 30 sign we just passed tells me we are in the northern tier of the country, and we're heading for US Route 101, which runs down the Pacific shore into California.

The Lincoln Highway was severed into several numbered roads, but almost two-thirds of it became US Route 30. The new road was identified, as every road in America is and has been since 1925, with a shield that encloses the number and, at one time, the name of the state. To avoid confusion, all signs showing named highways were taken down.

Where we live in eastern Ontario, planners a few years ago decided to remove apostrophes from road signs. What, the apostrophe takes too much time to print? Too much ink? The curlicue is aesthetically displeasing? Whatever the logic, the result was that Chaffey's Lock, where Wayne lived for a time, became Chaffeys Lock. The possessive apostrophe, which denoted the name of the person who had founded the town or built the lock, disappeared, though not without considerable outrage from the local citizenry. Likewise, the shift to numbered highways in the United States was not an easy one. As an editorial in the Lexington, Kentucky, *Herald* noted in 1927, "The traveler may shed tears as he drives down the shady vista of the Lincoln Highway, or dream dreams as he speeds over a sunlit path on the Jefferson Highway, or see noble visions as he speeds across an unfolding ribbon that bears the name of Woodrow Wilson. But how in the world can a man get a kick out of 46 or 55 or 33 or 21?"

The numbers stayed. After all, the original rationale for a federal highway system in the United States was national defence, and soldiers are not sentimental, at least not about other people's history. But a few Americans refused to see the old highway names disappear. On September 1, 1928, thousands of Boy Scouts fanned out along the Lincoln Highway to install concrete markers, one per mile, with a small bust of Lincoln and the inscription *This highway dedicated to Abraham Lincoln.*

A rock road from coast to coast; markers every mile to preserve the memory of a revered name: it's by these grand, sweeping gestures that I know where I am.

Lincoln Highway was decommissioned in 1928. Route 66 went the same way in 1985. The last major route constructed was US 12 on the Idaho side of Lolo Pass, completed in 1962. No new highways have been commissioned since, except the interstates.

In 1962, the year he won the Nobel Prize for Literature, John Steinbeck took a drive on the new interstate. "These great roads are wonderful for moving goods," he reported, "but not for inspection of a countryside. You are bound to the wheel and your eyes to the car ahead and to the rear-view mirror for the car behind and the side mirror for the car or truck about to pass, and at the same time you must read all the signs for fear you may miss some instructions or orders. No roadside stands selling squash juice, no antique stores, no farm products or factory outlets. When we get these thruways across the whole country, as we will and must, it will be possible to drive from New York to California without seeing a single thing."

Canada has no interstates. Roads are a provincial concern. It took various levels of government until 1950 to get together to build our one and only cross-country road—the Trans-Canada Highway—which wasn't finished until 1971. It is our version of Main Street across America: although you can take 1A bypasses around most cities now, Highway 1 itself still barrels through small towns and metropolises alike, stringing them together like beads on a necklace that stretches eight thousand kilometres (five thousand miles) from Atlantic to Pacific.

Route 30 reminds me a bit of the Trans-Canada that brought us west. It feels like a small miracle that this old American road is still here to be travelled, town to town, from one side of the country to the other. Although long stretches of it run parallel to or concurrent with interstates, this historic, eighty-one-year-old route has managed to avoid having its number hung up for good.

"What would you call this road, Wayne, if it didn't have a number?"

"The Twilight Creek Eagle Highway," he says.

"Really?" I'd been thinking of something more mundane: the Columbia Road, or Kelso Way. "Why?"

"After the Twilight Creek Eagle Sanctuary," he says, pointing to the sign near where we've pulled off to let a transport truck pass. "Want to go take a look?"

*　　*　　*

WE'VE pulled off Route 30 onto something called the Burnside Loop, which angles sharply down toward the river. After driving for a mile we come to the sanctuary, where instead of the milling eagles I expect to see, we find two forlorn-looking plaques looking out over a swampy lowland at river level. Here, one of the plaques informs us, is where the thirty-three members of the Lewis and Clark Corps of Discovery made their camp just over two hundred years ago, on November 26, 1805.

Canadians don't know much about the Lewis and Clark Expedition. We know Davy Crockett and Daniel Boone because of the television programs their exploits inspired, but Meriwether Lewis and William Clark did far more than those men to open the West to American expansion. In 1804, they were sent by Thomas Jefferson to explore the source of the Missouri River, cross the Rocky Mountains, and find an overland route to the Pacific Ocean. Along the way, they were to make note of anything "worthy of notice." They found a lot that was noteworthy: Lewis's journals alone filled a great steamer trunk.

"Great joy in camp," Lewis wrote on November 7. "We are in View of the Ocian, this great Pacific Ocean which we been So long anxious to See." To mark the occasion, Clark carved his initials and the date on a handy pine tree. Now they were moving back and forth across the river mouth, looking for a place high enough above the tideline to spend the winter. Like us, they hadn't booked ahead.

Out here in the wilderness, almost a year's travel from the Thirteen Colonies, the democratic principles of the freshly fledged nation prevailed. By a vote of the entire expedition—including York, Clark's black "manservant," and Sacajawea, the young Shoshone wife of one of the French-Canadian guides—the corps decided to make its winter camp on the south side of the Columbia, where elk were more plentiful, near what is now Astoria, at a place they named Fort Clatsop.

The Corps of Discovery scheme was inspired by Alexander Mackenzie, who trekked across Canada and reached the Pacific Ocean near Bella Coola, in what is now British Columbia, in 1793. Jefferson read Mackenzie's account of his trip avidly, passed the book on to Meriwether Lewis, who at the time was his personal secretary, and began planning an American version of it, with Lewis in charge. Mackenzie even carved his name and the date of his arrival—not in a tree, but on a rock. I like the idea that the Lewis and Clark journey, one of the defining myths of American history, had its origins in a Canadian expedition that few in Canada today remember.

Standing on the slippery platform of the Twilight Creek Eagle Sanctuary, at twilight, looking down at the great river where the expedition camped, I understand what it is that has fixed this journey so securely in the American imagination. We have a river, we have a small band of purposeful men floating down it, and we have an ocean. What could be more American than that? It is *Apocalypse Now.* It is *Huckleberry Finn.* Clark even had his single-named slave, York, with him. But unlike Huck's companion Jim, York isn't a runaway. In *Huckleberry Finn,* Jim is the one character for whom freedom meant something tangible; his eventual emancipation elevates the novel to the status of myth.

In the Lewis and Clark story, the loyal and obedient York is not escaping from anything. In fact, he is scarcely visible. He is given no voice other than that of an animal when he is amusing some Indian children and is mentioned barely a dozen times in the three years covered by the narrative, and then only matter-of-factly, as in "set out at 7 o'clock in a Canoo with Cap Lewis my servant and one man . . ."

Because York is denied any role other than that of a slave, the Lewis and Clark expedition, which was essentially a scientific and commercial enterprise, becomes a different kind of epic journey, one that also delineates and defines the American spirit. If Huck and Jim represent the fictional way Americans would like to see themselves—as simple, honest, and freedom-loving adventurers—then Lewis and Clark reveal the true nonfictional nature of their national consciousness: entrepreneurial and freedom-loving, except when it came to Manifest Destiny and slavery—in other words, the rights of others. When the expedition was over, York asked Clark for his freedom. Clark refused.

The setting sun is coming from the west, casting long shadows over the Seal Islands. I realize that this is my first real view of the Columbia

River. And that we have come here by land from Canada, after crossing the continent; in a sense, we have combined the journeys of Mackenzie and Lewis and Clark. I look around; there are several sizable trees, dripping with rain but suitable for carving. Unfortunately, I have left my Swiss Army knife at home; I didn't want to worry about it as I crossed the border.

★ ★ ★

*M*UTELY we drive through the gathering night toward the end of our second day on the road. The radio is off and Wayne is somewhere in his Lewis and Clark reverie, but even so, the air is filled with sound: tires on asphalt, wipers on glass, the bellow of a ship's horn on the river below, the wigwag of the railway track we just crossed.

True silence—natural quiet—is a rare thing. Gordon Hempton, an acoustic ecologist across the river in Washington State, has spent most of a lifetime searching for places where the sounds of nature might be recorded without man-made interruption. There aren't many left. He's made a few MP3 albums of the sounds of silence: "Forest Rain," "Spring Leaves," "Old Growth." I like the idea of listening to a forest growing.

On Earth Day 2005, Hempton decided to defend a bit of wilderness from all human-caused noise intrusion. His "one square inch of silence" is in the Hoh Rain Forest of Olympic National Park, 678 feet above sea level and a two-hour hike in from the nearest trail, the exact location marked by a small red stone placed on top of a moss-covered log at 47° 51.959′ N, 123° 52.221′ W. He even convinced airlines to reroute their flight paths around the park.

Hempton defines silence as "the total absence of all sound. But because the whole universe is vibrating, there is no true silence— though silence *does* exist in the mind as a psychological state, as a concept."

Wayne and I are silent, but it isn't the silence of solitude. Even without speaking, he is part of my mental space. I wonder what he's thinking, if maybe I should say something funny or smart. What kind of mood is he in? Should I bring up Christmas, how much I miss the kids? Or the novel that I so much want him to read. Maybe I should find something in the brochures to talk about, try to connect us with the river that is slipping by outside.

And what is Wayne thinking? Is he sitting in his silence the same way I sit in mine?

Probably not. Researchers at the University of California recently found that the amygdala, that almond-shaped structure nestled on either side of the brain, behaves differently in men and women at rest. When men are relaxed and quiet, the right amygdala is the more active one, while in women, it's the left. What's really interesting is the region of brain that the amygdala is talking to. In men, it's communicating with the visual cortex and the striatum, which controls vision and motor actions. In women, it's connecting to the insular cortex and the hypothalamus—the interior landscape. I'm thinking about our relationship; Wayne's wondering where he can pull over to pee.

"In human intercourse the tragedy begins not when there is misunderstanding about words, but when silence is not understood," Thoreau wrote. It's hard to believe he was never married.

After three months working alone on my book, I don't find it easy being trapped in this little Toyota with another person, even one I love more than I ever thought possible. How can I think in this Echo? Wayne won't be quiet for long. He has a penchant for golden oldies: he worked as a DJ in high school and knows all the words to all the songs up to about 1968. He has quite a good tenor, of the Gerry and the Pacemakers variety, so I don't mind sitting through endless verses of "The Sound of Silence," "Twenty-Four Hours from Tulsa," and "When I'm Sixty-Four." But driving through this blackness, I long for the Blues. Maybe a little Dr. John crooning "Such a Night," or Sippie Wallace doing "Suitcase Blues," Sister Rosetta Tharpe belting out "Didn't It Rain," or B.B. King. I can almost hear him . . . *Gonna roam this mean ol' highway until the break of day.*

It's not really a mean ol' highway. In fact, there's something about driving through the gathering nightfall in the rain that feels almost cozy. Not fearsome or alien, though I can see how some might see it that way. The damp darkness outside our windows is impenetrable; the headlights obliterate the landscape, force our eyes down wavering tunnels spiked with glinting needles of rain. There's a rhythm to the slap of the wipers that lets me sink into myself, just as Wayne has sunk into some contemplative place of his own. We are making this journey together, but separately, too.

★ ★ ★

WE'VE been vagabonding in America, meandering the day away, eating in the car, drinking water from our metal bottles. We're more than ready for dinner. We arrive in Astoria just as the street lights are making pale, yellow smudges in the misty rain, but even so the streets look dark and deserted. Few of the storefronts are lit up, and our hopes of finding a quiet, excellent restaurant fade.

The main thoroughfare, Commercial Street, which we're on, is a miracle of Victorian bakeshops, olde innes, souvenir and gifte shoppes, and the like. The Liberty Theater, built in 1925 and recently featured on HGTV's *Restore America* television series as one of its twelve American Treasures, appears to be dark tonight, and is likely to stay dark until spring. Ah, well. According to the Visitors Guide, the town fairly hums with life in the summer: visitors flock to the Fort Clatsop National Memorial, and on the waterfront, a "beautifully refurbished" 1913 trolley car runs between the port and the East Mooring Basin. But it's winter, and the town seems moribund. We drive through the business section without stopping and soon come to a huge, steel-girdered bridge that soars upward and off over the Columbia River, somewhere to our right. Almost directly under it, jutting out into the river, is the Cannery Pier Hotel.

The building was built as a fish cannery back when salmon runs in the Columbia River were the biggest on the coast and Astoria was the second-largest city in Oregon, after Portland. Most of the fish plants shut down in the 1940s. Although this building has been fully restored and turned into a boutique hotel, the area around it still looks fairly desolate in the dark. To get to the parking lot, we have to ease the Echo over a dilapidated dock that must still be on the town's to-be-improved list.

The hotel looks like a Mississippi riverboat moored to the dock, flags flying, lights ablaze, ready to cast off and float off down the Columbia. Merilyn goes in to negotiate a room while I sit in the car, twirling the radio dial to find a baseball game. Instead I get Miles Davis, so I turn off the wipers and let his smooth, muted trumpet ease the rivulets of rainwater down the windshield. When he was on the road, Davis used to send his wife, who was white, into hotels to secure them a room, figuring she wouldn't be turned away and might even get them a deal. I'm doing the same thing. The Cannery Pier looks expensive, and after our small flurry of spending in Seattle, Merilyn and I have decided on a limit of $100 a night for accommodation and another $100 a day for meals, gas, and various other necessities, such as books and wine. It's an arbitrary figure, but this is our first night and we think we should be setting ourselves a good example.

Merilyn comes back to the car smiling. "The woman at the desk was reading a book," she says.

I take that as a good sign. "What was the book?" I ask.

"I couldn't see the cover," she says. "She told me the rooms were $160. I told her we didn't want to pay more than $120, and she said, 'I can do that.'"

A hundred and twenty is more than a hundred, but maybe we can skip a meal tomorrow, or a quarter of a meal over the next four days. Instead of steak, fries, salad, and a glass of wine, I'll just have the steak, fries, and wine. A budget is a budget.

The foyer is a marvel of modern architecture, all plate glass and weirdly angled Douglas-fir beams bolted to gleaming hardwood floors.

I admire the view over the river, with the bridge sweeping overhead like an inspired brush stroke. Classical music plays softly from speakers hidden behind fabric wall hangings. The night clerk has gone back to reading in a soft leather chair by the window. A thick paperback with a glossy cover, but at least it's a book. She gets up and pours us each a glass of wine, "complimentary to our guests," she says. Merilyn doesn't drink, so I take hers, too, as we climb the carpeted stairs to our room.

It is spacious, with, as advertised, a fireplace, a narrow balcony overlooking the river, a claw-footed tub with a view, and, yes, Terry Robes hanging in the closet.

"It's gorgeous," Merilyn says, running the bath. I find a corkscrew on the side table and agree.

In the morning, we go downstairs for our free continental breakfast and carry it up on a tray to our room. We're not being anti-social; there are no other guests in the hotel. From our balcony, we watch a huge grey freighter slip upriver past the hotel, inches, it seems, from our wrought-iron railing, so close we can see sailors through the portholes having their bacon and eggs and hash browns. American coots and western grebes paddle about in the ship's wake. On an adjacent, equally dilapidated pier, a lone fir grows improbably from a pile of rotting boards. It looks like a Christmas tree. We note with approval that no one has crawled out onto the pier to festoon the tree with coloured lights and tinsel or heap fake Christmas presents around its base. Maybe I could like it here, after all.

3 / HIGHWAY 101

*M*y first impression of Oregon is that we have entered a no-nonsense state. Gone are Washington's chatty road signs: *Watch for Falling Rocks, Slippery When Wet.* The yellow diamonds now bark single words. *Rocks. Slides. Ice.*

I'm inclined to pay attention. Not much more than a week ago, safe in my Vancouver room, I anxiously followed the fate of the Kim family. James and Kati Kim and their two young daughters, Penelope, four, and Sabine, seven months, had spent Thanksgiving in Seattle, then continued on the I-5 to visit friends in Portland. On their way home, they decided to cross the coastal mountains near Grant's Pass in the southwestern corner of Oregon and spend the night at Gold Beach, before continuing south the next day to San Francisco.

When they turned their silver Saab station wagon off the I-5 onto what looked like a decent highway, early snows had already softened the landscape and whitened the road, so they were well lost by the time they realized they must have taken a wrong turn onto one of the myriad logging trails that meander through those rugged hills. They hadn't noticed the sign in the corner of the map: *Not All Roads Advisable. Check Weather Conditions.*

No one knew their itinerary. Days went by before friends and co-workers reported them missing. A full week after they'd run their gas tank dry to keep warm, the search began for the family. It wasn't long before a local pilot found Kati waving an umbrella as she ran up and down a road beside a giant sos stamped in the snow. The mother and daughters were hungry and cold but otherwise fine. On Saturday morning, James Kim had struck off on his own to find help. The Kims had no GPS, but they calculated from their map that they were only four miles from the nearest settlement. He left at daybreak, promising to turn back before sunset if he found nothing. He hiked down the road a bit, then decided to take a shortcut down the drainage bed of Big Windy Creek, past old-growth trees towering two hundred feet and more, over boulders and fallen logs, through virgin wilderness it's relatively safe to say no human had ever walked before.

Despite the freezing temperatures, he gradually stripped off his light jacket, a grey sweatshirt, a red T-shirt, a wool sock, leaving them as markers for anyone who might follow. The searchers tracking him found the clothes and indentations in the snow where he might have slept. On Tuesday, they figured he was still alive. On Wednesday, December 6, eleven days after the family had been stranded in the snow, James's body was found in the icy waters of Big Windy Creek. He had died of hypothermia after walking more than sixteen miles. The map was wrong. The nearest town was thirty-three miles away.

Wayne and I are sitting in the car, munching on a late breakfast of smoked chinook we bought at a fish shop in Astoria, trying to decide where to go next.

We have turned south onto Route 101, the most westerly highway on the continental USA, and are in a little park overlooking the Pacific, our first glimpse of ocean. We pore over the map. A budding oenophile, Wayne is keen to visit the Willamette Valley. We'd both like to see Portland, which, though it is a city (a category we've renounced for this trip), claims the distinction of being the greenest in the United States.

"We could take 26 up to Portland," he says, "go through the Willamette, then back on the I-5 and cross over to the coast south of Eugene." His finger is tracing circles around Redwood National Park.

The weather is lowering and there are breakers on the beach.

"Do you ever think about what we'd do if we got lost?" I ask. "Would we both stay with the car or would one of us try to find a way out?" It's like that lifeboat question: who do you throw overboard first?

Wayne sidesteps neatly. "We're not going to get lost," he says.

I haven't told him about the Kims.

"But if we do," I insist. I don't use the word "lost" lightly. I'm a mother; in the years after the divorce when my sons and I would cycle around the city we'd moved to, we often found ourselves in unfamiliar territory. "We're not lost," I'd laugh, to ease their minds and my own. "We just don't know exactly where we are."

"If we get lost, we'll call somebody," Wayne says, tapping the cellphone.

It was the cellphone that located the Kims in the end. Most of the area they were travelling through was out of range of a communications tower, but when a cellphone that's turned on goes in and out of a service area, it "pings," leaving an automatic signature at the tower. By combing the records of the towers the Kims might have passed, two dogged engineers found a ping, and by determining the roads within line of sight of that tower, the search was narrowed to Bear Camp Road, where Kati and the girls were found.

Our cellphone is never on. No one has the number. We use it only to call out, so why drain the charge by keeping it powered? We've told our family and friends we're taking the long way home. We'll be back when we're back. We could be stranded on some snowbound road for a month, maybe more, before anyone would think of looking for us.

"Let's stay on the coast road," I say to Wayne, closing the map. "We can loop up to the Willamette and back, then carry on to California. I want to see Gold Beach."

"Great," says Wayne. "And I'd like to see some wine."

★   ★   ★

*W*INDING for just over a hundred miles on either side of the picturesque Willamette River (pronounced "Will-*ah*-met" locally), the Willamette Valley is a relatively new region for Oregon wines. As the main destination for the 500,000 settlers who travelled the Oregon Trail in the 1840s, the valley, with its lush vegetation and fertile soil, was taught to say beans and carrots long before it was allowed to say grapes. Now, like the longer-established Umpqua Valley farther south, it is best known for its Pinot Noirs. The soil is, apparently, Pinot-friendly. I'm a Merlot man, myself, but am not averse to stepping up to a good Pinot if I have to.

Our idea is to cut east on Route 47, do a short raid through the Yamhill Valley (an offshoot of the Willamette), pull into a few local vineyards for some late-season *dégustation,* and then cut back west to the coast with a trunk full of vintage red that will see us into California. Alas, what we drive through looks more like pork and onion country than the state's premier wine region. We pass a few fields of vines and the occasional sign for a winery—Elk Cove, Kramer Vineyards, Domaine Serene—but mostly it is dry-looking fields, tumbling barns, rusting tractors and riotous fencerows. It looks a lot like eastern Ontario.

Since the 1960s, the number of wineries in the Willamette region has risen from nine to more than a hundred, but they all seem either elsewhere or closed and boarded up for the winter, the growers probably in California or Chile, depleting the competition's stock. We do stop at a wine market near McMinnville, a well-appointed establishment called Bellevue, with racks and racks of wines, a tasting bar, and a friendly, talkative manager named Patrick, who guides me through a tasting of six very nice local bottles, none of the names of which I write down.

The wines I like come from the places I've been. The small house we rented in the Côtes-du-Rhône, with its peeling wooden shutters that rattled throughout the mistral and nearly drove Merilyn crazy; the ten days we spent driving around Tuscany in a small silver convertible; a month camped in a desert in northwestern Argentina, drinking local Malbec around the fire at night. I can recall the night I first tasted wine from Oregon: it was in Boston, in a small restaurant across the Common from Cheers. Now, every time I taste it, I think of that trip and the friends we were with. Wine, for me, is more than immediate pleasure: it evokes layers of past experience, just as travel does.

"We don't get many Oregon wines in eastern Canada," I tell him.

"One or two," he says. "From the bigger producers. There are some very nice local wines that no one outside the valley ever hears about."

When he has guided me down a row of six selections, he asks me which I preferred.

"I think the one from Amity Vineyards," I say, selecting a bottle at random.

Patrick nods owlishly. "One of the bigger producers," he says.

He goes on to complain of a visit he had earlier in the day from a man who was getting married and wanted to hold his reception at the Bellevue, so that his guests could "sample" a wide variety of Oregon wines for free. Patrick pours me a Merlot. "Oregonians still have a hard-liquor mentality," he says.

"All North America does," I say, sympathizing. "You don't see John Wayne or Frank Sinatra bellying up to the bar and ordering a glass of Chardonnay."

"'In a dirty glass,'" Patrick laughs.

Portland was settled mainly by Scandinavians who worked in the timber and fishing trades, and for whom a good night out meant drinking vast quantities of schnapps before going to midnight mass.

McMinnville was one of those towns that William Least Heat-Moon says were placed on the map to fill a blank space, until the surge in interest in Willamette Valley wines in the 1980s made it quite prosperous. Nevertheless, there were still objections when local vintners on the town council wanted to put a cluster of grapes on the municipal emblem.

Patrick rails at length against the tyranny of Pinot Noir and presses more glasses of Merlot upon me. I have the impression that sales of Merlot have dropped since the movie *Sideways*. I buy an armful of Merlots and a few Zinfandels, mostly because they are inexpensive and I like the labels. Merilyn buys a packet of smoked hazelnuts, and Patrick throws in a chipped tasting glass with "Amity Vineyards" printed on it. "When they're chipped," he says, "I can't use them."

When we leave, Merilyn has to drive.

"You'll have to navigate," Merilyn says resignedly as I climb into the passenger side after stowing the wine in the trunk. She loves driving and is always eager to do her share of it, the only impediment being my hopelessness as a navigator. Unlike me, she likes to know where she's going before she gets there. The general rule is, if my instinct tells me to go one way, we should probably turn in the opposite direction. This makes for some awkward moments at intersections. Merilyn, in contrast, has developed the art of navigation into a virtual science. She is always saying things like: "Three minutes from now you'll see a large water tower with 'Forest City' painted on it, and a sign saying *Denning 38;* turn east there." To which I reply: "Would that be left or right?"

From the plethora of maps and brochures tucked away under the seat, in the glove box, and in the little compartment in the door panel designed especially to hold used Kleenex tissues, chocolate bar wrappers, and little plastic bottles of body lotion pilfered from hotel bathrooms, I select a map at random and study it carefully.

"When you get to the Pacific Ocean," I say, "turn left."

★   ★   ★

*M*ONTHS before the trip, I had a thought: Must get some brochures, check out the Internet, make a plan. I like to know
what's ahead, even if it morphs into something else. At home, I'm
the one with the tidy desk, pens in a row, books squared, something
I spend an inordinate amount of time justifying. Sometimes, I insist,
a messy desk is not a sign of a creative mind; it's just a disgusting,
messy desk.

Wayne is always telling me to stop thinking about the papers that
need filing and concentrate on my writing. I did that in Vancouver—
there's a manuscript in the back seat to prove it—and my plan to plan
this trip got pushed aside until it was almost too late. At the last minute, I dashed off requests to the tourism offices of the states we'd hit
first: Washington, Oregon, California. We were packing the car when
the bulging envelopes arrived.

From the tub in the Cannery Pier Hotel, I'd read the brochures
aloud to Wayne, who was sipping wine in the adjoining bedroom.
Along the Oregon coast, apparently, it's geology that dominates. "Listen to this," I called: "'Cannon Beach: nine miles of wide, walkable
beach . . . scenic beauty of the sea stacks offshore and headlands
onshore . . . sea creatures in tide pools.' There's something called Haystack Rock, the third-largest coastal monolith in the world, whatever
that is."

"Sounds like a garage band."

I ignored him and went on to the fine print. "A monolith is a geological feature consisting of a single massive stone. Says here the
Haystack is a 235-foot-high chunk of basalt. More than two thousand
seabirds nest on it."

I had his attention now. "Tufted puffin. Pigeon guillemot. Have we
seen those?"

I may be the organized one, but Wayne is better at keeping up his
life list. If I had my way, I'd make a note *every* time I met a bird, not
just the first sighting. I remember birding with Roger Tory Peterson

one cold, November day near his home in Old Lyme, Connecticut. I
drove us to the shore; he was over eighty and his wife wouldn't let
him take the wheel. "He'll get distracted by a bird and end up in the
Atlantic," she said. The wind off the ocean was bone-sharp; the clouds,
a weight overhead. I scanned the skies. Not much to see, I was thinking, when he raised his binoculars to focus on some ring-billed gulls
fighting over what looked like a french fry on the wharf. "I love gulls,"
he sighed.

But there aren't even gulls flying when we get to Cannon Beach.
The wind is blustery and the rain has started up again. I had visions of
wandering among the tide pools at the base of the Haystack, through
what the brochures call the Marine Garden, a 300-foot radius rich
with sea stars, iridescent anemones, and idiosyncratic crabs, creatures
so delicate that the whole assemblage could be obliterated in an hour
by careless tourists. "Walk only on bare rock," the brochure warns.
"Barnacles are animals too!"

No need to worry about dealing a death blow to a barnacle today. I
roll down the window to take a picture—the sun is shafting out from
under the clouds, a deadly, sulphurous yellow that defines the word
"inhospitable."

Monoliths rise from mercury waves all down the coast. Goonies
Rock. Arch Point. Otter Rock. Their slick shapes call out to be named.
Not far from where we turn back onto the coastal highway from our
Willamette detour is Proposal Rock, so named because some turn-of-
the-last-century romantic went down on one knee to a fair maiden in
the scrubby forest that sits like a bad toupée on top. To get up there,
not only do you have to climb a steep cliff, you have to cross a wide,
cold creek with your pant legs rolled and skirts hitched. How romantic is that?

After our detour to the Willamette, the weather does not improve.
Wayne dozes while I squint through the windshield at the central
part of Oregon's coastal highway. The waves are gelid, whipped into

grey foam against the monoliths. On a sunny day in mid-July, these beaches must be a lovers' delight, but in December, in a storm, they fill me with despair, even though I'm warm and dry and safe in our little car. At Cape Foulweather, the breakers pound as though they mean to end the world. And maybe they will. More than once, the Tillamook Rock Lighthouse, nicknamed Terrible Tilly, has had her light smashed by rocks flung 133 feet up from the sea floor by the waves. And then there's the Devil's Punch Bowl, an enormous basin formed when the roofs of two sea caves collapsed along this shore.

I keep my eyes on the road, on the endless slap-slap of the wipers. If we want to see the splendours of the Oregon Coastal Highway, we'll have to come back. In July. In a heat wave. In a convertible. I'll file the brochures. Planning will be a breeze.

★   ★   ★

*W*ITH the tapioca sun a pale, lucid orb in the upper right quadrant of the windshield and the Pacific Ocean on our starboard side, Merilyn is assured that we are heading due south, and I can relax. The effects of the wine are wearing thin.

"You were snoring," Merilyn says comfortably.

"I wasn't asleep," I protest. Navigator falling asleep is a grave offence for which we have yet to establish a suitable punishment. "Name the next five towns we'll pass through" has been suggested. "Drink less wine" has also come up. We've sent it to arbitration. Driver falling asleep is a much graver lapse, and it is part of the passenger's duties to prevent it, hence the stricture against a nodding navigator.

"Then you were awake and snoring," she says, "which is worse."

"Where are we?" Wrong question, coming from the navigator.

"Coming up to Florence," Merilyn says.

I look at the map. This entire coastline seems made up of one protected area after another: Beachside State Recreation Site, Yachats State Recreation Area, Neptune State Scenic Viewpoint, Carl G. Washburne Memorial State Park. To our left is the Siuslaw National Forest, a vast green area on the map that connects a little farther south with Elliott State Forest. If it is true that only about 15 per cent of American wilderness is protected by legislated parkland, most of that must be concentrated here, along the Pacific coast.

We are, I note aloud, passing through some very tall trees. They soar above us like rockets, their noses vanishing out of sight, their tangled, exposed roots trailing on the ground like ribbons of exhausted fuel. They completely dwarf the notion of what we easterners think when we think *tree*. At home, a log cabin might be made from forty logs; here, it seems, one log would make forty cabins.

The forest is primarily Douglas-fir, Sitka spruce, western hemlock, western red cedar, and tanoak. Every now and then we pass a stump that seems broad enough to build a house on, and I am rather surprised no one has. In fact, the nascent hobbit in me wonders if a person could simply carve out a western red cedar to make a house. A tree needs only 10 per cent of its outer cambium layers, a few dozen rings, and its bark, and it will keep sending sap up to its branches. A fifty-seven-foot-diameter sugar pine would give about fifteen hundred square feet of floor space. In fact, carving a house into a tree would seem to make more sense than felling the tree, sawing the wood into boards, and then reassembling the boards to make a house.

William Least Heat-Moon looked down this highway and saw four hundred miles of "clapboard-by-the-sea motels, Jolly Whaler buffets and clear-cut mountain slopes with tall stumps bleached into tombstones by the salt wind." Having read *Blue Highways*, I rather expected the coast of Oregon to be shoulder-to-shoulder cottages jammed between towns and quaint outports and former logging camps—more industrious, somehow. Compared with the megacity we drove through yesterday, this stretch seems almost deserted. To our right, glinting between gigantic trunks, is the sluggish ocean with its soupy light, into which we occasionally emerge when the highway swerves out around a scree of fallen rock and scrub. Then we hear the sound of surf and gulls. Always, to our left, the sentinel forest.

The trees are second-growth, of course, and there is a leafy under-storey of swordfern, salal, and huckleberry, encouraged by gaps in the forest canopy; their light-green leaves make the woods appear brighter and less cathedral-like than David Douglas found them in 1825. But there persists nevertheless an alluring sense of vastness, of endless-ness, of forest everlasting, of inexhaustible wilderness that was new and exhilarating to Douglas because it had ceased to exist in Europe long before the dawn of Romanticism, when nature was extolled as the model and source of all human virtues. It was that Romantic notion that had sent Douglas and Lewis and Clark and hundreds like them to places like this, to the ends of the earth, to find the spots on the globe where nature still reigned like an infinite deity, forever and aye, world without end, amen.

Such infinitude was a deception, of course, as these second-growth forests attest, bereft as they now are of wolves and cougars and grizzlies and spotted owls. Douglas and Lewis and Clark lived in a Romantic era—the whole notion of exploration is romantic—and Romanticism has more to do with what is going on in our own solip-sistic imaginations than it does with what exists on the west coast of North America.

WET SNOW adheres to our windshield as we approach North Bend, halfway down the Oregon Coast. We decide to look for a place to spend the night. A few motels appear on the right, and one of them looks clean and tastefully appointed. The front is well lit, the units seem cheerfully painted, the parking lot isn't cracked and weedy.

"That one seems nice," Merilyn says.

We drive on. This is how we choose a motel: we drive until just after it's too dark to see anything that isn't lit up; only then do we begin to watch for likely candidates. When we see one that looks good, we slow down and peer at it as we drive by, then continue on down the high-way for another ten or twenty minutes looking for something better. Then we give up, turn around and go back. This time, we drive all the way through North Bend to see if there is some kind of quaint inn on the waterfront, but the town's main drag offers up only factory outlets and drugstores. A sign over one of the shops says *Last Chance Liquors, Open 24 Hrs.* We turn back.

Merilyn is now the designated motel maven. I wait in the car while she goes into the office to see about a room. A large camper van is parked beside me. A rather well-padded woman sits in the passenger seat with a small dog on her lap, and both the woman and the dog stare at me through the window. Whenever I turn my head toward them the dog begins to yap, a high-pitched, shrill, infuriating sound that penetrates our car like an insane bell captain's cab whistle. The woman glares at me as though it is my fault the dog has gone berserk.

Merilyn seems to be taking a long time, which I assume to mean that there is a room available and she is negotiating the rate. Maybe there are several rooms and she is getting the keys to all of them and lining up an inspection. I smile at the woman, deliberately baring my teeth, which sends the dog into renewed paroxysms of demented fury. Then Merilyn comes back smiling and dangles a key from a square of masonite.

"What a lovely woman," she says, meaning the woman in the motel office, with whom I imagine she has been sharing recipes for morning glory muffins. "Our room has a view of the harbour. What's with the dog?"

★　★　★

*M*OTELS, by their nature, always seem a bit seedy, perhaps because they slink so close to the ground.

Wayne didn't like the looks of the one I pointed out as we entered North Bend—too vacant, too old-fashioned, he said—but I am happy when we turn around and go back. I have a good feeling about the place, which intensifies when I notice the 1950s cigarette machine outside the office door. It looks as though it still works.

"Betty," the woman behind the counter says. She has a broad face with poor skin, the pores large and the colour wanting oxygen. Her sweater is pilled, and the office smells of disinfectant. "They call me Bay Bridge Betty. I've owned this place for twenty-two years." She laughs. "I mean forty-four. See what happens when you get older?"

She takes down the key for number 15—"My best room," she says— and leads me down the narrow cement walkway, limping a little, as though her feet hurt. In the daylight, she tells me, we'll be able to see Coos Bay.

"I don't know what's wrong. It's never been so slow," she says, fitting the key into the lock. Only two other rooms are taken, one by a trucker, the other by an eighty-seven-year-old woman who comes up from California every winter. Her car is parked at an alarming angle outside her door, as if it had been heading over the cliff into the sea and she'd managed to stop it at the last minute.

"The woman's husband is gone," Bay Bridge Betty says in a way that makes me wonder if it was his choice or hers. "I promised to see to his wife. She's hemming some pants for me right now." I'm afraid she's going to take me to the room and show me the woman as proof, but she carries on to room number 15, where she flicks on the light switches and tugs at the flowered bedspread. "She makes me blankets, too. I do what I can for her."

The room is clean, perfectly adequate. Two neat double beds, a decidedly small-screen television, a long credenza, a small table and chair by the window. Standard motel fare. I take it without a quibble. Back in the office, I sign the register and hand her enough bills to cover the price she quotes, which isn't much. She slides the money into a drawer.

"Thank you," she says quietly. "We need you tonight."

FOR REASONS I don't quite understand—maybe it was the cigarette machine—I'm thinking of my father. He would have loved it here. He was a coffee lover and all through Washington and Oregon I've been noticing drive-through espresso bars, pert little sheds set off from the road where drivers pull up to windows to get their caffeine fix, coffee kiosks with names like Good to Go, Jumpin' Java, and Hail Mary's Espresso.

If there are drive-through banks, drive-through weddings and divorces, drive-through meals, why not drive-through espresso bars? Motor Moka was apparently the first: it opened in Portland in 1992. Now there's one every mile, or so it seems. Back home, there are only Starbucks, Second Cup, and Coffee & Company, all catering to the sit-down crowd, and Tim Hortons, where doughnuts are the draw as much as coffee. Canadians aren't in such a rush, I guess, at least not yet.

Tim Hortons (which used to be Tim Horton's) offered the original roadside cup of joe. The first outlet opened in Hamilton, Ontario, in 1964, and by 1967 it was a chain. But it was Starbucks that turned coffee into a gold mine. In 1971, three friends in Seattle—an English teacher, a history teacher, and a writer—decided to go into the coffee roasting business, selling the beans retail. The writer, Gordon Bowker, loved the novel *Moby-Dick* and wanted to call their new enterprise Pequod after the ship in Melville's story.

"Who would drink a cup of something called Pee-quod?" asks Wayne.

"I guess that's why in the end they named it after the *Pequod*'s first mate, Starbuck."

Sixteen years later, the trio sold out to Howard Schultz, who had been struck by the espresso culture during a trip to Italy. He added baristas to the bean sales and started building shops all over the country until today there are more than eleven thousand stores in the United States and another five thousand in forty-four countries, compared with a paltry two thousand for Tim Hortons. Schultz wasn't interested only in shilling coffee: his whole idea with Starbucks was to create a "third place," a spot other than home or work where people could relax with friends and a cup of good coffee. For the people of Oregon, that third place seems to be their cars.

"Oregoners sure must drink a lot of coffee."

"Oregonians, surely," Wayne suggests. We've settled in our motel room overlooking the bay, he with the crossword in the local paper, me with the computer.

"True or false?" I ask. "Coffee consumption is higher than it's ever been. Americans drink more coffee than Canadians."

"True," he says, "on both counts. Now can you unplug the computer, please, and plug in the kettle? I'd like a cup of tea."

"False. On both counts. Can you believe this? Coffee consumption in the United States today is *half* what it was in the 1940s. In 1946 these people were drinking forty-six-plus gallons each per year, compared with somewhere around twenty-five gallons today."

"What happened in the Forties? Besides the war."

"I'll give you a clue: 'Good to the last drop.'"

"Peak oil?" he says. "Hang-gliding?"

"No, you goose. Instant coffee."

My father invented instant coffee. A clever man without much formal education but with a creative imagination and a practical streak, he came up with all kinds of things he never patented: cupboard doors that hinged upward so you'd never bump your head, fast-and-easy comma-shaped bathroom towel hangers, and coffee you could make in a second just by adding boiling water. For months, he perked pot after pot of strong coffee, experimenting with ways of dehydrating the brew without ruining the flavour. He was still at the sticky-goo stage when Maxwell House came on the market with its fine powder. It was an instant hit. Packets of Maxwell House were put in soldiers' mess kits, and when they came home, that's what they wanted on the breakfast table—and in the lunchroom and at their local diner. Far from being chagrined that some American company had beaten him to the punch, my father wouldn't have anything but Maxwell House instant coffee in the house. "Those Americans," he would say, shaking his head. They were even smarter than he was.

But why the downturn in coffee consumption since the 1950s? There was no equal and opposite spike in tea drinking: tea has held onto its steady 10 per cent. The difference was soda pop. In 1947, Americans consumed around eleven gallons per person; now that's up over fifty.

Coffee hit its century low in 1995. Since then, it has been regaining ground, no doubt thanks to these drive-throughs. Today, 167 million Americans, 80 per cent of adults, say they sometimes drink coffee. The same proportion of Canadians claim an occasion cup of joe. But ask them if they drink it regularly, and 63 per cent of Canadians over the age of eighteen will admit to a daily habit, compared with only 49 per cent in the United States.

I have a hard time wrapping my mind around the notion of Canada as a nation of coffee swillers. Clearly coffee is an American drink—isn't it? It was the mainstay of settlers travelling the Oregon Trail, one of the primary overland migration routes to the West. Not all the wagon trains that left Independence, Missouri, made it as far as their final destination in the Willamette Valley—some cut off onto the Mormon Trail or the California Trail—but those settlers who did littered the landscape with names that attested to their preference in hot beverages. On the map of Oregon alone, I find Coffee Creek, Coffee Lake, Coffee Butte, Coffee Gap, Coffee Chute, Coffee Island as well as Coffee Pot Island, Coffeepot Crater, Coffeepot Basin, and Coffeepot Flat, more coffee place names than can be found in the entire 3.8 million square miles that is Canada.

Still, it's hard to argue with statistics and the *Coffee News,* the free weekly we picked up when we stopped for our daily decafs. Distributed at coffee shops in 225 cities in the United States every week, as well as in thirty countries around the world, *Coffee News* is the largest franchised publication in the world. With such hyperbole, it has to be American, right? No. It was started in Winnipeg, Manitoba, in 1988 by Jean Daum, a woman sitting alone during her coffee break with nothing to read but the sugar packets.

"How about a cup of coffee?" I call across the double double beds to Wayne. "I think we're out of tea."

I've set up a makeshift kitchen on top of the credenza: our two red plates, our travel mugs, the folding leather case with a single setting of silver flatware, a salesman's sample from the last century that Wayne bought me at an antique store one Christmas, in answer to my complaint that the cutlery in most restaurants might as well be plastic for all the heft it has in the hand. Lined up beside the coffee, cream, and sugar are my oatcakes and Wayne's Raisin Bran for breakfast, a couple of apples, the local hazelnuts I bought at the wine-tasting shop, and the last of the smoked chinook.

"Got any cookies?"

"Just oatcakes."

"Coffee's fine."

The pound of Kicking Horse decaf we bought because it was roasted near the headwaters of the Columbia is almost gone. I make us each a cup with the Melitta drip filter we always carry, boiling water in the kettle that I borrowed from Betty. I think of the settlers huddling around their fires within the ring of their prairie schooners, of the Union soldiers stirring a few crushed beans into their tin cups of water. Those men received eight pounds of roasted beans or ten pounds of green beans with each hundred pounds of rations. Confederate soldiers were reduced to drinking chicory, so whenever the two armies crossed, there would be an active trade: southern tobacco for northern coffee beans. When they bivouacked at night, writes John Billings, a Union veteran, in his memoir, *Hardtack and Coffee*, "the little campfires, rapidly increasing to hundreds in number, would shoot up along the hills and plains, and as if by magic, acres of territory would be illuminous with them. Soon they would be surrounded by the soldiers, who made it an inevitable rule to cook their coffee first."

I hand Wayne his coffee. I wonder if he knows the old Abyssinian proverb: When a woman gives a man coffee, it is a way of showing her desire. Maybe Anthony Capella made that up. I copied it from his novel *The Various Flavours of Coffee*, an erotic love story set in *fin-de-siècle*

London about a feckless dandy who takes a job with a coffee merchant and falls in love with the boss's daughter. His only talent is his palate: he's hired to create a vocabulary of coffee to rival that of wine—the hot nut aroma of a Java as water first hits the beans; the beeswax-on-leather aftertaste of a Yemeni mocha; the earthy, claylike flavours of coffees from Africa that evoke the stamp of naked feet on sun-baked ground.

Here in the American Northwest, coffee seems to be going the same way as alcohol in other ways, too. Drive-through espresso shacks have started offering hot girls along with their hot java. New joints are springing up that cater particularly to the male coffee aficionado: Bikini Espresso, the Sweet Spot. The staff are all female, young, and pretty. The service windows are elevated so that customers can look in at the short skirts and high heels. Some of the servers take time to fling a leg over the serving bar or strike a Playmate pose. They flirt, blow kisses, and vamp for the customers. At Cowgirls, the barista may be wearing a pink see-through negligee with matching panties. I've read there's talk of a Thong Thursday, a Saran-Wrap Saturday. Never satisfied with steak, they want their sizzle, too.

It's only Friday. I'm wearing my silk dressing gown, and not much else. "You want honey with that?" I purr.

"Sure," Wayne says, and puts down the crossword.

4 / EUREKA! CALIFORNIA

W<small>E</small> thought western red cedars were big trees, but when we cross into northern California we make the acquaintance of some true giants. Redwoods *(Sequoia sempervirens)* are a California specialty: few of them grow outside the state. In Redwood National Park, we leave the car and walk into the forest with our binoculars, though most of the birds are in the canopy, hundreds of feet above our heads. Only a few chestnut-backed chickadees and golden-crowned kinglets twitter in the lower branches. After a short stroll along what looks like an old logging road, we return to the car and drive to another parking area, where, when I open the car door, a Steller's jay perches on it a few inches from my head and peers expectantly into my face. Its feathers are a brilliant, iridescent blue that pulses against the forest's dark green. I try to figure out if it is so innocent of people that it is unafraid, or if it is so accustomed to people that it associates me with food, but it isn't giving me any clues. In return, I don't give it any food.

The park encompasses more than 150 square miles of old-growth coastal redwoods, about half those left on the planet. A century and a half ago, there were eight thousand square miles of old-growth red-wood forest in California alone, which means 99.5 per cent of the original dawn forest has been cut. Redwoods, also known as sequoias, grow to fantastic sizes and live for millennia. The largest tree in the world, the General Sherman in Sequoia National Park, is a redwood; its base is 102.5 feet in circumference, and it is thought to be 2,700 years old. The trees here in Redwood National Park are slightly smaller and younger, probably no more than 1,500 years old, mere saplings when Clovis drove the Visigoths out of France.

I gently close the car door and the Steller's jay flies to a nearby shrub and scolds me. There's a path and we follow it, eventually coming to the first big tree. It's fifty feet around if it's an inch, and so heavy it appears to be sinking around its own root ball, the way an obese man's ankles sink around his shoe tops. There isn't much we can do with it except stare, so we stare at it, then turn and follow the path deeper into the woods. This is a mistake, as there are paths bifurcating off the main path and we stumble along them, staring mostly up at the trees, until quite soon we are no longer certain how to get back to the car. Well, Merilyn is certain, but I insist on a different path and she follows under protest until neither of us knows where we are.

Merilyn has an apple and a packet of trail mix in her shoulder bag, and there is a path of sorts to follow. Walking through a forest, even on a path, is infinitely better than driving through it, especially if part of the purpose of the experience is to get lost. You can get lost faster, and stay lost longer. By the time we have meandered on intersecting paths for half an hour, I am hopelessly turned around, though I don't admit it, especially when the path takes us to the road.

"The car park is to the left," I say confidently.

"Then we should go right, right?" Merilyn says.

"Left," I say firmly.

"Let's just go right until we round that curve," Merilyn says. "If there's no car park, we'll turn around and come back."

Of course, the car park is around the curve. There is the traitorous Echo, waiting where it shouldn't be. I check the plates before inserting the key, but it's our car, all right. Merilyn somewhat pointedly asks me if I would like to drive.

Sticking to the coastline, we pass more big trees, a lot of seaside villages, brightly painted clapboard houses huddled against the rugged coastline. We encounter more cold, light drizzle, and a seaward wind that makes the fishing boats tethered in the harbours strain and rear against their hawsers like startled stallions. The water looks cold and thick. On the radio, we listen to a weather report that warns of snow squalls higher up in the mountains, with accumulations of two to three feet. Merilyn and I congratulate ourselves on having stayed by the water instead of cutting inland at Eugene, though at some point, we realize, we are going to have to turn east.

We pass a sign: *Eureka 10 miles.*

"I have a cousin in Eureka!" Merilyn announces excitedly, the way one might say, "Oh, I forgot to tell you, I won the Nobel Prize last night!"

"His name is Russell Thompson. He moved down to Los Angeles after the war and got into the movies, and now he's retired to Eureka!" I gather it's hard to pronounce Eureka without following it with an exclamation mark.

"Great!" I say. "Let's drop in to say hello!"

★   ★   ★

*M*Y American cousin is really my second or third cousin, I can never figure out which. He and my father shared a set of grandparents. We're not close, but we're blood.

My father, like many men, didn't seem to care much for the family he came from. They lived in Toronto, about an hour and a half away. We'd visit his mother and his brother, who lived in the apartment next to hers, almost every week. The air in the car was always brittle as we drove into the city and still edgy as we came out. Family put my father in a foul mood.

The only relatives he talked about with pleasure were Russell and Russell's sister, Dorothy, cousins he spent weekends with as a boy. Russell's birthday was in the same month as Dad's, and every March, the phone would ring long-distance. "It's Russell!" my mother would call out, breathless—"From California!"—and my father would rush to the phone as if he expected to win a round-the-world cruise.

Dorothy's birthday is the same day as mine, so I call her every September. She is full of stories: about another cousin who played piano in a sheet-music store and took off for San Francisco to play professionally; about the time Russell drove back to Ontario from California in a Cadillac convertible, top down all the way.

My American Cousin, the movie, opens with the cousin barrelling up to the family homestead in a flashy red convertible. His name is Butch and he is darkly sexy and safely rebellious in that James Dean kind of way. He's come to spend the summer in Canada, a place where NOTHING EVER HAPPENS, as the young female protagonist writes in bold across her diary. I felt the same way: real life happened somewhere else, somewhere like California.

Russell was lean and handsome, a lion tamer. In the eight-by-ten glossy in my parents' album, he wears skin-tight trousers, knee-high boots, and a white cutaway, and he is flourishing a top hat. I think he might be carrying a whip. When my parents talked about him, the conversation always started, "Russell, he's in the movies in California . . ."

What could be more glamorous than that? I met Russell only once, the summer I was thirteen. He drove up to Canada, and we visited him at Dorothy's house in the woods. The day was hot and clear, the water as blue as the ocean. We water-skied, my first time, and somehow the feeling of standing on the water, zipping across the waves, is what comes to me even now when I hear the word "California."

Since my father died, Russell has been sending me photographs, of himself and my father when they were kids, and later as soldiers, fighting for different countries. After the war, Russell hosted a Saturday-morning radio show on the Armed Forces Radio Service,

Let's Pretend with Uncle Russ. He sends glossies of himself leaning into a microphone with some famous actress or crooner glancing over at him with wry affection. From radio, he moved to television: he was a pirate on *The Shirley Temple Show,* a dead man on *Gunsmoke.* But it was on *Ozzie and Harriet* that he found his home. After the summer we met, he sent me an autographed picture of Ricky Nelson, signed "To Merilyn with love."

I haven't told Russell I would be travelling down this coast. I wasn't sure I wanted the old man he'd surely become to replace the golden Russell of my California dreams. But once I'd made the phone call, heard his voice, so rich and deep, that hint of a laugh waiting to split open wide, I couldn't wait.

"Eureka's not far," I say to Wayne. "Russell says we'll be there in twenty minutes."

*   *   *

*W*HY do I find the name Eureka so familiar? Yes, it's what Archimedes is supposed to have shouted when he discovered the trick of measuring the volume of an irregularly shaped object: "Eureka!" he exclaimed, jumping out of the bath: "I've got it!" But I don't think that's what's stuck in my mind.

Eureka (without the exclamation mark) is a small city on Humboldt Bay, in the heart of California's big-tree country; it got its name when gold was discovered by some classically trained forty-niner in nearby Trinity River during the California bonanza. The 1849 gold rush defined this part of California, draining so many people from southern regions that in one year the population of Los Angeles dropped from 6,000 to 1,600 and the population of San Francisco jumped from 800 to 35,000.

Mining and logging soon destroyed the forests around Eureka and the rivers that drained into Humboldt Bay. When the local natives, the Wiyot, protested the degradation, the citizens of Eureka hit upon a solution. In 1860, the local newspaper, the *Humboldt Times,* proclaimed that "for the past four years we have advocated two... alternatives to ridding our country of Indians: either remove them to some reservation or kill them." Eureka went for the second alternative. A group of citizens calling themselves the Humboldt Volunteers rowed out to a Wiyot village on Indian Island and slaughtered most of the Wiyot who were there celebrating in their annual World Renewal.

Bret Harte, then a twenty-four-year-old reporter for the *Humboldt Times,* wrote an account of the incident: "A more shocking and revolting spectacle never was exhibited to the eyes of a Christian and civilized people. Women wrinkled and decrepit weltering in blood, their brains dashed out and dabbled with their long, grey hair. Infants scarcely a span along, with their faces cloven with hatchets and their bodies ghastly with wounds."

Without the Wiyot to protest, the degradation continued. By the 1880s, when the gold ran out, there were eighteen sawmills ringing the bay, and the city was supplying lumber to most of the northern coast. So much sawdust was dumped into Humboldt Bay that salmon stopped spawning in the Trinity River. Scientists are still working on ways to get them back.

Scientists! That's how I know Eureka! A few years ago, the Sci Fi Channel aired a series called *Eureka.* The premise of the show was that the American government was secretly hiding all of its scientific geniuses in Eureka, not an easy secret to keep since the scientists kept inventing things like antimatter and telekinetic computers. In the series, things are always going awry. For example, in one episode, when they create a *Star Trek*–like transporter (it worked by decoding a person's DNA in one place and recoding it somewhere else minus the person's clothes, a complication not thought of by Gene Roddenberry), they inadvertently produce an über-Einstein kid who could launch missiles just by thinking about them.

"Did your cousin ever do television?" I ask Merilyn.

"Yes," she replies, getting a faraway look in her eye as if she's just turned on the old black-and-white set. "He was a regular on *Ozzie and Harriet.*"

I never really liked *Ozzie and Harriet,* but I don't tell Merilyn that. Ricky Nelson wasn't my idea of a rock star. I was a *Leave It to Beaver* kind of guy. But the difference was one of neighbourhood, not lifestyle. Like most kids who grew up in the Fifties, I formed my idea of what a typical North American family was supposed to be like from watching *Ozzie and Harriet, Father Knows Best, Leave It to Beaver,* and *My Three Sons.* Fathers who wore suits to work, mothers who were rarely seen outside the kitchen, children who dutifully did their homework on desks in their immaculate bedrooms and then came downstairs for roast beef dinners during which the problems of the day were calmly discussed, debated, and solved. Parents who listened to their children, went with them to basketball games, took an active interest in their lives. It was our version of the American Dream. Oddly, the fact that I didn't know a single real family that remotely resembled these television families didn't prevent me from believing that there was something wrong with *my* family, where homework was done wherever I could clear a spot, dinner was a half-hour argument over macaroni and cheese or fried bologna, and no one ever listened to anyone, least of all me. I thought, as I was meant to think, that it was us, not the Cleavers or the Nelsons, and definitely not America, who failed to measure up to reality.

"Did your cousin know the Beav?" I ask Merilyn.

"I don't think so," she says.

"That's okay, we'll go see him anyway."

★　★　★

MY American cousin greets us at the door of the neat olive-and-cream clapboard house behind its matching picket fence. He's wearing a red plaid shirt, the kind farmers and lumberjacks buy at Stedmans, and a comfy zip-up jacket.

"Russell?"

"And which one are you?" he asks, throwing his arms around me.

"Number three." The one who was rarely noticed, who got away with everything.

"You look like your grandmother Margaret."

Russell's hair is still black. He's wearing oversized rose-tinted glasses. I peer into his face, looking for my father, and I see him, a little. The dark almond eyes; the long coffin of a face. He speaks in CBC tones, sonorous and reassuring, as he leads us along a hall to his living room, which should be the dining room, since it gives onto the kitchen.

"The living room's full of old stuff," he apologizes, waving a hand at a pair of French doors. I glimpse what looks like a plush fainting couch.

We sit on a standard-issue sofa while he eases into his recliner. There is something odd about the floor: it doesn't meet the walls. Russell decided to cover the old linoleum flooring with new hardwood, which he bought at a Home Depot and installed himself. "But I didn't measure the room right so I didn't buy enough wood," he shrugs, as if he's talking about cocktail olives or soda water for the highballs. He started laying the floor in the middle and worked his way out, leaving a gap around the walls. He'll fill it in later, he says, "when I get around to buying more wood." Sitting on the couch feels like floating on a large raft in a very small pond.

The television is on. I watch the credits of a show, thinking I'll see Russell's name. That's what we used to do after an episode of *Perry Mason* or *Ozzie and Harriet*.

"I played a ringmaster," he laughs, when I tell him I always thought he was a lion tamer. "That was on Ozzie's show. The producer for *Perry Mason* saw it and asked if I'd play the same part in a mystery about the circus."

Russell is modest. Too modest for an American. It gives him away. I want him to flaunt a little. He knew Lucille Ball! Frank Sinatra! Frankie Laine!

I ask him if he's doing any acting, hoping like a thirteen-year-old that he knows Tom Cruise, maybe, or Julia Roberts.

"I just finished a movie," he says. "A small part. I didn't think much of it, to tell you the truth. The language—!" He shakes his head. I have no idea how old he is. Over eighty, I'd guess. If my father were alive, he'd be eighty-eight.

"Whatever happened to Ricky Nelson, do you know?" I ask.

"Died in a plane crash. Awful thing."

Russell gets up and goes into the kitchen to put on water for tea. He married a Japanese woman, Chiyomi, who owns Mad Hatter's Tea Party, a tea shop with banks of tea tins against the wall and a few small tables where she serves scones and fancy desserts. She creates her own teas: Russell offers us a selection, and Wayne chooses the Baby Grey.

The kitchen is immaculate. I feel comfortable here, though there is something odd about this room, too. There's not the slightest hint that food has ever been allowed, let alone prepared, in this kitchen: no pots hang from hooks over the island, no kettle on the countertop, no bouquet of spatulas and wooden spoons beside the stove. It is like a kitchen from the set of one of the commercials on *The Garry Moore Show,* or from *Ozzie and Harriet.* A fake kitchen. I half expect the back wall to open onto scrims.

The transistor radio above the sink is real, though. It's tuned to a show-tunes station. We stand awkwardly, waiting for the water to boil. We've gone over all the common ground, more than once. There doesn't seem much more to say. Then a song from the Forties comes on. Suddenly, Russell sweeps me into his arms and we swirl around the brightly lit kitchen, hands clasped, cheeks lightly touching, dancing in perfect step.

"Why don't you come home?" I whisper in his ear.

"I'd like to," he says, almost like singing, "but only if I could drive all the way in my Cadillac convertible."

★　★　★

*W*E leave Chiyomi's tea shop with a Christmas gift bag of Baby Grey, Chiyomi's version of traditional Earl Grey, which includes petals of a blue flower that reminds me of the Steller's jay we saw in the redwoods.

Tea, wine, smoked salmon; without really planning it, we are accumulating the makings of a fine Christmas Eve meal. The question is, Where we will be having it? Merilyn, unwilling to leave Christmas entirely to fate, has booked us for Christmas dinner at the El Tovar Hotel, on the south rim of the Grand Canyon. Since this is the twenty-third of December, we have what is left of today and tomorrow to get from northern California to central Arizona.

Rather than continue down the San Andreas Fault to San Francisco, we decide to cross the Coast Mountains here in the north and continue down the Central Valley at least as far as Sacramento, then cut over to one of the other highlighted routes on Merilyn's map, perhaps the one that would take us down through Yosemite and Death Valley to Las Vegas. We'll make that decision when we get there.

Before we left Eureka, Russell checked the weather report for the mountains and told us he had a spare bedroom we were welcome to use.

"Does it have a floor?" Merilyn asked.

Chiyomi laughed.

"What's a bit of snow," I said breezily, and though Merilyn seemed inclined to stay, we climbed into the Echo and headed up into the mountains.

The 299 to Redding is a red highway, which means it is not subject to seasonal closings. Merilyn checked. It follows the Trinity River, travelling against the current from Humboldt Bay up to Trinity Lake, a resort-ringed reservoir created high in the mountains by Trinity Dam.

Hordes of forty-niners swarmed to the Trinity River when California was nothing but a northern extension of Mexico's Baja province. I imagine its banks lined with grizzled prospectors swishing gravel in tin pie plates, but in fact, this roadbed was excavated by a nefarious practice known as hydraulic mining. Rushing water from the river was funnelled into a metal pipe coupled to a canvas hose with a nozzle that, when turned on, shot water at the rate of 150 cubic feet per second. The nozzle was mounted on a tripod like a Gatling gun and trained on the riverbank in order to wash thousands of tons of rock and paleo-gravels, not to mention trees, sod, insects, and small mammals, into sluices from which the debris, theoretically minus its gold, sloshed into the river, clogging its passage, destroying salmon redds (spawning beds), making outlets such as Humboldt Bay unnavigable, and in some places raising the riverbed by as much as sixty feet. Hydraulic mining was officially banned in the late 1800s, but it went on much later than that. Canadian novelist Michael Ondaatje writes in *Divisadero* that as late as the 1940s there were still "five thousand full-time gold miners along the banks of the Yuba and Russian rivers," using Anaconda hoses and gas-fuelled dredges "to suck up whatever remained on the river bottoms."

We are travelling through the Shasta-Trinity National Forest. I see the sign and wonder if, in the daylight, we'd be able to see Mount Shasta. At 14,179 feet, it is the second-highest peak in the Cascades. It is snowing now, suddenly—heavy, wet flakes that cling to our windshield. Avalanche snow. We can see only a few feet ahead of us as the road twists and corkscrews up the mountains. At Weaverville, we briefly consider a detour to Trinity Lake, but most of the resorts are seasonal, and, we tell ourselves, those that are open would have long ago been booked for Christmas. We press on to Redding, heading down the eastern slopes into the Central Valley, a seventy-five-mile-wide fertile plain squeezed in the centre of the state between the Coast Mountains to the west and the Sierra Nevadas to the east, with the Cascades and Mount Shasta at the top like a stern paddler at the high end of a very long canoe.

Redding, a city of some hundred thousand souls, is bigger than we expect, too big to tackle this late at night. We turn south onto the I-5, rejoining it for the first time since Washington. All we want is a place to sleep that will be easy to get to and out of in the morning. Soon we are well south of Redding.

"Anderson. That looks small. Surely there'll be something nice and reasonable here," Merilyn says.

She checks out a few chain motels, but with the storm, no one is offering a discount tonight. We settle at last into the Valley Inn, which is privately owned but looks as though in happier times it used to be a Days Inn. The place is so unremarkably dreary that it could stand for all cheap motels everywhere: one bed, one lamp, one reproduction painting (usually Van Gogh's *Starry Night,* sometimes Monet's *Yellow Irises*) hanging above the coffee-maker tray on the credenza. I often wonder why motel owners don't put reproductions of local paintings on their walls. Perhaps they think they'd be stolen. Or that if people want to see the local landscape, they can look out a window, but if they want to see what the night sky above Arles, France, looks like through the eyes of a complete lunatic, they'll have to rent a motel room.

Are we supposed to like it that all motel rooms are the same? Maybe it has to do with what Patricia Hampl, in *Virgin Time,* calls "the anonymity at the core of all travel"—we are not meant to feel like our usual selves in a motel. But I suspect the idea is to make us feel *more* at home, as though we're sleeping in the same bedroom night after night, under the same floral bedspread, over the same grey mottled carpeting, with the same blond-wood night table and matching sideboard, the same malfunctioning clock radio, our coats hanging from the same stainless-steel coat rack. And the same smell, something between underarm fungus and hospital disinfectant. The same outlet mall next door, waiting for us as familiarly as a corner store. If we wake up in the wee hours to go to the bathroom, we don't have to turn on the light to find our way, we can stride confidently through the dark and know exactly when to reach out for the bathroom doorknob.

Had we followed Highway 101 all the way down the Pacific coast, past San Francisco, we would have come to San Luis Obispo, the site of the world's first motel—the Milestone Mo-Tel—which opened in 1925. The charge for a two-room bungalow complete with kitchen and an adjoining garage was a dollar and a quarter, but Merilyn probably would have got that down to seventy-five cents with extra pillows. Nineteen twenty-five isn't that long ago: my father was born in 1925; Wyatt Earp was still alive. *The Great Gatsby* was published that year, as was *Mein Kampf.* In 1925, George Bernard Shaw won the Nobel Prize in Literature, and Calvin Coolidge declared that "the business of America is business."

"America," wrote Doris Lessing, "has as little resistance to an idea or a mass emotion as isolated communities have to measles and whooping cough," and, true enough, from San Luis Obispo, the motel business spread across the continent like head lice in a kindergarten. By 1940, there were twenty thousand motels in America; by 1960, there were sixty thousand, all mom-and-pops. The mom-and-pop motel was the quintessential American idea: quick, inexpensive, and infinitely expandable. All you needed to start one up was a strip of roadside property and a few cabins. The shortage of building materials during the Second World War made motel owners squish the string of cabins into one long row house with a common foundation, wiring, and plumbing system. But the war also mobilized the American middle class, put them all in cars, and put them to work building hundreds of new highways (originally for troop transport to, or flight from, the coast), blue veins that spread into out-of-the-way places where the only things to see were hot springs or grizzly-bear habitat or a ghost town, and the only place to stay was a mom-and-pop with a name like the Dew Drop Inn or Peek's Motel or the Desert Palm Motor Court.

In 1956, President Eisenhower signed into law the Federal-Aid Highway Act, which created the interstate system and rang the death knell of the old highways as well as the mom-and-pop motels.

Gradually, the small roads were superseded by multi-lane through-ways with turnpikes and overpasses and cloverleafs that bypassed every town, killing the small motels that fringed them. New corporate chains were built along the interstates; massive, multi-storey edifices, with signs rising above them like lighthouses, visible across six lanes of traffic going sixty miles an hour. We saw dozens of them as we dropped down the I-5 from Redding to Anderson: Best Westerns, Holiday Inns, Quality Inns, Days Inns, Hampton Inns, Vagabond Inns, Clarions, Super 8s, La Quintas, Best Values, Econo Lodges, Travel-odges. Illogically, unlike the mom-and-pops, they cluster like flies near cities and towns and spread out to hide in rural regions, where someone might actually need a place to stay.

The room we are assigned is so demoralizing I suggest we go out to find a restaurant before we even open our suitcases. Unpacking seems so permanent.

★   ★   ★

*M*IDNIGHT is what it feels like, though it's only a little after eight. It is dark and cold, too cold for California, and we haven't eaten since lunch. We're usually good about finding interesting places to eat—not so good when it comes to choosing a place to stay. For fifty miles I've been saying, "That looks promising," or "How about the one up ahead, the one with the blue lights?" but I can't get the timing right and we're past before the words are fully out. "Do you want me to turn around?" Wayne asks. It sounds like a challenge to me. What if the place is no good? We'll have stopped for nothing, lost more time. I hear my father barking at my mother as we drive through northern Ontario, past cluster after cluster of holiday cabins, and I say what my mother always said, "No, it's fine, let's keep going, there'll be something better ahead."

Driving across the coastal range also reminded me of driving across northern Ontario. Rocks and trees, trees and rocks, the road a string carelessly curled across the slopes. Mist when we started out, snow at the highest elevations, and through it all, endless, rugged forest. I've been astonished by the wilderness, not only here, but all through Oregon and Washington State. Apart from the urban gauntlet we passed through that first day, we've seen few towns and even fewer homesteads carved into the bush. I had imagined the United States to be thoroughly populated. Not like Europe, perhaps, where every scrap of land is owned and worked, but not like Canada either, where the population density works out to only three people per square kilometre. We rank 226th out of the 237 countries in the world. The United States is 176th, with a density of thirty-one people per square kilometre. They must all live in the East, because driving through those mountains we saw no houses, no lights, no cars on the road. At least the signs became more hospitable once we crossed into California. After Oregon's terse declarations, *Watch for Falling Rocks* seems almost conversational.

Anderson has about it a whiff of northern isolation, too. It advertises itself as a city, but if it is, we can't find it. On its website, where I look to find a restaurant, its greatest claim to fame is its revitalization program. The sign coming into town says *Home of Anderson River Park*. It has a river. It has old buildings. But does it have a decent restaurant?

The streets around our motel are drab and all but deserted. Wayne and I both tense as a knot of youths bursts out of the darkness and shoulders past us, laughing. Finally, after walking for blocks, we spot the Family Restaurant.

"Sounds good," I say, trying for optimism.

"As long as there's food," Wayne grumbles. "My stomach's dropped down into me arse." Now it's his cousin in Newfoundland speaking.

We open the door and a warm fug of grease reaches out to haul us in. The place isn't busy, but the waitress waves us to a booth near the other occupied tables, clustering her clients together. We eye the food on their plates as we pass, then order hamburgers from the stained menu. It seems the safest thing. The plates, when they arrive, are heaped to overflowing. Who can eat this much food? What's wrong with it that the restaurant is so anxious to get rid of it?

We sit in a booth, surrounded by enormous people eating Brobdingnagian mounds of freedom fries and chicken-fried steak. We haven't noticed the size of Americans particularly, although they are, according to the statisticians, the plumpest people on the planet. Over 60 per cent of adults in the United States are overweight, compared with something around 35 per cent in Canada (the Canadian stats are self-reported, so it may be wise to add a few percentage points).

Across from us, two gigantic men and their obese women fuss over a roly-poly baby who seems to belong equally to them all. It is impossible not to eavesdrop: their conversation fills the room, squashing us into silence.

They have just come from a prison where they were preaching to the infidels. I wonder if it was Folsom State, which isn't far from here. Folsom was one of the first maximum-security prisons in the United States, and it is the second-oldest correctional institution in the state, next to San Quentin. Americans seem to like prisons. Californians especially like prisons. Thirty years ago, California had twelve prisons and fewer than 30,000 prisoners. Today, after decades of tough-on-crime legislation, the state has close to 175,000 inmates living in thirty-four correctional facilities. One in every two hundred California residents is being corrected. And this statistic doesn't include the tens of thousands incarcerated in county jails. The annual cost of these corrections to California taxpayers is about $10 billion a year, almost exactly what the state spends on its public university system.

Johnny Cash made Folsom State famous by writing "Folsom Prison Blues" and by singing a couple of concerts there. "They were the most enthusiastic audience I have ever played to," Cash said. But not so enthusiastic about church, apparently. Our restaurant neighbours caught one of the inmates with a paperback inside his hymnal.

"Jesus will get him for that," the biggest mountain-of-a-man chortles, shaking his head with what looks like glee at the thought of this felon burning in eternal hell. I can't help wondering what the book was. *Catch-22,* I hope. Maybe *In the Belly of the Beast.*

The baby starts to fuss. The chortler lifts her onto one enormous paw and flies her like an airplane over the table, swooping over the half-eaten food until she throws up a stream of greasy white that arcs across their plates.

I turn away. It's an odd place to say it, but I miss my family. Tomorrow is Christmas Eve, and I have no idea where I'll be. They couldn't reach me if they wanted to.

I shift my gaze to the corner booth, where a gargantuan police officer is tapping at a computer while a prepubescent girl with all her baby fat intact talks non-stop about her mean and nasty school friends. The man never once looks up, not even when she suddenly goes quiet.

"I wish I could talk to my mom," she says finally.

"She's out of your life," he snaps, squinting into the screen, "and that's a good thing. She can't screw you up."

I wonder, for one horrified moment, if that's how my children think of me. "The Family: They Fuck You Up" is the title of one of my favourite issues of *Granta* magazine.

"Remember that issue of *Granta* about families?" I say to Wayne, looking for consolation.

"Yeah, the title was taken from a line in a Philip Larkin poem." He's going to recite it. He always does; he has that kind of memory. I pull my coat closer and wrap my arms around myself in the corner of the booth.

But he doesn't. We exchange a soulful look. He's missing the children, too.

5 / **ROUTE 66**

*W*HEN we leave Anderson in the morning, there is still snow on the ground, but nothing to be alarmed about.

We decide to buy food so that we can have dinner in our room and stop briefly for supplies in Sacramento, following the signs to the historic district of the state capital, thinking we'll find some quaint local offerings, but the streets are roped off, the houses tarted up like a theme park and populated with shops selling tourist T-shirts and caramel popcorn. We get a coffee and muffin in a Starbucks, where the clerk tells us about a grocery store that might be open.

Perhaps because it ends with "o," I half expect the city to look like what I expect of Monte-Cristo or Capistrano, an early mission turned into a secular city, and am surprised to find how ordinary it is. It was never a mission, of course: it was named for its location at the confluence of the Sacramento and American Rivers and was founded by John Augustus Sutter, who built Sutter's Fort on the spot in 1844. It was his workers at Sutter's Mill on the American River who, in 1849, while taking a lunch break, found the gold nuggets that started the California gold rush.

When we pass the State Capitol, a white pillared and domed Roman Corinthian edifice, I tell Merilyn it looks like the White House.

"I've never seen the White House," she says. "Have you?"

"Just in pictures. Look at the back of a twenty-dollar bill."

"Really?" she says, taking her wallet out of the glove box. "You're right. How weird."

"Why weird?"

"Putting the president's house on your money. I can't imagine Canada putting a picture of 24 Sussex Drive on a twenty-dollar bill, can you?"

"What *is* on a Canadian twenty?"

"I have no idea. Good grief," she says, "why do we know more about American money than our own?"

"And what's with that strange pyramid with the all-seeing eye hovering over it on the one-dollar bill? Was the country founded by a group of Masons?"

"Did you know," says Merilyn, not willing to be upstaged, "that there are people in the States who track dollar bills online by registering the serial numbers?"

"No," I say, "they don't."

"They do," she says triumphantly. "It's called 'Where's George?'"

"As in George Bush?"

"No, silly, as in George Washington."

"Ah," I say, "I guess it's a Republican thing."

This conversation gets us through most of downtown Sacramento, until I park in front of the only grocery story in town that is open on this Christmas Eve Sunday. *Will* be open, I should say. People dressed in parkas—parkas! don't they know this is California?—are lined up outside the door. We join them, stamping our feet and exchanging shrugs and grins with the others until the doors swing wide and we whoosh inside on a tide of moms and dads here to pick up the turkeys they thoughtfully ordered weeks ago.

"Nice to think the El Tovar is going to do all that for us," Merilyn says, though she doesn't sound all that pleased.

When we regain the I-5, our small cooler replenished, we continue south. I find myself doing Grade Five mental arithmetic as we drive. It is a curse and I hate it, but I can't stop myself. Every time I see a road sign with a distance marked on it, I have to figure out how long it will take us to get there. The first sign we see, for example, is *Stockton, 85 miles.* We are driving fifty-five miles an hour. It is 12:45. What time should we arrive at Stockton? Click, click, whir, whir: 2:07. According to the next sign, Stockton is now twenty-two miles away. We are still travelling fifty-five miles an hour. It is now 1:43. What time will we arrive? Click, click, grind, grind: 2:17. What? We've lost ten minutes already? Has the town moved? Did we pass through a time-space anomaly?

We arrive in Stockton at 2:15, close enough to my calculations to debunk my theory that we've been abducted by aliens and returned to the Echo with tiny burn marks and no memory of how they got there. Stockton is due east of San Francisco Bay, where the Sacramento River from the north and the San Joaquin River from the south meet and empty. From here on, we're in the San Joaquin part of California's Central Valley, passing through one of the richest food-producing regions in the world. There is hardly a fresh vegetable consumed in North America that doesn't come from this valley, most likely from its southern portion, which produces more than two hundred kinds of fruits, nuts, and vegetables. From the I-5, we can see acres of packing sheds and rows of canneries lining the side roads and railway lines. Even now, in late December, the landscape is quilted in shades of living green.

It appears to us as a vast, luscious Eden, but in fact, the San Joaquin Valley is more like a film set—the product of large-scale human engineering at the expense of natural habitat. When Pedro Fages, the Spanish governor of Alta California, first laid eyes on the San Joaquin River in 1774, he found its banks a verdant oasis in a vast, seemingly sterile desert. A hundred years later, a series of dams and canals had drained the river's wetlands, pulled water down from the Sacramento River into the San Joaquin, and redirected it into the desert to create arable farmland. By 1931, so much water was being siphoned out of the San Joaquin that the river was reduced to a trickle, but the valley itself was a fertile fruit belt controlled by a handful of agribusinesses.

Joan Didion, in *Slouching Towards Bethlehem*, writes that the small towns between Sacramento and Bakersfield "seem so flat, so impoverished as to drain the imagination. They hint at evenings hanging around the gas station and suicide pacts sealed in drive-ins. An implacable insularity is their mark." Even the guidebook warns us of the area's "lack of visual appeal." But Merilyn and I are country people; we like hanging around gas stations and, to a certain extent, we are comfortable with insularity, which does not lead to suicide pacts all that often. If you want to count suicides, you'll have better luck in the cities.

We pass miles and miles of feedlots, fenced compounds in which mud-coloured cattle stand idly around like prisoners on smoke break. These are factory farms or, more properly, Concentrated Animal Feeding Operations (CAFOs), and they're enough to turn one off milk. It isn't simply a matter of visual appeal; animals in CAFOs are confined and given hormone injections to promote growth and productivity, pumped full of antibiotics and vaccines to prevent the spread of diseases, and then we eat the super-dosed meat. Back home, we buy our meat from local farmers or a small butcher, but here on the road, we can't avoid mass-produced beef, pork, and chicken, either outside our windows or on our plates. Ninety-nine per cent of the meat produced in North America is produced on factory farms.

"I miss our chickens," Merilyn says, looking forlornly at the feedlots.

Each year we raise two dozen chickens for meat and a dozen more for eggs. We buy them as day-old chicks, pamper them to maturity, let them roam freely about the gardens and grounds, house them at night in a dry, airy coop, collect their eggs, and, when the time comes, kill and dress them ourselves on a big wooden table we set up in the orchard. Not so long ago, that was normal for most people living in the country; now when we tell friends about our chickens they look at us as though we've just stepped out of a wormhole from the nineteenth century. Small-time farmers are fast disappearing. In 1967, there were still one million family pig farms in America; now there are a little over a hundred thousand, a measure of the extent to which factory farming has taken over the family farm.

After the feedlots come row after row of fruit trees, some of the orchards identified by signs near the road: peaches, oranges, plums. But not all are neatly labelled. After spending some time with a puzzled look on her face, Merilyn finally exclaims, "Almonds! These must be almond trees! Oh, let's stop!"

We get off the interstate at the Lost Hills exit, gas up, buy some fruit at a canvas-covered stand beside the station. No almonds, but the two women manning the stall tell us that we'll pass some nut orchards if we take Route 46 toward Wasco. When we see the sign—*Wasco: Home of the Long White Potato*—we are on a straight highway between vast, amazingly tidy almond orchards. We pull off onto a narrow lane leading into the trees. I park about a hundred feet in, and we eat our lunch—bread and cheese and wine for me, fruit and water for Merilyn. Sitting in the car with the doors open, among the almond trees, she is ecstatic. Unable to drink cow's milk, she often substitutes a milk-like product made from almonds, so this place is, for her, what the Willamette Valley was for me, a kind of spiritual motherlode.

The almonds were harvested at least two months ago. Before the harvest, the orchard grounds would have been swept clean of ground litter, and mechanical tree shakers would then have moved down the rows, shaking the ripe fruit from the branches. The nuts were left on the ground to dry for a while and then sucked up, again mechanically, and augered into trucks.

By now, the orchard has been fastidiously cleaned of nuts, but the leaves have since fallen and there is a familiar autumnal mustiness in the air. Flocks of birds make their way through, heading noisily north, and we take out our binoculars. There are Brewer's blackbirds and a great many yellow-rumped warblers and white-crowned sparrows. When we finish our lunch, we get out of the car and walk farther up the lane, looking into the treetops for more birds, breathing in what to us is the springlike air. Suddenly Merilyn points excitedly to the ground: a sweep of almonds, apparently spilled from an overloaded truck, lies alongside the road. We gather handfuls, take them back to the car, and eat them, a little furtively. They are fresh and sweet and go well with the chocolate we bought in Sacramento.

We are not far from Bakersfield, on what Jack Kerouac, in *On the Road,* called "the floor of California, green and wondrous." That was in 1947, when he was approaching it from the east, having picked up an Okie hitchhiker in Tucson, Arizona, who said he was a "moosician" who'd had his guitar stolen and was on his way home to Bakersfield to collect money from his brother, some of which he would give to Kerouac. Kerouac's companion in the novel, Dean Moriarty (Neal Cassady in life), had lived in Bakersfield and "wanted to tell us everything he knew about Bakersfield as we reached the city limits." Moriarty shows them a succession of pool halls, railroad hotels, diners, rooming houses, Mexican and Chinese restaurants, even park benches where he had picked up girls. "Dean's California," Kerouac writes, was "wild, sweaty, important, the land of lonely and exiled and eccentric lovers come to foregather like birds . . ."

Merilyn and I are perhaps a little exiled but not the least bit lonely as we sit here in the orchard, munching on almonds and serenaded by foregathering birds.

* * *

*M*Y face is turned east, at last. It feels right, as though we're finally heading home, but oddly wrong, too. This transcontinental journey is most often told east to west, following the actual course of American history. Simone de Beauvoir, Vita Sackville-West, all the visiting Victorian ladies, the explorers, the pioneers, set off from the Atlantic into the setting sun, and now we're driving toward them all, meeting their ghosts.

At Bakersfield, we put the Pacific at our backs and set our sights on the eastern seaboard. We're on Highway 58, part of what used to be called the National Old Trails Road, a loose connection of Indian tracks and wagon trails that led from Maryland through middle America and the deserts of New Mexico and Arizona to California. Around the time the Lincoln Highway was conceived, someone had the idea of turning these trails into the Ocean-to-Ocean Highway, but by 1927, only eight hundred miles had been paved. Surprisingly, the stretch we are coming to, the road that crosses the Mojave, was among the best.

The Old Trails Road fell apart, literally, when Highway 66 was built in its place. But just as the Boy Scouts weren't willing to see the old Lincoln Highway disappear, the Old Trails had its saviour, too: a Missouri woman named Arlene B. Nichols Moss, who decided to mark the Trail with statues of pioneering women.

I am in awe of this American penchant for the monumental. This is a republic that carves presidents into mountainsides, a country that builds a Grecian temple to house a thirty-foot-tall Republican, a nation at war for most of its history that erects a ten-foot-high, 275-foot-long granite wall to honour soldiers who fought in the one it lost. The cause doesn't seem to matter: they love to wear their hearts on their sleeve.

Arlene Moss was a Daughter of the American Revolution, a member of a peculiarly American and passionately patriotic group of women, each of whom could "prove lineal bloodline descent from an ancestor who aided in achieving United States independence." It was the DAR that, in 1939, refused to allow Marian Anderson, the black contralto, to sing in its concert hall, prompting Eleanor Roosevelt to arrange a live performance on the steps of the Lincoln Memorial where, twenty-five years later, Martin Luther King, Jr. delivered his "I have a dream" speech.

We have no Daughters of the Repatriated Constitution in Canada. My mother belonged to the church auxiliary and the

Woman's Christian Temperance Union. Women of my day joined feminist collectives.

That's not to say the DAR hasn't done good work. Arlene Moss, for instance, not only rescued the Old Trails from complete extinction but honoured women pioneers by mounting a statue called the Madonna of the Trail in each of the twelve states the old road passed through. Interestingly, Arlene's inspiration came from a monument raised to Sacajawea, the Shoshone woman who helped get Lewis and Clark through the Rocky Mountains. She was also the first woman to register a vote in North America and the first American woman to be honoured with a larger-than-life public portrait, which in the monument-prone United States is high honour indeed.

"How would you feel about taking a detour down to Upland?" I ask tentatively. "It's only about seventy-five miles."

I want to see the Madonna of the Trail for myself. The ten-foot-tall pioneer mother clasps a baby in her left arm while clutching a rifle in her right; her young son clings to her skirts, which trail through the prairie cactus and sage, scraping past arrowheads, barely missing a rattlesnake coiled in the grass. From the pictures, it's not a pretty portrait, all jutting angles and desperation. These square-jawed baggy-eyed women have their hands full, their skirts hobbled as they trudge grimly forward. They don't look valiant so much as put-upon.

Wayne is staring blankly ahead. I wait.

"That's an hour and a half," he says finally. "Probably more with traffic. Each way. At that rate, we'll never get far enough tonight to make it to the Grand Canyon in time for Christmas dinner."

Maybe we can stop and visit the one in Springerville, Arizona, or in Albuquerque, New Mexico. All the way home, I'll be staring into the faces of these women, driving against the hard wave of their determination.

I wonder what kind of monument Canadians would raise to their pioneer mothers, were they inclined to public displays of sculptural affection. We have few statues to women, and the ones we have seem domesticated by comparison. The five who fought to have Canadian women recognized as "persons"—Emily Murphy, Irene Parlby, Nellie McClung, Louise McKinney, and Henrietta Edwards—are gathered at a tea party. Laura Secord, though famous for her desperate midnight hike through the woods to warn the British that the Americans were invading, stands demurely near a bridge over the Ottawa River.

The most heroic statue of a woman that I can think of is mounted on a quiet, residential corner in our national capital. It depicts an American scene: a Vietnamese woman running with a child in her arms. You can almost smell the napalm, hear the rolling thunder of the American fighter-bombers. It honours civilians, not soldiers: "In memory of those who have lost their lives in their quest for freedom."

THERE'S NOT much to see out the window. This desert used to be strung with small towns, crossroad villages like Bagdad of the film *Bagdad Cafe,* in which a man and a woman, driving across America, have an argument and the woman leaves her husband and stays to work at the cafe. But those places are gone, pulverized by heat and indifference. It's a lonely stretch of road. Not much out there but scrub turning to desert and lava fields so scorched-looking they make the desert seem lush by comparison. In the distance, a bank of windmills, like sparse daisies, stand planted on a ridge.

I'm reading the map, on the lookout for the National Old Trails Road. Most of it is gone, buried under other highways, straightened and groomed out of existence. A lot of it survives only as ATV tracks and abandoned trails. But in some parts of the country, bits have been returned to the old designation. I see a gentle loop that starts at Daggett and continues to Essex, which is just a spit away from Needles, where we hope to spend the night. If there's time and Wayne seems in the mood, I'll suggest a detour. It won't take us as far out of our way as Upland would have. It starts near the Pisgah Crater, named for the mountain that God commanded Moses to climb so that he could see the Promised Land. This Pisgah is a fairly young volcano, as volcanoes go: its cone rises only a few hundred feet above the desert.

Whoever named it must have been an unredeemable optimist. I can hear his grim-faced pioneer wife muttering in the background: Some mountain! Some promised land!

* * *

*W*HEN people are asked to name a famous American highway, chances are they'll say Route 66. I first heard of it in the 1960s, on the television series *Route 66*, starring George Maharis and Martin Milner as two young boyos travelling around America in a Corvette. Before that, the road was immortalized by John Steinbeck in the 1930s, by Nat King Cole in the '40s, and by Jack Kerouac in the '50s. The long, meandering highway was begun in 1925 to forge a continuously paved link between Chicago, Illinois, and Barstow, California, joining hundreds of hitherto disconnected small towns and dirt back roads, following river and even creek beds, heeding its own serendipitous logic as it sifted down through Arkansas and Oklahoma and the Texas Panhandle before finally swinging west through New Mexico and Arizona. It was finished in 1934, just in time for the exodus of Oklahoma farmers heading to California in search of a new beginning. "The mother road," John Steinbeck called it. "The road of flight."

At Barstow we leave Highway 58 and get on the I-40, which has obliterated the Mother Road across much of America. Although the I-40 bears little resemblance to that mythical highway of the 1930s, it's still a prepossessing ribbon of daylight, threading the Mojave Desert, lined with cactus and mesquite. Not a place to run out of gas, get a flat tire, or have an argument with your wife. As I recall, there are no knock-down, drag-out fights between the Joads in *The Grapes of Wrath*. Driving through country like this gives you a firm grasp on what's important.

It certainly did for Steinbeck. The vast, westward migration of some 250,000 destitute farm workers became his life's subject. In 1936, he was hired by the *San Francisco News* to write a seven-part feature about the massive influx of American migrant workers into the Central Valley. He called the series "The Harvest Gypsies," and although it began as an objective report on the plight of the homeless and the helpless, it quickly became a polemic against the industrialized agricultural system that flourished as a result of engineered water and economies of scale, a system that reaped huge profits for owners but paid migrant workers starvation wages and brutally punished anyone who even thought about forming a farm workers' union (which Cesar Chavez finally achieved in 1966).

"It is difficult to believe," Steinbeck wrote in that series, "what one large speculative farmer has said, that the success of California agriculture requires that we create and maintain a peon class. For if this is true, then California must depart from the semblance of democratic government that remains here."

In *Grapes of Wrath,* Steinbeck often steps outside the fictional world of the Joad family to present detailed descriptions of Highway 66, as well as first-person chapters by used-car salesmen or truck-stop waitresses. These realistic riffs were Steinbeck's way of bringing his readers to the understanding that what they were reading was not fiction invented out of thin air by an abstract artist, but a true account of a serious crisis in American history. By putting a face on the working class, he paved the way for the eventual success of Chavez and the United Farm Workers Organizing Committee in their struggle for human rights. It is fitting that when Chavez went on a hunger strike to protest migrant workers' living conditions in 1968, he received a letter of support from Martin Luther King, Jr. Among King's last public words before his assassination was the verse "Mine eyes have seen the glory of the coming of the Lord," with its implied next line: "He is trampling out the vintage where the grapes of wrath are stored."

When the Joads crossed the Colorado River in their overloaded Hudson truck, they looked down on the section of California through which we're now travelling. They saw little but "broken, rotten rock winding and twisting through dead country, burned white and grey, and no life in it." The landscape hasn't changed. I wouldn't say there is no life in it, but it is certainly diminished life, toehold life, life the Joads must have understood.

Near the Pisgah Crater, we turn into what looks like an abandoned quarry or an open-pit salt mine, with a dirt track running down into a hole carved through an exposure of reddish-brown stone. Thick thorn bushes cover most of the ground. We get out and pick our way through them to the top of the quarry to look southwest, toward the setting sun. The sand still holds some heat from the day, and although a cool breeze is coming at us over the desert, we are not cold. We can hear birds, tiny peeps and quiet, cricket-like flock calls, a small family group making its way through the low shrubs and grasses, but we cannot see them.

Merilyn and I separate for a while, the first time we've been out of each other's sight for days, and I find a small cup-nest set deep in a leafless Anderson thornbush that must be that of a cactus wren, a wren the size of a robin (most wrens are not much bigger than chickadees) that I would very much like to see. But there is no sign that the nest has been used lately. I call Merilyn over, and she reaches delicately into the thornbush, extracts a dun-coloured feather, and hands it to me, a gift. It is, after all, Christmas Eve.

* * *

MUCH about this parched interior landscape seems familiar. I've never been here before, but staring through the windshield at the empty desert, I realize I've been seeing it all my adult life, in the photographs of Dorothea Lange, Walker Evans, and Robert Frank.

I reach back into the rubble of the back seat and lift out the camera.

"Want me to stop?" Wayne asks.

"No," I say. "I'll just roll down my window."

In the latter half of the Thirties, the Farm Security Administration hired some of the best photographers of the day—Dorothea Lange, Ben Shahn, Russell Lee, Walker Evans—to roam the country, documenting the devastation wrought by the drought. The photographers were sent out with detailed shooting scripts: "Crowded cars going out on the open road. Gas station attendant filling tank of open touring and convertible cars." The kind of pictures I like to take.

Walker Evans had already compiled his own list of picture categories, which rivals Jefferson's directive to Lewis and Clark in ambition and scope. It's a useful list for any traveller out to understand a country:

People, all classes, surrounded by bunches of the new down-and-out

Automobiles and the automobile landscape

Architecture, American urban taste, commerce, small scale, large scale, clubs, the city atmosphere, the street smell, the hateful stuff, women's clubs, fake culture, bad education, religion in decay

The movies

Evidence of what people of the city read, eat, see for amusement, do for relaxation and not get it

Sex

Advertising

A lot else, you see what I mean.

But Dorothea Lange is the photographer I associate with this dry corner of America. It wasn't far from where we turned east off the I-5 that Lange took her iconic portrait, "Migrant Mother." It's 1936. A woman sits surrounded by her children, one in her arms, one leaning against her shoulder, another huddled at her back. She is thirty-two, a mother of seven, one of the destitute pea pickers who flocked to the Central Valley after the land they worked in the Midwest simply blew away.

In Lange's photographs of the pea pickers, the cotton pickers, and the rest of the environmental refugees flooding west, the people are all but indistinguishable from the land: their skin is just as creased and parched. In "Jobless on Edge of Pea Field, Imperial Valley, California," a man crouches on his haunches, bone-thin and desperate, though his eyes are still sharp, his chin jutting into the breeze. Hope has vanished altogether from "Man Beside Wheelbarrow." He buries his head in his hands, his back against a brick wall that fills the frame, as if it goes on forever.

To me, though, the most desolate, the most hopeless of Lange's photographs is "The Road West." The top third of the picture is a strip of scoured sky bisected by the narrow end of a funnelling highway, the asphalt widening as it approaches the viewer until it takes up the entire bottom of the frame. I've made it sound as if the road were coming toward you, which it could be, but when confronted with the photograph, what you see is a road receding into an endless, pointless distance. There are no people. No cars. Nothing is coming. Or going. Beside the photograph in Lange's book *An American Exodus* is a quote from someone Lange met on the road: "Do you reckon I'd be out on the highway if I had it good at home?" This is Tom Joad's road west, "silent, looking into the distance ahead, along the road, along the white road that waved gently, like a ground swell."

It's the heat that turns a road into an undulating river. But in December, what lies before us is flat and grey as a roadkill snake.

Twenty years after Lange shot "The Road West," Robert Frank took a similar picture in the New Mexico desert between Taos and Santa Fe. It was 1955, and he and Walker Evans, funded by a Guggenheim Fellowship, were on a road trip to document America. They wanted to show how the nation had changed since Lange and Evans had photographed it in the Thirties, to document "the kind of civilization born here and spreading everywhere." As Geoff Dyer points out in *The Ongoing Moment,* a masterful extended riff on photography in the United States, "America was becoming a place to be seen from a car, a country that could be seen without stopping."

In Frank's road picture, the horizon is still flatlining, the road still swelling, but in the distance, a small black car approaches. The image no longer feels hopeless—someone is coming!—though the night is still empty and bleak. Kerouac mentions this picture in his introduction to Frank's book *The Americans* (which, wouldn't you know it, was released first in France): "Long shot of night road arrowing forlorn into immensities and flat of impossible-to-believe America."

Only twenty years separates those two pictures, yet they are a world apart. As Dyer notes, Lange's photo "is about distance, remoteness; Frank's is about covering ground." It's been fifty years since Frank was here. There's not one car on the horizon; there are hundreds. A wall-to-wall highway of cars. Covering ground is still what it's all about: getting there fast, and first.

Wayne and I have covered a lot of ground today. Hours ago, we spoke to a fireman at the Starbucks in Sacramento who told us the Grand Canyon was a good twelve-hour drive away.

"You can do it in a day," he said, "but it's a push."

We've been driving ever since. Now and then I lift the camera to the window, taking pictures of the wind turbines lazily turning on the hills above the desert, the sunset over the Mojave, signs that tell us how far we have yet to go. I stare down at the images, clicking through them, giving my eyes a rest from the endless desert, stalling our progress for a while. The soul walks, they say. I give it a bit of a breather.

We imagined we'd find a quaint and quirky place to stay in the desert, dreamed of getting up to do a little birdwatching on Christmas morning, but there are no towns, not even the ones named on the map. When Simone de Beauvoir went by bus from California to the Grand Canyon fifty years ago, she saw rustic shacks selling curios, wagon wheels propped against walls, ghost towns and diners and tourist inns. All traces of that past have been obliterated, the motels boarded up or knocked down when the interstate sucked the traffic through without stopping. Gone are the solitary ghost towns with their mouldy wooden shacks, their old theatres with faded posters. In the half century since de Beauvoir was here, another layer of history has crumbled to dust, asphalt laid like a gravestone in its place. Only the landscape never changes.

Bleak thoughts, and now we're travelling at a snail's pace. Construction on the I-40 has reduced it to one lane.

"How about getting off onto the National Old Trails Road for a while?" I suggest. Wayne must be tired of the interstate, too. I watch him spin through his mental mathematics.

"Okay," he says. "It can't be any slower than this."

We veer south onto the loop of narrow road. Here, surely, we'll stumble upon a classic motel with a diner off one side selling hamburgers and cherry Cokes. But there is nothing. No cars. Not even a road sign. For a hundred miles in all directions, the map on my lap is alarmingly blank, save a few sparse labels: *Bristol Lake (Dry). Cadiz Lake (Dry). Danby Lake (Dry). Calico (Ghost Town). Soda Lake (Dry).* Only desert, as far as the eye can see.

*   *   *

*W*INDOWS down, driving at night, I feel the desert cascade into the car, hitting us in all five senses at once: I am falling in love with the desert. The mineral scent of cooling sand; the play of stars above an intuited horizon; the roar of an unfathomed emptiness, as though we're following the lip of a bottomless canyon; hair beating against my ear, and the hydraulic hum of the tires on rough pavement; the cyanide taste of almonds.

It feels good to be off the I-40. "I hate how those interstates bulldoze through hills and fill hollows with gravel trucked in from as far away as economically possible," I say to Merilyn, "don't you?"

"Why are your thoughts always so negative?" Merilyn asks. "My mother used to say, 'When you hear hoofbeats, think horses, not zebras.' But when you hear hoofbeats, you don't think horses *or* zebras, do you?"

She's right. Occam's razor: the law of parsimony. The most obvious answer is usually the right one. I don't seem to be able to think parsimoniously.

"You think the Four Horsemen of the Apocalypse, don't you?"

"I guess so," I say, using an Americanism. All Americans in British novels say "I guess so" and "You bet."

But I do respond to the parsimony of this desert. After the thoroughfares of the West Coast and the lush but artificial landscape of the Central Valley, this desert is my first taste of the real America, the unspoiled landscape I hadn't been prepared for, and I like it. It's so un-American. Deserts always surprise me, the way they look dead but are actually teeming with secret life. I have always loved them, the way their lack of clutter forces you into yourself, strips away inessentials like ego and even history. Deserts as antimatter. I once spent two months digging fossils in the Gobi Desert, and I remember lying awake at night looking out into the darkness, watching the desert surface ignite into a billion tiny explosions as grains of sand were bombarded against one another by the constant wind, like particles in a proton accelerator, and marvelling at the soft violence that surrounds all living things. It was the same in the High Arctic, another desert, where I would stare across the ice for hours, happily giving myself to its pure immensity. "The desert is a vast world," Edward Abbey wrote, "an oceanic world, as deep in its way and complex and various as the sea."

Nothing bad has happened. No one has bonked us on the head and stolen our hubcaps or shot at us. I knew a violinist from Nova Scotia who said she'd moved back home from California, where she'd played with the Los Angeles Symphony, because as she was coming out of a grocery store one day a bullet had bounced off the roof of her car. "I left that day," she said. "I still had the groceries in the car when I got to Cape Breton." Nothing like that has happened to us.

"Do you hear that?" asks Merilyn quietly.

"Yes," I say. "Coyotes."

Desert peoples refer to coyotes as God's dog, perhaps because the animals seem to have appeared out of nowhere. I pull over and we get out. From somewhere off in the darkness comes a faint, discordant yipping, a plaintive sound that carries no threat, like the sound of a train whistle diminishing in the night. I consider answering their call, but I don't, not wanting to identify myself as an interloper from a foreign pack. If I can't belong here, I can at least sneak through undetected.

"It's beautiful, isn't it?" Merilyn says, leaning against me, looking up into the sky.

"It's beautiful everywhere," I say, wanting to believe it, reassessing it all—the soaring Douglas-fir forest; the placid Pacific; the brotherly mountains and now the desert. "We've seen a lot in just four days. It will take us a while to assimilate it."

"By which time we'll have seen a lot more."

"We're really into it now, aren't we?"

"No going back," Merilyn says. "Shall we go on?"

"You bet."

She gets back into the car and I linger behind, beyond the glow of the tail lights. Let the coyotes smell my mark.

*　*　*

*M*Y thrill on clear winter nights is to douse the headlights and drive down our road with only the moon on the snow to guide the way.

"Let's drive blind," I say now, and Wayne switches off the lights.

The sand glows like December drifts. Far to the south a pale light twinkles. If it's a car, it will take hours to reach us. But maybe it's a star.

Something glows on the road in front of us, too.

We're over it before we can see what it was, something painted on the road surface. Then another one. Wayne stops and turns on the lights.

"Route 66" is stencilled in white paint on the black asphalt, the numbers tucked inside their old, curvaceous, police-badge frame.

No statues here: they've branded the road itself, like a steer they're afraid will run away.

"People must steal the signs," Wayne says.

What people?

We get out, leaving the car parked in the middle of the highway, lights off. There's nothing coming, not from any direction. We stand under the dome of stars. I wonder if they're the same stars we'd see if we were at home.

"It's Christmas Eve," I say after a while, pushing the words out into the silence. "Everyone's probably safe at home." My voice sounds small. It sails off into the darkness without resistance. Even the insects are settled for the night.

Wayne is rummaging in the trunk. He pulls out a bottle of wine and the chocolate truffles we bought in Sacramento.

He slides the cork out of the bottle.

"Wait!" I open the glove compartment and lift out my camera. "Go stand on the Route 66 sign. With the wine."

I crawl into the driver's seat and flick on the headlights. Wayne squints. He is standing between the two sixes, holding up the wine in one hand, his glass in the other. Then he thinks better of it, takes a long drink, refills the glass, and resumes his pose.

I snap a picture. Wayne is a pale ghost hovering on the road. I lean back into the darkness of the car and snap a couple more.

I'm cheating, I know that. When Garry Winogrand travelled across America on his Guggenheim, ten years after Robert Frank, he took his pictures through the windshield, too—while he was driving. The hood of the car, the dirty glass, the dusty dashboard are all part of the composition, which creates an odd effect: the road that seemed so vast in Lange's and Frank's photographs seems familiar in Winogrand's hands, just another highway to anywhere. Viewed from the seat of a car, the endless desert shrinks to the size of a movie screen, neatly framed. Something that can be understood, ignored. The yearning is still there, but the forlorn, gentle randomness of Frank's roaming is cranked now to an edgy frenzy. It isn't hopelessness or the urge to move on one feels in these photographs, so much as impatience, an unwillingness to stop.

But we have stopped. I stow the camera in the glove compartment and join Wayne on the road, where we sip the last of the Willamette wine and hold truffles in our mouths until they melt.

"Happy Christmas," we say at exactly the same time, which makes us laugh, and then we kiss.

6 / GRAND CANYON, ARIZONA

$\mathcal{M}$Y head hurts. We started Christmas Day with fresh-squeezed orange juice and some cheap bubbly we bought in Anderson but didn't drink, the setting being too downscale for even faux champagne. Even here, it doesn't seem to have agreed with me. We're in Needles, California, which feels at this moment like a town of addicts, though I know the place is named for the sharply pointed spires of rock we can almost see from our motel window.

We have driven 2,250 kilometres, some 1,400 miles, since we left Vancouver. Last night, we decided we owed ourselves a treat. Instead of a Motel 6 or a Super 8—or "Suppurate," as Wayne quips at every opportunity—we pulled into the parking lot of a brand-new Best Western. The plump young woman at the desk did not seem pleased with our late-night arrival.

"I just want to get home to wrap my Christmas gifts," she grumbled as she reached for a key.

I smiled and, without argument, accepted the price she offered. It was Christmas, after all.

We nosed into the parking spot in front of number 4. Beside us was a shiny black Harley. Wayne grunted, man-speak for "This isn't going to be good." The window in front of the motorcycle glowed blue. As we walked past, I glanced in: a porno flick.

I didn't even put the key in the door. "It's Christmas!" I moaned, turning back toward the office and calling over my shoulder, "This won't take long, I promise."

Wayne does not believe in switching rooms. You take what you're given, that's his motto. No matter if it's across from the ice machine or beside the elevator or over the all-night bar. He sees it as a kind of karma: you get what you deserve. He'd rather stay up till 3 AM railing—"What? Do I look like a bum? Like I don't appreciate a good night's sleep in clean sheets in a decent bed?"—than ask the desk clerk to see another room.

"Oh, no," I groaned when we pulled up outside number 18. It was tucked beneath a staircase blockaded with lumber and bags of concrete. I imagined air hammers and power drills in the morning.

The girl gave me another key. No neighbours, no construction.

"This looks good," I said cheerily.

"What did you say?" I learned to read lips as a child, watching American movies dubbed into Portuguese. I think I missed a couple of Wayne's words at the beginning, but that was the gist.

"I said, This looks good."

We were yelling. A sign outside the room was buzzing like a giant hornet.

"One more time," I begged.

"It's Christmas Eve," I said to the plump young woman. Even I could hear the whine in my voice. There was room at the inn, obviously, but what we wanted was a *decent* room. "We're a long way from home," I pleaded. "Please. Do you have something nice?"

She put her hand over the telephone mouthpiece. When I came in, she was saying, "Look, I'll be there as soon as I can, you get started, you can do that much, can't you?" She leaned over, took number 25 off the hook, and threw it on the counter.

"Thank you," I said, but she was already back on the phone, giving instructions as to what went in the stockings, what under the tree. She must have had her babies when she was twelve.

"This is fine," Wayne said, challenging me to disagree.

And it was. A second-floor room that looked out over a row of palm trees to the desert and, if we stretched, those rocky spires. Yes, it was at the top of the stairs, and yes, everyone in the place would pass by our door in the morning, but how many people would be staying in a motor hotel on Christmas Eve?

"And it has Internet!" I said. "We can Skype the kids and it won't cost us a cent."

Except that I couldn't get the Internet to work.

I dialled the front desk and asked how to hook it up properly.

"I wouldn't know," the disgruntled young mother replied. "I've never been in any of the rooms."

IN THE morning, we pack our bags, rinse out the champagne glasses, and return the key. A different woman is sitting at the desk, an older woman, which makes me happy. I want that plump young woman to be home with her kids. *I* want to be home with my kids.

When I get in the car, I tie the red ribbon from our Sacramento shortbread around the rear view mirror.

"There," I say brightly. "Now it feels like Christmas."

Though it doesn't, not at all. Christmas morning is supposed to be sticky buns and coffee with Baileys and stockings full of toys and treats and silly, sentimental, useless stuff. Then presents, really good presents, with turkey perfuming the air for hours, the kids huddled over a jigsaw, or around the piano, or suiting up for the toboggan hill.

I cast about for something else to prop up my mood. We watch birds for a bit, I do a few Sudokus, stare out the car window. My head still hurts. I consider asking Wayne if he'd like me to read him my novel, but instead I pull out the newspaper I picked up in the motel office. We haven't seen or heard the news for almost a week.

"The Denver airport is completely snowed in," I report, scanning the headlines. "Las Vegas has been hit by a blizzard for the first time in a hundred years. That's not far from here, is it? Nothing about Canada, but in Minnesota, there's no snow at all. It's the warmest December since 1931. How weird is that?"

"Sounds like El Niño."

Never travel south in an El Niño year: how could we have forgotten that traveller's rule? To be fair, the boy child of world weather has been a bit of a brat: he shows up whenever he feels like it, every two years, maybe seven, which isn't exactly something you can plan for. Typically, in El Niño years, the weather in the southern part of North America is wet and cold, while the north is treated to a warmer-than-usual Christmas. And there it is in big, bold print: temperatures across the northern United States are six to twelve degrees above normal, which means our kids probably haven't pulled out their down-filled jackets yet.

There's a cold draft blowing up my summery skirt. I turn on the car heater, close my eyes, and rub my temples.

We have made a terrible mistake. We headed south to avoid snow on the Prairies; now here we are in Arizona, without the kids, freezing in the desert, a champagne headache on Christmas morning: it's all wrong, wrong, wrong.

★　★　★

WE cross the Colorado River into Arizona at the same place the Joads crossed it, going the other way. They would have been stopped by armed guards, employed by the factory-farm owners to prevent union organizers from entering the state; we stop of our own accord to take a closer look at the river.

Even after coming down through the Grand Canyon, the Colorado River is still a major watercourse, about two hundred feet across, I'd guess, curving somewhat desultorily around a bend to the east, past an expensive-looking, Spanish-style house with white stucco walls and a red clay tile roof. Since there doesn't seem to be anyone around, we walk down the sloping drive to the river's somewhat precipitous bank and look over the edge. The reeds Steinbeck noted are still there, leaning and waving downstream. The river glints in the morning sun, and we shiver beneath the highway in the shade of the metal bridge. We keep forgetting it's December.

We climb back to the car. At Kingman, Route 66 takes a loop north to a town promisingly called Peach Springs, but we veer instead onto the I-40 and press on. Speed is the thing now. We have to be at the Grand Canyon by five for our dinner reservation. "Speed," wrote Jean Baudrillard, the French post-structuralist who visited the United States in 1985 and, like me, fell in love with the desert, "creates pure objects." I take it he meant that when you're moving at speed, your eye doesn't have time to focus on inessentials: you see a tree as an isolated object, not as a living organism surrounded by other living organisms. It isn't pine or spruce or oak, it just registers as *tree.*

"We'll turn north at Williams," Merilyn says.

"What about Flagstaff, Arizona?" I say. "And don't forget Winona."

"We'll have to get our kicks at the Grand Canyon," she says, although it doesn't sound as though kicks are likely to be in our future.

It's Christmas Day. I wonder what our kids are doing now. It's nice, we tell ourselves, to be "free of all that," driving through this desert, looking at creosote bushes and prickly pear cactus instead of Scotch pines and Christmas presents, and for a kilometre or two we actually believe it.

"We'll phone the kids from the Grand Canyon," Merilyn says.

"How will we know where they are?" I ask.

"They all have cellphones," she says, almost sadly. Having a cellphone is like being bedridden: you can always be reached.

"Are we still in the Mojave?" I ask, and she checks her maps.

One desert tends to look a lot like another, unless you look particularly closely. Technically, Arizona's Mojave is a transition des-ert between the Sonoran Desert of southern California and southern Arizona and the Great Basin, north of the Grand Canyon. It is defined by the presence of the Joshua tree, *Yucca brevifola,* a squat, cactus-like plant that nonetheless deserves to be called a tree: it has a woody stem, and can grow to fifty feet even in the arid desert. Some of them live a thousand years. It was named by the Mormons, who thought its stumpy, upturned limbs made it look like Joshua praising God as he led the Children of Israel through the Sinai Desert. If this tree is pray-ing, I think, then it is praying for rain.

"Stop!" Merilyn yells. "Stop the car! Stop the car!"

"What is it?" I ask, pulling over to the side of the road, not an easy thing to do on an interstate.

"Back up! Quickly! Not too fast!"

My brain is clumsily trying to decipher these contradictory injunc-tions while simultaneously slowing down and checking the mirror for oncoming transport trailers.

"Bird," she says softly, as if it could hear. "Oh, a nice bird."

"Nice bird" is code for "I don't know what it is but we haven't seen it before." I quickly back up slowly until we are abreast of a largish, grey-and-black bird sitting on a fence wire about thirty feet in from the roadside. At that moment, the bird flies down into the grass beyond the fence and we groan, but when it flies back up and perches on the wire again, we madly focus our binoculars. It's about the size of a robin, but is grey with white shoulder patches, a black tail, a hooked beak—

"Shrike!" we shout simultaneously.

Loggerhead shrikes are extremely rare in our part of Canada. Peterson lists the bird as "diminishing; gone from most of its range east of the Mississippi River." A native, in summer, of the Great Plains and southern Prairies, the loggerhead moved eastward, turning up in Ontario in 1860 as more and more forest was cut down for cropland, creating the kind of open-meadow habitat (we call them farms) that shrikes and coyotes prefer. Shrikes live on mice, smaller birds, and grasshoppers, kabobbing their prey on the thorns of hawthorn and buffalo thorn trees.

As its new habitat succumbed to the twentieth century, the log-gerhead shrike population dwindled. But we tend to forget that a bird spends only half its life in the north; Arizona is where it winters, and here it seems to be doing just fine. As we drive, we see two more log-gerhead shrikes, more than most Canadians see in a lifetime of looking, both of them perched on fences lining the road, hopping off regularly to forage for food in the desert.

We feel as though we have just been given a Christmas present, which is a good thing, because we didn't give each other Christmas gifts this morning. We haven't really talked about it, but we seem to have tacitly agreed that the trip is the gift.

"I hope you didn't get me anything," Merilyn said before we left Vancouver, "because I didn't get you anything."

I had planned to stop somewhere and buy her something expen-sive, as it is an axiom of gift giving that the later you leave buying the present, the more expensive it has to be. I did bring a backup from Kingston, so I was happy enough to say, "Of course I have something for you, but it can keep until our anniversary."

The whole gift-giving part of Christmas makes me unaccountably sad. I have memories of walking slowly through department stores in late December with a dollar, looking for something wonderful and thoughtful to buy for my mother. I'd lean against the glass jewellery display case (by which I mean the case displaying glass jewellery) in Woolworth's and look at clip-on earrings and brooches in the shape of floral wreaths and despair at the inevitability of it.

Parents get even by asking you what you want for Christmas, and then dividing your answer by ten. I remember going through a Sears catalogue when I was eleven or twelve, circling the things I'd like. Sears Roebuck was a big American department store and sold the kind of things the Cleavers would give the Beav for Christmas. I was fascinated by the page displaying a range of Chemcraft chemistry sets, the ads showing a studious boy in a striped T-shirt and a brush cut (he even looked like the Beav) pouring something from one test tube into another, a look of intelligent concentration on his face.

The really top-of-the-line set, the one I asked for, cost $49 and was as big as a tabletop; it had at least twenty-five chemicals, with names like sodium ferrocyanide and phenolphthalein, and included a rack of eight test tubes, a pair of glass pipettes, a graduated cylinder, a retort, and a spirit burner with its own jar of spirits. A thick booklet described hundreds of experiments, some with acids that would eat through metal, others with foul-smelling substances that would clear a room in seconds, still others involving combinations of harmless ingredients that, when mixed in the wrong order, would explode in your face.

If this were *Leave It to Beaver,* there would be a long family discussion over pot roast about responsibility and trust, the value of a scientific education, and the need to clean up after oneself, and then the mother would smile at the father and the Beav would get the chemistry set. In real life, there was no such discussion. The set I got was the least expensive. About the size of a cigar box, it cost $12.95 and contained six chemicals, one test tube, a set of tongs, and a candle. There were only two or three experiments I could perform. I did one on Christmas morning: I combined a blue-coloured chemical, probably cobalt chloride, with water and got—hey presto!—blue water.

As a consequence, I tend to over-gift when it comes to my daughters. I'm the same with Merilyn. She always says that what she wants is a simple Christmas: the whole family at the table, the turkey, the small, sensible tree, the stockings over the fireplace, a light snow falling outside the windows, and the recording of Dylan Thomas reading "A Child's Christmas in Wales" on the stereo. Every year she tries to put a limit on how much we spend on presents; one year, she suggested that all the Christmas presents be handmade. Everyone was thoroughly delighted. After the others went home, I gave her a pearl necklace and she gave me a Montblanc fountain pen.

I look over at Merilyn in the seat beside me and see Christmas sadness. I want to give her the world, but I didn't even remember to bring the Dylan Thomas CD.

WILLIAMS APPEARS as little more than an exit ramp. We turn north and begin the climb up from the desert floor to the rim of the Colorado Plateau, a huge chunk of sedimentary rock thrust up from the sea floor 250 million years ago. More recently—20 million years ago—its northeast end heaved up another six thousand feet, causing the rivers running across it to run faster and dig deeper into the plateau's soft sedimentary rock. The biggest of these was the Colorado: it ran so fast and cut so deep that it formed the Grand Canyon in just over a million years, carving out a gorge a mile down and ten miles across that exposed layers of rock dating back almost 2 billion years, half the age of the planet.

That I have never seen the Grand Canyon I count as a serious mark against any claim I might have to being a well-travelled individual. I think I flew over it once on a flight from Los Angeles, but it might have been some other gorge, or I might have been asleep and dreaming. (It is unbelievably huge; if the entire population of Earth were packed like smoked oysters into a cube, that cube could be hidden in the Grand Canyon.) Seeing the Grand Canyon is supposed to be humbling, as though its immensity just might save us from the sin of pride, of thinking we're too big for our britches.

It might even save us from dying. In 1958, novelist Edward Abbey was visited at his campfire in Arches National Monument, in southeastern Utah, by a Bavarian in lederhosen with a case of Löwenbräu beer under his arm; it was such an unlikely occurrence that Abbey made room for him and they began to talk. The Bavarian opined that America should have joined with Hitler during the Second World War to fight the Russians and went on to list a string of arguments in support of anti-Semitism.

"I could have opened his skull with a bottle of his own Löwenbräu," Abbey writes, "and was powerfully tempted." But, he says, he didn't have the heart to do it. "After all, he hadn't seen the Grand Canyon yet."

As we drive, the sagebrush gives way to chaparral, then to thicker stands of piñon pines; the ground around them is sandy, with little tufts of cranky-looking grass sticking up here and there. It reminds me strongly of northern Ontario. I remember reading somewhere that every thousand feet you climb in elevation is the equivalent of travelling eight hundred miles north in latitude. The Colorado Plateau is seven thousand feet above sea level, which means we've been spirited approximately 3,800 miles north since leaving Needles, which puts us, in effect, in boreal forest verging on tundra, somewhere around Whitehorse, in the Yukon.

As if to prove my point, it even starts snowing—thin, wispy threads of white that whisk like spilled sugar across the highway.

*   *   *

*M*Y heart sinks. Snow? In Arizona? Sitting in our little Echo in my summer clothes, I feel ridiculously unprepared. For the weather. For this trip. What were we thinking, setting off without a plan?

There are an alarming number of tour buses on the road, giant double-deckers, their windows packed with faces. Cars with large plastic boxes guyed to their roofs vie for lane space with camper vans and Winnebagos. I suddenly realize that although we have a reservation at the El Tovar Hotel dining room for Christmas dinner, we have not booked a room, either at the El Tovar or anywhere else.

It never occurred to us that all of Arizona and half of Japan would want to spend Christmas at the Grand Canyon. In the snow. Snow is a novelty here in the South, I suppose. It reassures me only a little that there is as much traffic coming toward us as there is heading our way.

"Maybe these are all day trippers," I say feebly, turning on the cellphone.

It is early afternoon. I open a travel guide and start calling hotels in Grand Canyon Village. Nothing at the El Tovar, nothing at the Hampton Inn, the Marriott, the Holiday Inn, or the Days Inn. All the tour buses and family vans must have booked ahead, probably as far back as a year ago. Finally, at something called the Bright Angel Lodge, described in the brochure as a "rustic main lodge, guest lodge and cabins forming a picturesque village on the South Rim of the Grand Canyon," I snag a room.

"Someone who booked ahead must have died," Wayne says.

"Is that the best price you can give us?" I ask the clerk. There is a guffaw at the other end of the line. "Okay, we'll take it, we'll take it."

Wayne and I exchange glances. We feel like Joseph and Mary arriving in Bethlehem a day late and finding the manger still available. "What's wrong with the manger?" they must have asked themselves.

We skim through Grand Canyon Village, a strip of chain hotels and restaurants, and head on to the rim, to the Bright Angel. I try to be cheered by the name, to stall my descent into what feels like post-Christmas depression, though Christmas Day isn't even half over yet.

"What the...!" Wayne exclaims. He is hunched over the steering wheel, manoeuvring at a crawl past the hordes of tourists that take the road for their sidewalk, which they must since the sidewalks are packed tight. It looks like Coney Island in July or Whistler on the day the lifts start up. Swarms of tourists stroll among the trees and along the walks, mill in front of the hotel, sit on benches and curbs and on the bare ground itself, as if they're waiting for a parade to begin.

"Whose three-ring circus is this?" he says, then, always careful to attribute a quote, he adds, "Carl Sandburg."

The main lodge is surrounded by a vast parking lot crammed with cars. We snake up and down the aisles until we are half a mile from the hotel.

"I'll find something—you go check us in," Wayne says, dropping me at the entrance.

I hurry in, worried now that the laughing clerk has given our room to someone else as punishment for my cheek. The lobby is a seething mass of bodies in hiking gear sitting on backpacks and drinking water out of plastic bottles, apparently waiting for room cancellations or no-shows or patrons with attitude. I take my place in line in front of the check-in desk and stare up at the cathedral beams of the ceiling, trying to quell my anxiety. I feel a surge of desperation as the clerk searches for our name, a rush of euphoria when he finds it. By the time I see Wayne hauling our suitcases into the lobby, I am such a stew of emotion I don't know whether to kiss him in triumph or cry with relief.

We thread our way along a gangway of souvenir shops to a side exit that opens into a covered causeway that leads to the door of the guest lodge, a term that to my mind implies a long spacious lounge made of logs with quaint rooms giving off indoor balconies that overlook a massive central stone fireplace. It turns out to be a semi-subterranean maze of dark, dank, wood-panelled corridors with numbers keyed to the site map in my hand.

Our room is in corridor E-6. The door is chipped and dented and sits loosely in its jamb. It has a vent at eye level, like the one in our cellar door back home. When I unlock it, the door swings halfway open before bumping into a bed. The room is barely larger than the two cots and battered dresser it contains. All the light comes from a fixture in the ceiling, which, like the walls, is covered with wood panelling painted a regurgitated shade. There is a musty smell of mould. Above the beds, a small window looks out onto a path at ground level. Legs scissor past a drift of dirty snow. I can't help it; I start to cry.

"It's not that bad," Wayne says hopefully. It's so unlike him to be optimistic that I know it really is very, very bad. "It's only for one night."

"But it's *Christmas* night!" I wail, giving in to sobs.

"We'll have a great dinner and go for a stroll, and by the time we get back we'll be too tired to notice the room. We'll push the beds together," he adds, sounding inspired, "and get candles at the gift shop."

"Is there a bathtub, at least?" A hot bath is my solution to just about everything. It's the only place I don't think.

Wayne opens door to the bathroom. It's relatively clean. There is another window, and a small tub underneath it. Maybe I could sleep there. I look back into the bedroom and shudder.

"I don't think I can stay here."

"But it's the last room," Wayne points out.

"I don't care," I say. I cup my hand over my eyes to shield them from the overhead light. "We'll have dinner, then drive somewhere until we find a better room. We'll drive all night if we have to."

"What about seeing the Grand Canyon?"

This gives me pause. Of course: that's why we're here. I look out the window. It's not like me to give up so easily. I feel myself resisting and relenting at the same time.

"It's not quite dark yet," I say at last, the glass-half-full part of me in ascendance. I wipe my eyes, blow my nose, straighten my shoulders. "Okay, let's go for a walk, then come back here and change for dinner. Maybe I'll feel better by then."

* * *

*W*HEN Nathaniel Hawthorne visited Niagara Falls in the summer of 1835, he was filled with dread that the falls would fail to live up to his expectations. So haunted was he "with a vision of foam and fury, and dizzy cliffs, and an ocean tumbling down out of the sky," that he stayed in his hotel room for three full days before finally steeling himself to confront them. Why rush to be disappointed? he asked himself.

We aren't going to stay in our room for even three minutes. We step outside the guest lodge and turn left onto an interlocking paving-stone path that runs beside a low parapet, not knowing quite where we are going—and there, to our utter astonishment, is the Grand Canyon. The sudden shock of it renders us speechless. There is the stone parapet, about knee-high, there is a ragged cliff edge on the other side of it with a few scraggly trees growing out of bare rock, and then there is—nothing at all. The setting sun illuminates the opposite face like a reading lamp trained on an enormous stack of books. Our eyes travel down to the distant bottom of the canyon, where a thin trickle of silver, the Colorado River, meanders among soaring chimneys and hoodoos. How immense is it? the mind wants immediately to know. Niagara Falls could be at the bottom of the canyon and it would be all but unnoticeable from where we stand. We would point down and say, "Oh look, is that a waterfall over there?"

The canyon follows a fault line where two vast chunks of North America came together (Niagara Falls is on another). The silt-laden Colorado River cut down through the fault like sandpaper through balsa wood. Each layer on the canyon walls represents the bottom of an ancient ocean; when there was no ocean, and therefore no accumulation of sediment, there is no rock. This absence of rock is called a nonconformity. We are living in a nonconformity now, since the top of the canyon is a limestone slab that is already 230 million years old and has nothing on it but a tsunami of tourists with their requisite hotels and restaurants.

Once we have taken in what is there—the pale earth tones, pinks, greys, and siennas of the various strata; the play of light and shadow on the ledges; the trees gripping sheer rock faces with their gnarled roots; the distant specks that are birds (gulls? peregrines? condors?) riding thermals above the river—we slowly begin to appreciate what isn't there. There is far more absent from the Grand Canyon than there is present. In fact, the Grand Canyon is one colossal absence, billions of cubic metres of sedimentary rock carved away almost overnight by that thin silvery trickle of water we see enlivening the canyon floor.

Indeed, it *is* a trickle compared to what it once was. In its heyday, when John Wesley Powell led the Powell Geographic Expedition down it in 1869, the Colorado River flowed through the canyon at the rate of 250,000 cubic feet of water per second. Powell found the rapids so treacherous that half his crew deserted after three months. The water, in Edward Abbey's words, "flowed unchained and unchannelled in the joyous floods of May and June, swollen with snow melt. Boulders crunching and clacking and grumbling, tumbling along the river's bedrock bed, the noise like that of grinding molars in a giant jaw."

From our vantage point on the parapet, it doesn't look like there's much grinding and clacking going on. We walk along for a while, hardly taking our eyes off the canyon, watching the pinks turn to purples and the greys to black. Snow is still falling, but gently, as though someone has upended a great scenic snow globe of the Grand Canyon and then righted it again. Eventually we come to an impressive four-storey log structure with wings stretching out almost to the canyon's rim. Through a row of lighted windows in the main building we see white-shirted waiters setting up tables in a huge dining room; through another window, an enormous Christmas tree soars to the top of an atrium. People wearing expensive sweaters sit casually about in the lobby, reading, talking quietly among themselves, sipping drinks. We have come to the El Tovar.

"Let's go in and confirm our dinner reservation," Merilyn says, her voice trembling.

One of the appeals of travel is that we get to live our fantasy lives for a brief spell. Merilyn wants to live in a hotel. When she was seven her family moved to Brazil, and they lived in a hotel for several months while their apartment building was being constructed, a rather nice hotel, with wide, carpeted corridors, a dining room with its own pastry chef, unsalted butter that came in small curls on a silver platter, a grand piano on a raised dais, doormen at the revolving doors, and by the elevators on each floor, tall, umbrella-stand-sized ashtrays filled with white sand with the hotel's initials pressed into the surface.

It isn't the luxury of living in a hotel that attracts her, I think—not the fact that she would never have to cook or serve food, or repair a screen or wash a floor or a dish again (which would be my first thought)—but rather the quiet efficiency of hotel management, the sense of everything running smoothly because everything is in its proper place, and in good repair, and the staff all know where it is, and when you look, it really is there: the iron is in the closet, in its little wire basket; extra pillows are in the linen closet, beside the neatly folded and pressed (!) sheets; the salt and pepper shakers are always full and free-flowing, the coffee is always hot, the croissants always fresh, the poached egg always perfectly poached (the white solid but the yolk still runny), sitting proudly on its mound of perfect, pan-fried hash browns. Not all hotels are like that, of course, but a surprising number of them are, and you can tell you're in one the minute you walk through the door. As soon as we enter El Tovar's lobby, with its thick carpet, its chandeliers and cushioned sofas, the soft classical (not Christmas) music coming from hidden speakers, the concierge's desk in one alcove and the front desk across from it, I know this is a hotel where Merilyn could live.

The El Tovar was built in 1905 by the Atchison, Topeka and Santa Fe Railroad. The ATSF hired Charles Whittlesey to design the hotel and Fred Harvey to build and staff it. Whittlesey, a Chicago architect, imagined the Grand Canyon setting to be vaguely alpine and conceived the hotel as a kind of overgrown Swiss chalet. It was originally to be called the Bright Angel Tavern, because it was situated at the head of the Bright Angel Trail, but in the end it was named the El Tovar after Pedro de Tovar, the Spanish conquistador who led a scouting expedition out of New Mexico in the grip of one of the most powerful exploration myths of America: the search for the Seven Cities of Cibola.

When the Moors were overrunning Spain in 1150, seven bishops from Mérida fled with the church's gold, jewels, and religious relics to a distant land, where they founded two cities made entirely of gold: Cibola and Quivira. Nearly four hundred years later, a Franciscan friar named Marcos de Niza claimed to have seen one of them in what is now New Mexico. In 1540, the Spanish governor of Mexico sent a huge expedition under Francisco Vázquez de Coronado to find it. Guided by the friar, Coronado travelled up the west coast to what is now southwestern Arizona. De Niza's "city of gold" turned out to be a small Zuni pueblo village, the walls of which contained mica, which flashed like gold in the setting sun.

Just to make sure there wasn't something more, Coronado sent two smaller expeditions farther north. The one led by Pedro de Tovar made it into Hopi territory, where he heard about a large river that flowed westward to the Pacific, but he never bothered to check it out. It was the Colorado. I find it interesting, and amusing, that the hotel we are standing in was built by the Santa Fe Railroad, which didn't go to Santa Fe, and named after Don Tovar, who never saw the Grand Canyon.

"Why don't we ask if they've had any cancellations?" I say to Merilyn.

"Do you think?" she says, her face brightening for the first time today. Then it clouds again. "I did call about an hour ago. And we already have that other room."

"It won't hurt to ask," I say, leading her to the front desk. I'm still going to let her do the talking. The clerk is a young, officious-looking man in a black suit with a bronze pocket badge that says "Ronnie." When Merilyn asks him if he has a room, Ronnie gives her an admonitory look and asks if we have a reservation.

"No," Merilyn says. "But when I called earlier someone told me you might get a cancellation. Would you check?"

"I have checked," Ronnie says, but he clicks the keyboard on his computer anyway and looks at the screen. "Half the people in this lobby have asked me the same ques—Well, I'll be," he says, incredulous, "a cancellation just came in this second. Seems we do have a room, after all. I can let you have it for $166."

Merilyn looks at me. "It's awfully expensive," she says, and I'm afraid she's going to try to get a better rate. People from the lobby have begun to rise out of their chairs, murmuring ominously. I hear the clerk at the next wicket telling another couple that a cancellation has just come in.

"We'll take it," I tell Ronnie before the others can reply.

By the time we have checked in and brought our luggage over from the Bright Angel, and I have brought the car around to the El Tovar parking lot, it is dark. I can see Merilyn's shadow moving behind the curtains of our room as she sets up our acquired goodies for a pre-Christmas-dinner repast. The room is on the second floor and has a view of the kiva, which will be splendid in the morning. But now night has fallen and it is still snowing gently; to my right I sense rather than see the huge void that is the Grand Canyon at night. Thomas Wolfe, arriving in 1938 at this rim at about this time in the evening, described the canyon as "a fathomless darkness... fathomlessly there." But I find it comforting, perhaps because it is so much like being beside a large lake after dark, the water holding the warmth and filling the air with a life-infused almost consciousness. The words "Thank you" occur to me, and I address them silently to the canyon.

* * *

*M*Y expectations of the Grand Canyon have been shaped by books. I peer over the rim and see searchlights; I look back and see the El Tovar in flames. It's the view from Vita Sackville-West's novel *Grand Canyon,* a futuristic fantasy when it was published in 1942, though it doesn't seem quite so far-fetched now, after 9/11. Sixty years ago, no American would have considered the possibility of being attacked on home soil, let alone at the brink of the Grand Canyon, the gaping symbol of American grandeur. In Sackville-West's story, it becomes America's last trench.

Sackville-West's characters are in the desert on holiday, as are we, and the scene she sets is eerily similar to the one I see around me, except that the porters and maids are no longer Navajos in costume, their long black hair tied up in red ribbons. And nowhere do I see the huge outdoor dance floor she describes: "parquet from California forests laid in patterns at the canyon's edge."

Sackville-West was British and obviously had no patience for American hubris. As the tourists retire to their beds, Germans swoop down from Canada to bomb the American forces huddled on the desert plateau. The manager, a villainous spy in cahoots with a worldwide Nazi alliance, sets the hotel on fire, turning the lovely log structure into a flaming beacon for the bombers.

I look at the logs now and see them as so much kindling, look at the path down into the canyon where Mrs. Temple scurried with the other guests, trying to outrun the blast.

I long to walk alone down that slender trail, to sleep at the water's edge on a bed of ferns, to follow the river night after night on foot or float its length in a canoe. That would feel real. I think of Powell, the first white man to see the canyon from the bottom. Like all white explorers, Powell christened everything he saw: Music Temple, Marble Canyon, Flaming Gorge, Split Mountain, Bright Angel River. The names, though fantastical, don't begin to represent the overwhelming strangeness of what is really here, the soaring spires and gaping arches we can barely make out from the rim.

Maybe if I could see it from Powell's perspective, looking up from below, I would feel like I was seeing the Grand Canyon. But gazing down into its enormity, I go blank. I can see the depth of the hole in the earth, the striations of colour, but I can't take it in. I float like a gnat on the edge. I am minuscule; it is monstrous. How can we establish any kind of relationship?

When Simone de Beauvoir visited America in 1955, six years after the publication of her feminist landmark, *The Second Sex,* she saw a Grand Canyon akin to Disneyland. "The most ingenious efforts have been made to transform a natural marvel into a kind of amusement park," she wrote. There was a tower at one end where a person could look through a slit and see the canyon upside down or manipulate its image on huge sheets of glass. On an upper terrace, telescopes offered views of the canyon and the violet-and-red plateau that is the Painted Desert beyond: glimpses of landscape sold off for a nickel. Now there is an interpretive centre with lectures and dioramas, which seem relatively non-invasive compared with the Skywalk, a U-shaped glass bridge the Hualapai Indians have extended seventy feet out from the western edge of the abyss.

"The tourist is offered every possible artificial means of taming these exuberantly natural spectacles," wrote de Beauvoir. "In the same way, people in America consume 'conditioned' air, frozen meat and fish, homogenized milk, canned fruit and vegetables, they even put artificial chocolate flavour into real chocolate. Americans are nature lovers, but they accept only a nature inspected and corrected by man."

"What's the good of having a canyon if you don't exploit it?" the manager of Vita Sackville-West's hotel argues. He may be a turncoat, but he's American in his bones.

I expected to be profoundly moved in the face of this grandeur. To be swept off my feet. But nothing happens. The canyon feels fake, like one of those buildings with windows painted on a blank brick wall.

"Very impressive," Wayne says, "but why did they put it so close to the hotel? That's a quote, I don't remember from whom."

But who are we to talk about fakery? When we went back to the Bright Angel to move our things to the El Tovar, I approached the reception desk with heaving breaths.

"I can't stay here," I gasped.

The clerk looked at me with concern. "A lot of people have trouble with the altitude," he said solicitously. "No problem. There won't be any charge."

I nodded, and put my hand to my chest. The fake asthma attack already felt real.

Now the whole day feels fake. Two atheists celebrating Christmas at a natural phenomenon tarted up for tourists, a geological wonder

I seem to see only through the eyes of dead writers. I turn away in disgust.

I can't even do that without being reminded of Howard in Richard Ford's story "Abyss." Howard, an otherwise decent real estate agent from New England, has ducked out of a conference in Phoenix to drive to the Grand Canyon with Frances to continue their ongoing illicit affair. Frances steps over the low wall to take a picture, the same low wall that I am standing in front of. One minute she's there; the next, she's gone. Howard steps over the wall, too, to see how far she has fallen, then quickly steps back, as if in that motion, everything can be returned to what it was. He's on the right side of danger, but nothing is the same.

"What you did definitely changed things," he says to the absent Frances.

Wayne and I understand Howard and Frances. We understand in the worst possible way how what we do changes things. The life we have now is built, at least in part, on sadness and pain, not only ours. We feel it most keenly at Christmas, when what we want more than anything is for our family to be safe together under the eaves. But our notion of family is not the same as our children's, and here we are, thousands of miles away from them.

I return to the El Tovar to dress for dinner and to join Wayne for a preprandial. It was good of him to allow me these moments alone, though I could tell he worried about my mood and my being so close to the cliff edge. A woman is playing Christmas carols on the grand piano in the lobby: the strains of "O Come, All Ye Faithful" penetrate our room even after I close the door. We call the kids, one by one, and wish them a merry Christmas, discovering that, in fact, it *is* merry, even without us. We open a bottle of good champagne and, linking arms awkwardly across the bed, clink our hotel glasses.

On the table is the gift I bought Wayne just before we left Vancouver: a silk tie with a repeating pattern of a Haida raven, the trickster-hero who brought the sun, the moon, and the stars to life.

Wayne brings out a small velvet box. Inside are a pair of gold drag-onfly earrings. I've always loved dragonflies. Dive-bombers, I call them. They show up in the spring just after the blackflies. I'll be working in the garden, swatting and swearing under my breath; then the dragon-flies arrive, swooping close, devouring the cloud of flies at my mouth.

"There were dragonflies on Earth a hundred million years before the rock outside our window was formed," Wayne says. "They survived two mass extinctions."

On our way to dinner, Wayne wearing his new tie and I in my ear-rings, we stop in the gift shop, where we see the dragonfly motif on necklaces and pottery, a stylized double-bar cross.

"What does it mean?" I ask the clerk, a nice-looking young man, smart and well-spoken, though he is keen, I sense, to be elsewhere.

"For the Navajo, dragonflies are symbols of pure water," he recites, then warms to us a little and leans forward, as if to share a secret. "Some say they represent renewal after a time of hardship."

*　★　*

*W*AITERS in the El Tovar dining room the next morning are wearing white shirts, black trousers, and long white aprons tied behind their backs. They move efficiently among the holidayers—families, mostly, and older couples dressed in matching heavy-knit sweaters.

"But they aren't Harvey Girls, are they?" Merilyn confides when our young man has deposited my stack of waffles and Merilyn's poached egg atop a heap of—alas—daintily cubed but darkly deep-fried hash browns.

"Meaning?" I say.

"And you'll notice our meals are not served on blue plates."

"I wonder, my dear," I say gently, "whether the trip is proving too much for you."

"Not at all," she says. "I have a point. The Fred Harvey who built this hotel was the first chain restaurateur in America. In the 1860s, he got the railway to let him build restaurants in all its stations. Tired of rowdy male waiters—"

"Our waiter is perfectly tame," I interject.

"—he advertised in East Coast newspapers for 'Young women, 18 to 30 years of age, of good character, attractive and intelligent.' He paid them $17.50 a month plus room and board and gave them a train pass to the restaurant, where he dressed them up in black dresses with Elsie collars and hems no more than eight inches off the floor, and called them Harvey Girls. They were credited with civilizing the West: they ended up marrying all those cowboys and getting them to settle down. There was a Judy Garland movie about it, the one where they sing, 'Folks around these parts get the time of day from the Atchison, Topeka, and the Santa Fe. All aboard!' It's been running through my head all morning."

"Thank you," I say, wincing, "now I've got the earworm, too."

"In those Harvey Girl restaurants, the daily specials were served on blue china, hence the term 'blue plate special.' See? I did have a point," she concludes, carefully scraping her egg onto a side plate, leaving the hash browns in their puddle of grease.

The dining room is a vast, L-shaped affair, full of dark, heavy furniture. Some of the tables are long, with room for a dozen or more diners. Ours is a table for two tucked away in a quiet corner, with a view through the windows of the Grand Canyon, into which a light skiff of snow is softly falling. On each of the walls is a large, colourful mural depicting scenes from the life of one of the four Indian tribes that originally inhabited the area: Hopi, Navajo, Apache, and Mojave. I am facing the Mojave mural, which shows a group of men wearing feather headdresses, doing a bird dance to give thanks for a good corn harvest. Around them as they dance, a flock of red-winged blackbirds clean up the loose corn in the fields. The dancers are thanking the birds that no corn is wasted.

"Interesting," says Merilyn. "European settlers shot blackbirds for eating their grain."

After our waffles and egg, we walk part of the way down a trail leading to the bottom of the canyon, then turn back to trudge up again to the top, against the flow of younger hikers skipping jauntily downward with the aid of walking sticks and gravity. Some are on donkeys, sad-looking grey beasts (I mean the donkeys) that step thoughtfully close to the edge of the trail as they pass us. We had contemplated the donkeys at the lip of the canyon, but the matter was settled, as far as I was concerned, by a small sign advising that no one weighing more than 170 pounds was allowed to ride. The whole scenario begins to look like an allegory of aging, the young gambolling down the slippery slope, the decrepit clawing their way back up.

Just when we stop to collect our breath, a largish, whitish bird with black wings flies over our heads and lands on a promontory a few hundred feet behind us. We have our binoculars and field guide, and after some page shuffling, we concur: a Clark's nutcracker, our first. William Clark first saw the bird on August 22, 1805, on the Columbia River. He thought it was "of the woodpecker kind," but Lewis thought it was more like a jay. To settle the dispute, Lewis had York shoot half a dozen of them and collect their skins. Years later, the eminent ornithologist Alexander Wilson named it Clark's crow, but it isn't a crow, it's a nutcracker, which is what it's called now.

I like it that Lewis and Clark seem to be tracking us east.

After puffing our way to the top of the canyon, we pack our bags and what's left of our Christmas goodies and check out of the El Tovar. Reluctantly. We think about staying an extra day, but the expense and the busloads of tourists that continue to arrive decide us against it.

At the Visitors' Center, we pick up a checklist of local birds: I put a mark beside the Clark's nutcracker. We are on the fringe of a small group listening to a lively lecture on Grand Canyon geology delivered by Geology Jim, a tall, thin man in a ranger's uniform. At one point, Geology Jim throws a beanbag the size of a grapefruit forcefully to the terrazzo floor and shouts, "Bang!"

"Imagine," he says, fixing each of us with a fanatical glare, "that this beanbag is a raindrop." We try. "Rain hits the desert with incredible force, much harder than it hits land covered with vegetation because there's nothing to stop it, and over time it does a lot of damage. We like to think that rain is good in a desert, don't we?" We nod obediently. "But like most things in nature it's both a bane and a blessing, depending on how you look at it."

7 / THE MARRIAGE ROAD

*W*HAT we see of Page, Arizona, doesn't inspire us to search for a gourmet restaurant, and anyway, after our splurge last night, we have to get back on budget. We find a cheap motel and, for dinner, make further inroads into our Christmas goodies from the comfort of our room, which looks out across an alley to the back of a grocery store. After the splendour of the El Tovar, Merilyn is looking a bit glum, so during the meal I tell her about a theory I'm developing about motel-room towels. My theory is that motel towels start life as hotel towels, large and thick and white, with unfrayed borders and neat corners, and when one enfolds oneself within them after bathing they hardly seem to get wet. Big, expensive hotels buy them, and after washing them a few dozen times, they replace them with newer, thick, plush towels and sell the old towels to smaller, less expensive hotels. Then, after a few more washings, these smaller hotels sell them to even smaller hotels, maybe to the chain hotels, the nicer chains, which, when they are done with them, sell them to the economy-line motels. Eventually the towels are sold in auction lots to the sub-economy strip motel chains like the one we are in. By then they are grey and stained and so thin as to be transparent, cut down into ever smaller sizes and roughly re-hemmed. They now hang limply over racks in small bathrooms, wincing at the sounds of plumbing and the smells of drains, surviving on their faded memories of happier times, when they had nap.

Merilyn looks at me sadly, as though to say, The Four Horsemen on the rampage again, are they?

"We have really nice towels at home," she says glumly.

Some motels can take the nap out of people, too.

IN THE morning, I walk to the grocery store in the strip mall to buy some breakfast things. I take a blue plastic handbasket from a stack by the door and walk up and down the aisles with it over my arm. Cereal. Milk. A sad-looking peach. I scrutinize the meagre cheese selection for cheddar, but all they have is something called Kraft American. Merilyn asked me to look for Scottish oatcakes, but curiously there don't seem to be any on the shelf with the nachos and party dip.

"Excuse me," I say to the woman at the checkout. She is young, thin, her dark hair tied back except for a fringe that covers her forehead down to her eyebrow studs. Her eyeliner is so flawless I suspect it is tattooed. "Do you have any oatcakes?"

"Oat what?" she says, looking alarmed.

"Cakes."

"Cakes don't come in until after," she says.

"After what?"

She shrugs. She has nails to buff.

"What about demerara sugar?"

"Baking supplies is aisle 5."

"I looked there. You just have white and brown."

"Then I guess no," she says. "Is this all then?"

I take the cereal and milk and Kraft American out of the basket, wondering what besides the poor peach I can get for Merilyn. The hash browns are all frozen: they're thin, shaped into patties, but I don't think we can heat them in the coffee maker. "I don't suppose you have any almond milk?"

This time she doesn't even look up. She's hitting the cash-register keys hard. *Get this wacko out of here before he goes postal.*

"Is there a good place around here to see California condors?" I risk, keeping my voice conversational. Her finger hangs poised over the cash register. I wonder if there's a 911 button. "It's a kind of bird. A vulture. There are supposed to be lots of them in this area—I just wondered if there was a specific place where we could see them."

"You tried down at the dam?" she says. "They're all up and down the canyon. You'd probably see them for sure at the Navajo Bridge." She looks at me. "What? We did a school project on them. You want a bag?"

"No, thanks," I say. "And thanks."

"Uh-huh."

AFTER BREAKFAST, we drive down to the dam. Unless you know its history, there's nothing particularly remarkable about Lake Powell. It's a fake lake, created in 1957 by the Glen Canyon Dam. In one of his sadder essays, "Down There in the Rocks," Edward Abbey, sitting on a boat on Lake Powell, tries unsuccessfully not to think of what is down there, hundreds of feet below the surface: "Glen Canyon as it was, the wild river, the beaches, the secret passages and hidden cathedrals of stone, the wilderness alive and sweet and charged with mystery, miracle, magic." This is Abbey in elegiac mood, in metaphysical funk, mourning his lost love. "All that was living and beautiful lies many fathoms below, drowned in dead water and buried under slime. No matter. Forget it."

Good advice. We get out of the car and walk across the road. I look down over the dam, past the power cables, scanning the canyon for condors. It's a long way down. The walls, jagged layers of dark Navajo

sandstone, draw the eye to where the turbulent waters of the Colorado River tumble out of a tube roaring with delight, I imagine, at their
release after having been pent up behind the concrete wedge of the
dam. No condors ride the thermals above the churning water.

"Before damnation," as Abbey calls the time before the Bureau of
Reclamation made it lie still for jet skiers and houseboaters, the Colorado was a great river. Now it's the most dammed river in the United
States. The Hoover Dam, at the far end of the Grand Canyon, was the
first. Completed in 1935, it stores up water for Las Vegas in Lake Mead
and was at the time the largest electric generating plant in the world
(it is now the thirty-fourth largest). Protests from the Sierra Club and
from citizens such as Seldom Seen Smith, the hero of Abbey's novel of
eco-terrorism, *The Monkey Wrench Gang,* prevented the bureau from
turning the entire Grand Canyon into a gigantic reservoir, but even so
the river bumps into a dam every hundred miles along its 1,470-mile
course from the Rockies to its outlet in the Sea of Cortez. Between
here and there, 95 per cent of its water will have been siphoned out
of it, and the 5 per cent that is left when it crosses the Mexican border
evaporates in the desert before it can get to the Pacific. The mighty
Colorado River no longer reaches the sea.

We could cross the river here, but instead we circle back to Route 89
and head for the bridge where the grocery girl said we might see a condor. A California condor might be just the thing to cheer me up.

CALIFORNIA CONDORS once covered about as much of the continent
as we will on our trip. They were sacred to the West Coast natives for
millennia: an archaeological site in West Berkeley, California, that
dates back three thousand years yielded a complete, articulated condor skeleton arranged and buried exactly like the human corpses
found at the same site. In eastern native cultures, wild turkeys were
substituted for humans in ceremonies that once involved human sac-
rifice and ritual cannibalism. Here in the West, that honour was given

to the California condor, the bird most likely to have been the spark for the Thunderbird myths.

But the condor population has been in decline for many years, probably since the last ice age, which didn't favour large animals with a lot of surface area and specialized appetites. Not that condors were fussy eaters; so long as something was dead, they'd eat it. The *coup de grâce* was European settlers, who reviled condors and shot or poisoned them at every opportunity.

By 1981, there were only nineteen California condors left in the wild; five years later, despite a vigorous program of removing eggs and chicks from wild condor nests and raising them in zoos, there were only five California condors living outside captivity. The best estimates were that the species was one bad meal away from extinction.

That's when the Condor Recovery Program, organized by the Los Angeles and San Diego Zoos, began collecting the last remaining adult condors from the wild and raising them in special breeding facilities, called "condorminiums." The last five condors on Earth became egg-laying machines. As the eggs hatched and nestlings matured, they were released into the wild in national parks throughout California and Arizona. While researching my book *Vulture*, I spoke with Mike Wallace, the condor specialist at the Los Angeles Zoo and leader of the Recovery Program, who told me that his long-term plan was to have three hundred birds reintroduced to the wild by the end of the twentieth century. By now, as Merilyn and I approach the Navajo Bridge, that plan has been accomplished, and wild condors are once again flying over wilderness areas where they haven't been seen for thousands of years. Sixty have been released in the Vermilion Cliffs Wilderness Area, which lies ahead of us.

We park at the south end of the bridge and walk out to the midway point. Another couple is already there, looking upriver with binoculars. They appear to be what Edward Abbey called, unkindly, New Yorkers: in their sixties, wearing pressed khaki and stout hiking boots. Abbey would have looked around for a Winnebago to sneer at, but I can see their car, a sedate sedan, parked not far from ours. And I, too, am wearing khaki and hiking boots.

"Peregrine falcon," the woman says when we come up to them. The man points to a spot along the cliff face. We can tell from the quality of their Bausch & Lomb binoculars that they are serious birders, and by the fact that they don't talk except to convey information. And sure enough, there is the falcon, perched on a narrow ledge about halfway between the river and the lip of the canyon, above an arrow of white guano that identifies the ledge as its regular roosting spot.

"Have you seen any condors?" I ask the woman.

Over her shoulder, I can see Merilyn gesticulating wildly for me to come and come quickly. She has continued walking along the bridge and is almost at the far end. I excuse myself and hurry down to where she is pointing triumphantly to a black object resting on one of the bridge girders, slightly below the road level. At first I think it's a raven, but when I focus my binoculars, I realize with a jolt that it's a California condor. There is no mistaking its bald, goofy-looking pate, its baleful eye, and the way it sits hunched on the girder, as though shrugging its black shoulders at the world and only incidentally keeping its featherless neck warm. It's odd how vultures manage to look repulsive and comical at the same time. The bird appears uninterested in us, probably because we are still breathing. There are bold white squares on each of its shoulders, painted with the number 50. All released condors have radio transmitters implanted in their shoulders and under their tails so that their movements can be traced telemetrically, and they are numbered so they can be monitored visually, too.

"Hello, Condor 50," I say to it. No response, unless its eye becomes slightly more hooded. In my notebook, I have a list of all condors released in Arizona since 1992. As much is known about the bloodlines of these condors as about most racehorses. Condor 50, male, hatched at the World Center of Birds of Prey in Flagstaff, April 9, 2001, released in the Vermilion Cliffs Wilderness Area on December 9, 2002, along with a female (Condor 41), four days younger. I scan the cliff faces with my binoculars, but there is no sign of her.

On our way back to the car, we tell our fellow twitchers about Condor 50.

"Yes," the woman says, "we saw him when we left the car. He's here every day. He's quite a handful, when he wants to be. Last year, down in the canyon, he tore a hole in a camper's tent and stuck his head into it looking for food. I guess captive-bred condors aren't shy around people."

"This is my first," I tell her. "A beautiful bird."

She beams. "If you want to see condors, you're in the right area," she says.

We thank the couple and head back to our car, where, before heading up the highway, I take out our checklist and put a satisfying tick beside "California condor."

It's barely nine o'clock in the morning, and as far as I'm concerned, it's already been a good day. After witnessing the wreckage of a great river, it's good to see something that we as a species have done right.

★　★　★

MEANDERING, that's how we're travelling. Going toward whatever destination presents itself.

"We'll make a plan as we go along," I say cheerfully.

"Or not make one at all," Wayne counters.

"Right." It is one of those marriage moments when we acknowledge the difference between us without feeling it an abyss.

We're on the other side of Marble Canyon, in the Arizona Strip, a wedge of five million acres tucked between the Colorado River and the Utah border. The road swings close to the rise of monumental red buttes known as the Vermilion Cliffs.

It's still cool, but the sun is out, drawing oxblood and ruby from the stone. I roll down my window and snap pictures that I erase as soon as

I see them. This landscape resists the frame. And yet, it feels familiar precisely because it has been so frequently framed, in endless commercials for tough trucks and as the backdrop for all those Hollywood westerns that made an icon of the American wagon train conquering the West.

I think of those first white travellers, plodding for days across this red plateau, stopped in their tracks by sheer walls of rock dropping to the Colorado. They couldn't know that if they turned left, they'd be faced with the vast chasm of the Grand Canyon. The lucky ones turned right and came to a place where the plateau knelt down to the water, at a crossing that became known as Lee's Ferry, a narrows that gives access onto the Arizona Strip.

"Look! A house!" I exclaim.

"Where?"

"Under that big stone."

Close by the foot of the cliffs, a red tongue of rock licks out over a wall of roughly stacked adobe, held together by nothing but hope. Scraps of wood painted Arizona turquoise crazily frame the low openings of a window and a door.

"Somebody lives here?"

"I doubt it." The shack looks like something Wile E. Coyote might have built from a cheap Acme kit that included a bottle of water and a bag of sand. "Look, there are more."

Under every overhanging hoodoo, a crumbling ruin of mud brick, here and there a thin cedar pole. We make out a house, maybe a chicken coop, a shed, an animal pen, an outhouse with its back to the road.

"There's a town marked on the map," I say. "Cliff Dwellers Lodge. Could this be it?"

In the desert, we are discovering, the definition of "town" loosens to embrace the faintest human breath. Cliff Dwellers Lodge is not a village, not a settlement, not even a lodge. It is a pause in the grey coiling road, the spot where Blanche Russell's car broke down one day in the late 1920s. Blanche was a dancer with the Ziegfeld Follies. When her husband, Bill, was diagnosed with tuberculosis, she hung up her tap shoes and drove him west in search of the hot, dry climate the doctors said would be the cure. The Navajo Bridge was brand new then, so they crossed the Colorado at the same place we did rather than a few miles north, at Lee's Ferry.

They weren't much past Marble Canyon when their old Ford broke down at the foot of the Vermilion Cliffs. Blanche, looking around, must have thought it might not be such a bad place to hole up for a while. It was definitely hot and dry. She threw a tarp against the biggest of the wind-carved rocks and set up house. There was nothing around for miles except homesteads abandoned to the drought, a sprawling herd or two of longhorns, and people like the Joads on their way to somewhere else. Blanche and Bill collected stones and pressed the endless sand into adobe bricks, shaping rooms as they felt the need. Passersby who stopped to gawk were invited to help in exchange for a meal. Before long, Blanche was running a diner, serving sightseers who came up by bus from the Grand Canyon. She installed a hand-operated gasoline pump when tourists started driving out in their cars to see the North Rim for themselves. And she sold water from Soap Creek and pigeons she raised in a coop to Mormons travelling the Honeymoon Trail to St. George to have their marriages sealed.

I like to think of Blanche and Bill ending their days in this splendid ruddy isolation, but they lasted only a decade. Blanche sold her collection of makeshift structures to a local rancher who turned the restaurant into a bar during the war, then passed it on to a couple who kept the place going into the early 1950s, when the nuclear bombs the government set off in the Nevada desert shook the ground so profoundly that Art Johnson, who was charged with keeping up the place, thought it would surely fall on his head.

It's hard enough to imagine settlers crossing these barren plateaus, almost impossible to imagine anyone staying. No telephone. Radio only on a good day. Tourists now and then. Nothing but arrowhead hunting to pass the time—and watching the windswept curve of boulder that was roof, wall, and sometimes both, wearing steadily away, shimmying now and then to a blast that could be neither seen nor heard.

People seem to take up such places by accident. I hear the story of Blanche Russell from Wendy, who owns the new Cliff Dwellers Lodge, which we find around the next bend in the road: another spread of low buildings made of stones tumbled from the cliff, but cobbled together in a more organized and reassuring way. Twenty-six years ago, Wendy came here for the summer to wait tables at nearby Marble Canyon Lodge, fell in love with a river guide named Terry Gunn, and never left. Now they have a son whom she home-schools rather than put him on a school bus at six in the morning for the slow, convoluted drive into Page.

Bob, who brings us weighty plates of eggs, sausages, and hash browns at the lodge restaurant, is another itinerant, a self-described couch surfer who worked both rims of the Canyon and sometimes down in Flagstaff, mostly living in his truck until he stopped in at the motel one day and stayed. Now he presides over the kitchen that serves the best road food we've had yet: the hash browns are good, not perfect, though they are real potatoes, grated and fried with fresh onions, just a little underdone.

"Why didn't anybody at the Canyon tell us about this place? Or Marble Lodge?" I ask Wendy. When we inquired at the Grand Canyon, everyone said the same thing: Page'd be your best bet.

"Travel rule number 21," Wendy laughs. "Never ask a local."

The combination general store, fly shop, and gas bar attached to the lodge offers an astonishingly varied display of groceries, hardware, sports clothing, fishing gear, and, yes, books. We have nowhere to go, nothing we have to do: we met our only deadline two nights ago at the El Tovar. We are definitely on freefall holiday now. We each buy a hiking shirt impregnated with uv block against the blazing sun. We're in the desert, after all. We go up and down the aisles, pick up sunscreen and mosquito repellent. Wayne lets loose a little yelp when he spots *The Monkey Wrench Gang*. I discover the Mormons.

Rediscover, I should say. I first met them in the guise of two very cute boys in slim black suits who drank numerous glasses of water in my parents' living room for most of one sunny afternoon. I was fourteen, home alone. When they knocked on the door and I invited them in, they turned and looked at each other as if their prayers had just been answered.

We are firmly in Mormon country here on the Arizona Strip. Lee's Ferry was built in 1871 by John Doyle Lee, a Mormon settler with nineteen wives and sixty-seven children. Into the early 1900s, his was the only ferry crossing the Colorado between Moab, Utah, and Needles. (Before Lee built the ferry, the river was forded at the Crossing of the Fathers, which is now under Lake Powell.) Lee's seventeenth wife, Emma, managed the ferry while her husband was off with the Mormon militia, fighting the United States Army for authority over the Utah Territory, which the Mormons had organized as a kind of theocratic democracy under Brigham Young. They were fighting the influx of non-Mormon settlers, too, sometimes masquerading as marauding Indians in order to frighten them off. At Mountain Meadows, a wagon train from Arkansas was raided and the men, women, and children who surrendered—120 people—were murdered. Seventeen children under the age of eight were spared to be distributed among Mormon families, while the corpses of their families were left to rot in the sun. Nine men were arrested for the killings, but only Lee was convicted, then executed by firing squad at the site of the massacre.

The cute boys didn't tell me that. Wendy does. There must be a dozen books on her shelf about the Mormons.

"I'm hooked," she says. "The Honeymoon Trail ran right close to here."

For a religious sect that encouraged multiple marriage, they certainly didn't make it easy. To marry, a Mormon settler had to travel from his homestead somewhere in the midwest to the town of

St. George, tucked in the far southwestern reaches of Utah. Here the faithful had built a glistening white church of plastered sandstone, a castellated Gothic affair that was the first temple dedicated west of the Mississippi River. It is still the oldest operating Mormon church, with eighteen "sealing rooms" in which marriage rings are exchanged. In the 1800s, that journey, by foot, horse, or cart, could take weeks. As the young couples moved along the trail, they'd stop to chisel their names into boulders and cliff walls, the same impulse, I suppose, that prompted Alexander Mackenzie and Lewis and Clark to carve their names in trees. For years, Wendy's husband, Terry Gunn, has been recording Mormon graffiti with his camera: *Ed Finney 1882. Adams, Joseph, from Kaysville to Arizona and Busted on June AD 1873. Ferrin, Zobedia Nov. 12 1882. 1885.*

Each new betrothal meant another trip on the Honeymoon Trail. John Doyle Lee must have passed this way eighteen times. Although the Church of Jesus Christ of Latter-day Saints officially disavowed polygamy in 1890, the practice of "plural marriage" and "spiritual wives" continues among splinter fundamentalist groups, both in the United States and in Canada. I think of the polygamist Mormons of Bountiful, British Columbia, recently in the news as a haven used by Warren Jeffs, one of the FBI's ten most wanted fugitives, accused of arranging marriages between his adult male followers and underage girls. Jeffs is apparently husband to more than fifty women.

"To be interested in American identity is to be interested in marriage," Nancy Cott concludes in *Public Vows: A History of Marriage and the Nation.* The same might be said of Canada, or of us—no doubt about it, marriage affects identity. As the Harvard historian points out, the so-called Christian model of lifelong monogamous union between one man and one woman wasn't the standard on this continent until just over a hundred years ago, a pretty short history for what politicians like to call one of their "traditional" values. Among First Nations peoples, marriage and divorce were often fluid. The first Europeans adopted the practice of "bush wives," a version of bigamy. Among early settlers, women were at such a premium that land-hungry bachelors would line up at railway stations to whisk single girls off to the mayor's office so they could stake a larger claim as married men. Americans were seen as particularly wild and woolly. In fact, many of the strict marriage laws in early Canada—no deviation, no divorce, no remarriage—were put in place specifically to protect us from the corrupt, immoral influence of the United States, a civic fence erected against a boisterous and bawdy neighbour.

"A viable society depends on stable families, which depend on stable marriages," trumpeted an editorial in the *Calgary Herald* last summer, supporting Prime Minister Stephen Harper's announcement that Canada's Parliament would consider reopening the same-sex marriage debate in the hopes of reversing an earlier decision that allowed gays and lesbians to marry. (On July 20, 2005, Canada became the fourth country in the world and the first country in the Americas to legalize same-sex marriage nationwide.) At the same time, in the United States, President Bush was calling for a ban on gay and lesbian unions, invoking the sacred spectre of "family values." But the truth is that marriage, especially here in the Wild West, was not a tradition so much as a metaphor for voluntary allegiance and permanent union, the moral bedrock of the freshly minted United States of America. No wonder polygamous Mormons were hunted down and arrested: they were terrorists in the bedrooms of the nation.

"Ready to get back on the trail, pardner?" I say to Wayne. Something about the desert has put a John Wayne twang in my talk.

"You all have a good time now," Wendy says as we head for the door.

"We will," Wayne and I reply in unison.

"We already are," I add, taking his hand. Ride for a week in a buckboard to seal my marriage to this man? Sure. We're never so happy as when we're on the road.

Wendy laughs. "I can see that."

*W*HEN we leave the Cliff Dwellers Lodge, we drive up onto the steppes that rise toward Utah from the Grand Canyon's north rim. It feels as though we are climbing a stairway to a very large church. *Repent, sinners; redemption is at hand.*

Deserts have always been associated with redemption: Brigham Young chose Utah over the California coast; Christ wandered off into the desert to deal with Satan; Moses redeemed the Children of Israel from the bread of affliction by parting the Red Sea and leading them into the Sinai Desert.

Much of early American literature is about the need for redemption. American culture is, despite its Hollywood glitz, a very religious culture. The five books held to be the American classics, what critic Harold Bloom refers to as "the secular Scripture of the United States of America"—*Moby-Dick, The Scarlet Letter, Walden, The Adventures of Huckleberry Finn,* and *Leaves of Grass*—all deal with various quests for redemption: Ahab intent on ridding the world of evil (incarnate in the white whale); Hester Prynne redeemed of the sin of fornication through punishment, penance, and good works; Thoreau wanting Nature to redeem the careworn human spirit; the slave Jim redeemed from bondage by the actions of one kind soul. Bloom refers to Whitman as the redeemer of American poetry.

In fact, everything in America seems to be about redemption, even that which is ostensibly about something else, like losing weight. In 2006, a 410-pound man named Steve Vaught decided to walk from California across the United States "to drop a few pounds and find joy," as Steve Friedman writes in *Backpacker* magazine. Before Vaught even got out of California, however, he ceased to be a simple fat man walking and became thefatmanwalking.com, with a website, a ghost writer, and two documentary filmmakers following him as he waddled off into the Mojave Desert. He eventually made it to New York, 114 pounds lighter and a lot wiser. His story, writes Friedman, is one of "suffering and redemption writ extra, extra large."

Perhaps this obsession with redemption comes from America's puritanical beginnings. ("Puritan" was originally a term of abuse. The Puritans preferred to call themselves "the godly.") According to this breakaway sect from the Church of England, mankind was by nature depraved and every circumstance was viewed as the judgment of an absolute and demanding God. The result, over centuries, is a state of confusion about the difference between a condition and a punishment: being obese isn't just the result of overeating or a sluggish hypothalamus, it's a punishment for gluttony. Those who are obese should feel guilty about it, and so losing weight becomes a quest for redemption.

Social psychologists studying the differences between Eastern and Western ways of thinking have found that, whereas Eastern cultures are capable of attributing small causes to great events (think butterfly wings causing hurricanes), in the West we tend to equate the size of the cause with the magnitude of the event. Thus John F. Kennedy's assassination could not have been carried out by a lone gunman; it had to be a conspiracy involving top members of the government and the CIA. Similarly, 9/11 was not a catastrophe engineered by a handful of zealots; it was the opening salvo in a war between the United States and Islam.

I was in Whitehorse, in the Yukon Territory, on September 11, 2001. At six in the morning, I was at work at my desk, a week into a four-month stint as writer-in-residence at the Whitehorse Public Library, when Merilyn telephoned from home and told me to turn on the television. I was four thousand miles from New York and in a different country, and yet I felt the attack as though it had been aimed at me.

Jonathan Raban, in *My Holy War*, writes that the reaction in Seattle was similar to mine: this catastrophe could have happened anywhere. "The plane-bombs," he writes, "were squarely directed at the great abstraction of 'America,'" and that great abstraction, we know, includes Canada. Ottawa and Toronto were on the alert, and Merilyn, at our house between those two potential targets, felt no safer than any American citizen. Nor did I feel safe all the way up in

Whitehorse: later that day, two Korean Air Lines planes that failed to respond properly to being hailed were force-landed in Whitehorse by United States Air Force fighter jets from Alaska. As Canadians, we were *implicated* in the attacks. "September 11 was different," Raban argues, "because it was so clearly and insistently about us." In Canada, we felt that "us" included us.

But Canadians didn't necessarily *respond* the way Americans did. That night, at a town meeting in Whitehorse, ministers and First Nations leaders took turns urging North Americans not to turn the incident into an excuse for war. After the meeting, I went to a bar with some friends and fell into conversation with Leo, a small, wiry man in his fifties, with steely grey hair, paint-spattered blue jeans, and a Grateful Dead T-shirt. He was from Ohio but had been living in White-horse for five years, working as a contractor. He wasn't having any of this turn-the-other-cheek stuff, he said.

"Last year," he told me, "I had a guy renting a room in my house. One night he was having a party and I knocked on his door and asked him to quiet down, and he started pushing me around. He was a big guy, and he hit me pretty good over the head a couple of times, and I thought, This guy is going to knock me out and then he's going to finish me off. I had my cordless phone in my hand and I managed to dial 911 and then I just jabbed the phone as hard as I could into his rib cage, and by this time another guy who lived downstairs had heard the commotion and come up and pulled the guy off me, and the police came and took him away. Anyway, now I keep a baseball bat right by my door, and a slingshot with rocks. The guy in the basement used to be a bouncer in Quebec, and he told me the trick with the baseball bat is to coat it with Vaseline. If a guy starts acting up, you poke him in the chest with the end of the bat, and when he tries to grab it from you his hand will slide off because of the Vaseline, and then you hit him."

I nodded, but told him I was a little vague about his point.

"My point is," he said, "that after that, I said I'm never going to let anyone get me like that in my own house. They can beat me up in the street or in the bush or in a bar downtown, and okay, I can take it. But if anyone tries to beat me up in my own house, I'm going to kill them. And that's how the United States feels right now."

The events of 9/11 gave the United States a kind of reprieve, a chance at redemption, as any ill feeling other countries harboured toward it was held in abeyance while America mourned. It was as though America were an unpopular, belligerent neighbour whose wife had just died. Slack was cut for it. Judgment was withheld, for a time. How would it react? A man whose wife has died might take the opportunity to reconsider his ways, view his former bellicosity in the new light of his bereavement. Or he might lash out again at his neighbours. There was that moment of grace while the rest of us watched, holding our breath, ready to either welcome the man into the fellow feeling of the neighbourhood if he repented, or else shrug and turn away if he didn't, murmuring that we had tolerated the fellow only because of his wife.

And so, it seems, we are driving through the backyard of a neighbour who keeps a baseball bat by the door and a slingshot with rocks. A neighbour aching for redemption.

★　★　★

*M*OMENTS ago, we were in desert. Now, when we see the sign saying we are entering the Kaibab National Forest, we laugh: the trees are chest-high, scattered across sand.

"They call this a forest?" we say, almost in unison.

But the road climbs swiftly and the trees take on girth, and soon we are in a dense pine woods. It's as if for a moment we only dreamed we'd driven south and instead have reached northern Ontario. Then, just as suddenly, the road coils sharply down from the strangely forested plateau. When we reach desert level again, we come upon two enormous yellow snowplows pulled off to the side of the road. Two men in orange safety vests lean against their trucks, smoking cigarettes. Their forms waver like a mirage.

"I have to get a picture of this," I say to Wayne, and he slows to a stop. The men eye our Ontario licence plates, as though we are two Trickster coyotes come to bewitch them.

"What are you guys doing here?" I can't keep the laughter out of my voice. Snowplows? In the desert? Are they kidding? These machines are built for a four-day blizzard in Montreal.

"Big storm on the way," the younger one says.

"You get a lot of snow here in the desert, do you?" Even Wayne is snorting under his breath.

"Enough," the older one says.

"Do you mind if I take your picture?"

"Sure. I guess." He looks at his partner, who shrugs in the universal language that says "Crazy tourists."

Our plan is to make a loop of three canyons—from the vastness of the Grand to the sheer red cliffs of Zion and on to the carved pinnacles and spires of Bryce—then head north and east to Arches National Park, where Wayne wants to pay tribute to Edward Abbey. Then we'll turn south through Mesa Verde, Taos, and Santa Fe to pick up Route 66 again at Albuquerque. This detour will take us up through Utah, across to Colorado, and down into New Mexico, circling the Four Corners, the only place in the United States where four states share a common point.

We cross into Utah at Fredonia, which we recognize from a distance by the gigantic "F" on the hillside.

"Just like Hollywood," Wayne notes. "Follywood."

The town was settled by Mormons. Some say the name is a commingling of the English "free" and the Spanish "doña," meaning "free woman," apparently referring to the Mormons' many wives. More likely it is just another town that took its name in the early 1800s, when Samuel Latham Mitchill was trying to get Americans to give up the name United States of America in favour of Fredonia as a more appropriate appellation for the Land of the Free and the Home of the Brave. Eleven states now contain towns called Fredonia, and for a very short time—forty days to be exact—there was a Republic of Fredonia in East Texas, declared in 1825 by a settler named Haden Edwards after he received a land grant from the Mexicans. Haden's plan was to conquer all of Texas and split it with the Cherokee.

I wish Mitchill had succeeded in his name-change campaign. It is a low-grade but constant irritant that this nation, squashed between the forty-ninth parallel and the Rio Grande, has appropriated for itself the name of an entire continent. Two continents, in fact. When Canada was created, it was considered part of the larger land mass known as America. (When Alexis de Tocqueville was sent by the French government to visit the American prison system in 1831, he understood that to mean both the United States *and* Canada.) When the United States began to call itself America, Canadians recoiled, as if we'd been annexed, as we have been, linguistically at least.

Fredonia—or Freedonia—has become something of a running joke in the United States. In the 1960s, Woody Allen, as a host on *Candid Camera,* asked people in the street, to hilarious effect, what they thought of Freedonia's bid for independence. (Rick Mercer in recent years took a page from that book to create his series *Talking to Americans.* In one famous segment, Mercer asks George W. Bush— the presidential candidate who claimed, "You can't stump me on world leaders"—for his reaction to an endorsement by Canadian Prime Minister "Jean Poutine," to which Bush replied in all seriousness that he was looking forward to working with the head of state.) In the 1990s, the American satirical magazine *Spy* went further, successfully convincing several members of Congress to issue statements condemning "the ethnic cleansing in Freedonia."

Alas, the only nation of Freedonia is the fictional one conjured by the Marx Brothers in *Duck Soup.* "Land of the Spree and the Home of the Knave," as Groucho puts it. In the movie, this tiny, obscure, autocratic nation—nothing at all like the great United States of America—is suffering from severe financial difficulties. Government leaders ask a wealthy widow, Mrs. Teasdale, for a loan to keep the country afloat, which she agrees to with the proviso that Rufus T. Firefly (Groucho Marx) run the country. On his first day in office, Groucho bursts into song: "If you think this country's bad off now, just wait till I get through with it."

"Must be George W.'s favourite movie," I say to Wayne.

*   *   *

WHEN Sharlot Hall, Arizona's "poetess laureate," as she was known, came along this route in 1911 in a covered wagon, she recorded seeing bison in the red canyons of the Vermilion Cliffs, "big-humped and shaggy-maned and moving lazily down the trail," the scattered remnants of a herd introduced in 1906 by Buffalo Jones and Uncle Jim Owens, who thought the area would make excellent farming country. The semi-wild buffalo thrived for a time but soon ate themselves into an empty pantry, and the herd diminished. There are still some around, but they are not in evidence today.

What we do see are mule deer. Close relatives of the more familiar (to us) white-tailed deer, mule deer are so named because their large ears reminded someone of the ears of a mule. The males stand rigidly poised in the gravel clearings, staring hard at us as we pass, while the females go on kicking at the thin layer of snow that covers the desert floor. They have few other predators to worry about, wolves and grizzlies having long since been eradicated from these hills. There are still mountain lions in the forested areas, and coyotes might take the odd fawn. Ravens have been known to kill large ungulates by pecking at the eyes and anus. But the deer we see don't appear to be leading particularly suspenseful lives.

*   *   *

MAUVE clouds roll in from the north, turning the sky that distinctive bluish-grey slate we know so well from home. We have left the desert and are in farm country, rolling hills dotted with Muffets of hay, sleek horses, well-tended houses and barns. There is snow on the fields, on the road, in the clouds racing up behind us.

"Let's skip Zion," I say when we get to the turnoff that leads west toward Hurricane and the national park. "Looks like there are a couple of nice inns near the entrance to Bryce."

Neither of us says it, but the clouds over Zion are distinctly threatening. If we were in Canada, we'd say they looked like snow.

In the years we were courting, I knew that as soon as the weatherman called for snow, or sleet, or hail, or even heavy rain, Wayne would be at my door. "Let's go for a ride," he'd say. The bigger the storm, the more his eyes would sparkle. My own capacity for risk—he'd say adventure—is not up to his, but even so, I'd laugh and haul on my coat, throwing a couple of chocolate bars and a candle into my pocket, just in case.

Instinctively, I pat my pockets. They're empty, but it doesn't matter: we're heading north, where the sky is clear blue.

On the map, the road is traced with a dashed green line, which means this is a scenic route. It passes through the Dixie National Forest; if we keep going, we'll end up in Salt Lake City, and for a few minutes we consider that option.

"I wouldn't mind seeing the Mormon Tabernacle," I say. "I'd like to hear the choir."

But we've already made the decision to avoid cities, so when we come to the turnoff for Bryce, we take it, heading east on Route 12, advertised as the "Journey through Time Byway." Bryce Canyon itself is several miles down a narrow side road. A road, I notice now, that is highlighted in pink. *Closed in Winter.*

"We'd only be able to get as far as the park headquarters. The hotels all look closed, too."

"Anything else coming up?"

"The town of Tropic."

"That sounds promising."

Tropic is tiny, the size of the village where I grew up. Five hundred souls and counting. But it has a bakery, so we stop.

"Just sold my last loaf," the man behind the counter says.

We buy a Danish of indeterminate age and two small packets of hot, fresh-roasted cashews, which are neither. "The light bulb in the machine burned out," the man explains.

We ask if there are motels further down the road.

"Yep," he says, "but you'll have to stop in Escalante. You'll never get over the mountain in the snow, not with the storm coming."

"How much snow are they predicting?" we ask, thinking smugly, Come on, we're Canadians!

"About two feet."

We exchange surprised glances. That's real snow, no matter where it falls.

But as we leave Tropic, the sky clears, the desert resumes, and we congratulate ourselves for our decision to carry on. We are brilliant. We are making one excellent decision after another. From our blessed hands, even the cashews taste warm and freshly toasted.

★ ★ ★

*W*E drive between red canyon walls that loom above us, looking almost sculpted in the way their crenellated tops resemble chimneys and battlements, their crowns and lower talus approaches fringed with evergreens. There's St. Petersburg's Winter Palace! There's the Mormon Tabernacle in Salt Lake City! There's Vienna! There's the Royal Bank of Canada on Sparks Street in Ottawa! Everywhere is somewhere else. Despite the snowflakes swirling like shrapnel in the gyrating air around us, the sun is still shining and the mini-greenhouse of the car interior is warmed by it. We forget that we are absurdly underdressed. Our Echo is invincible. We can see the black specks of birds floating on thermals above the cliffs, but they are too far up for us to identify, even when we get out of the car and look with our binoculars. Not condors: either eagles or red-tailed hawks, we agree, diving back into the car.

It's not that cold, we tell each other as we both reach to crank up the heat.

Even in the thickening snow, there is no mistaking the string of mountain bluebirds perched on telephone wires as we travel along Route 12. We slow down and count them: twenty-three on one loop, fifteen on the next. They have snow on their backs.

"Bluebirds of happiness," Merilyn says. At home we see only eastern bluebirds, and never more than one or two at a time.

She turns to me. "I am very, very happy," she says. "How about you?"

"Delirious," I tell her, hardly daring to take my eyes off the road to smile into hers. "Happy as a lark."

8 / ESCALANTE, UTAH

*W*E press on, a tinge of urgency now in our pace. It is decidedly dusk, and I calculate that without incident we can be in Escalante by ten after six. There's a museum there that looks interesting, Merilyn says. The snow is falling heavily, a curtain drawn across the valley to our left.

"Funny to think that we came this far south to avoid driving through snow," Merilyn muses, her tone not as light as she'd clearly like it to be.

"Yes," I say, "but we're in Utah. It's the best snow in the world."

Back in Page, we watched a televised weather report that told us there is still no snow at all in the northern part of the continent; snowmobile dealers and ski resort owners are jumping out of windows. Here, meanwhile, it's a fair bet that those two snowplow drivers are revving their engines and checking each other's flashing blue lights. We are gradually but assuredly climbing, the weather becoming increasingly wintery. I weave the car back and forth on the highway to test the traction of the tires.

"Wayne, stop that," Merilyn says.

"I'm just checking to see if the road is slippery."

"Of course it's slippery," she says. "There are two inches of snow on it."

"It's not bad," I say. "We have snow tires."

"No, we don't. We have all-season radials."

"What are those lights down there?" I ask, changing the subject. Downslope to our left are the lights of what looks to be a small town.

"Probably cars that have spun out of control and gone off the road," Merilyn says, then relents. "Maybe Escalante."

A dark shape appears at my side window. Before my mind can say "Deer!" it veers toward the car. A sickening thump, and the road in front of us disappears as a pelt of coarse, grey-brown hair presses against the windshield. The road reappears, there's a breath, and another thump as the deer comes down on the trunk. It takes me another fifty feet to rein the car to a stop. We are marooned in the middle of the highway. I keep my foot on the brake and look at Merilyn. She is staring at me.

"Thank God it didn't come through the windshield," she says, her voice shaky.

"I didn't see it until it was too late," I say, idiotically.

"You didn't have a chance," Merilyn says, staring straight ahead out the window. We are both in shock.

The engine is still running, the headlights glaring cockeyed into the snow. Even more idiotically, I say, "I don't think there's any damage to the car."

"That's not possible," Merilyn says.

"I know."

In the rear-view mirror I can see the deer on the side of the road, struggling to its feet, falling, getting up again, Bambi trying to get his footing on ice. I move the gearshift into reverse, absurdly thinking I can help. When I look again, the deer is gone. I get out of the car—the door opens, thank goodness—and walk to the back to look for the deer. We are on a deserted stretch of snow-covered road, high wooded hills to our right, low sloping valley to our left, a fringe of trees along the roadside where the deer must have been lurking before we came along. But where is it now? Surely the impact has at least broken its legs? But there is no sign of it, no blood on the road, no tracks leading up into the darkness. Nor are there any marks on the car's trunk. This is one of those freak accidents, I tell myself with relief, in which the car is not damaged and the deer is not hurt. But my heart is still racing, and I have a sick feeling in my stomach.

I walk around to the front of the car. The entire hood is crumpled in on itself, as if the Fremont troll had sat down on it. The driver's-side fender is crushed, the grille broken. The right windshield wiper pokes awkwardly into the night sky. The left headlight is smashed, but the bulb, dangling in its socket at the end of its cord, still shines valiantly. The car looks mutilated, but the engine is running. I think the tires will turn without rubbing against the wheel wells. We can drive; we even have lights, of a sort.

"What do we do now?" I ask when I'm back in the car and have given Merilyn an account of the wreckage.

"We have to report it," she says.

I've never hit a deer. I once hit a raccoon. It staggered in its hump-backed fashion out of some tall grass beside the road, not far from our house, and it was its hump that I hit. You think you have time to stop, you think you have reflexes and instincts and peripheral vision and hand-eye coordination. You actually have none of these: you see the raccoon, you tell yourself it isn't going to run out onto the road, it does, and you say, "Hey, get out of the—," and there is that sickening clunk as undercarriage hits bone.

There is a story by Barry Lopez in which he describes driving across the northern United States. Every time he sees a road-killed animal, which is often, he stops to drag its carcass off the highway into the verge. Animals should die with dignity, he says, or at least have some posthumous dignity after an ignominious death by transport truck or family sedan. I suppose I have something of the sort in mind when I go back to check on our mule deer. But it isn't there. There aren't even any tracks. I look again up into the swirl of snow that closes in like a shroud between us and the trees, and see nothing.

I put the car in gear and inch forward, watching for smoke, listening for shrieks.

"Let's hope we can make it to Escalante."

WELCOME, SAYS the sign on the first motel we come to. *Open Year Round.* The motel is a ranch-style row of modern units along an unroofed, pressure-treated deck set at a right angle to the highway. There is something that looks like a convention hotel across the road but this isn't the time for comparison shopping. No cars are hitched to the boardwalk, no tracks mar the snow in front of the units. The place looks quiet. This time we both go into the motel office, a low affair attached to a bungalow near the entrance to the parking lot, Merilyn to negotiate the room and me to call the local sheriff.

A large, middle-aged woman comes into the office through a Dutch door behind the desk, bringing with her the smell of pizza and the sound of a television game show. She seems distracted, as though mulling over a tricky Double Jeopardy! question, until we tell her about the deer; then she perks up and calls another woman, who comes in from the back. "This is my sister," the first woman says. The sister is younger. She has dark hair and is wearing a yellow-and-white floral-patterned housedress. I wonder if they are Mormons, if "sister" is code.

"I know someone who'll take care of that deer for you," says the sister. "Was it a doe?"

"No idea," I say. "We need to call the sheriff."

The first woman looks at me with a blend of surprise, concern, and mild disdain.

"We have to report the accident so our insurance will pay for the repairs," Merilyn explains.

The sister shrugs and composes the sheriff's number. She talks for a minute, then hands the phone to Merilyn. I feel left out of the sisterhood.

"He's going out to look for the deer," Merilyn says when she hangs up. "He wants us to wait in our room until he comes to take our statements."

Two hours later, through the window of our unit I see a burly, farm-faced man in a Smokey the Bear outfit walking around our crumpled Echo with a clipboard. When I go outside he introduces himself as the deputy sheriff. The name tag on his jacket says "Jared Porter." I invite him in for a coffee. We've had our dinner of smoked salmon and hummus (I abstained from drinking wine), the last of our Christmas hoard, but we still have some of the good coffee we bought in Sacramento. We don't tell Jared that it's decaf.

"I didn't find the deer," Jared says after writing down our particulars on his clipboard, "but looking at your car it's obvious you hit *something*. Maybe you'll come back with me in the truck and show me exactly where the incident took place?"

I look at Merilyn in alarm. It suddenly occurs to me that the deputy is not taking for granted that what we hit was a deer. For all he knows it could have been a tree or a cyclist (in a snowstorm? why not?) or someone walking along the side of the road. I feel as though I am crossing a border to somewhere remote.

I put on my coat and hat. We need to find that deer.

Five minutes later, Jared and I are driving slowly west along the highway where I think I remember hitting the deer. Jared's Chevrolet Tahoe is so high off the ground I feel slightly giddy, as though we're flying. I can barely see the road over the Tahoe's hood. The windshield wipers clear a cone of darkness ahead of us, faintly illuminated by the truck's headlights. Jared is watching the roadside through his side window while talking to a dispatcher on his radio. Between the deputy and me there's a computer on a swivel stand, and above the deputy's head is a handle that turns a spotlight mounted on the roof of the truck's cab. Jared plays the light over the shoulder of the road and up the steeply rising embankment, revealing rocks and deadfall and occasional lumps of snow that do not resemble a deer. We've been over this stretch a couple of times, each time the snow a little deeper. I'm beginning to get worried. Was it farther out, perhaps? A different road? I tend to talk when I'm worried. I want to tell the sheriff about the motel owner who offered to have the deer taken care of. Whoever it was has obviously beaten us out here and made off with the deer. Or the bicycle, the sheriff is no doubt thinking.

"I guess the deer was unharmed and has run off into the woods," I venture. I wonder if there is a "no body, no murder" rule for deer collisions.

Jared makes no response. I decide to clam up. I've watched the reality cop shows. Anything I say can and will be taken down and used against me in a court of law. Suddenly, Officer Jared stops the truck and jumps out. I can hear the voice-over: *Suddenly, Officer Jared stops the truck and jumps out.* I follow from my side, surprised by my freedom. I could run off. Jared is stooping over the road and brushing aside three inches of snow. He picks up a small piece of amber plastic about the size of a yogourt tub lid.

"This is from your headlight, I would guess," he says. He pokes around in the snow and finds two or three more pieces, some amber, some clear. I notice he doesn't put them in an evidence bag. "This is where you hit it. But where the heck is it gone?"

He believes me. I feel like putting my arm around his shoulder, if I could reach it, in a manly embrace. He takes a flashlight from his jacket pocket and walks up into the forest, leaving me standing in the middle of the highway. With the truck running.

He believes me.

Given the lack of evidence, says the voice-over, *Officer Jared has no choice but to let the suspect go.*

THE NEXT morning someone named Leslie from the insurance company's Toronto office calls. She suggests we get the car towed back to Canada to be repaired. This strikes Merilyn and me as absurd. Merilyn passes this observation on to Leslie. "We're in *Utah*," she says. Leslie says she'll look at a map and call us back.

"I wonder what property prices are like in Escalante?" Merilyn muses, obviously thinking of Blanche Russell and her mud-brick house.

I take my coffee out onto the deck in front of our unit. A foot of fresh snow hides the car's disfigurement and makes a still, white lake of the parking lot. In a field between the lot and a row of blank-faced bungalows, a boy of about twelve is wheeling doughnuts on an ATV, driving at full speed for fifty feet, then jamming on the brake and cranking the handlebars so that the machine goes into an uncontrolled spin. He does this over and over, a look of fierce anger on his face, as though the ATV is a bucking bronco and he's trying to break its spirit. I wonder what he really wanted for Christmas.

"Let's just pack up and go," I say when I'm back inside.

Merilyn looks dubious. "What if we get caught in another snowstorm?" she says. "What if the car breaks down in the middle of nowhere? We don't even know what is wrong with it."

Just then, Leslie calls back. This time she says the car can be towed to a Car Star repair shop in St. George, Utah, a hundred and twenty-five miles behind us. She adds that if we can get a garage mechanic to certify that the car is safe to drive, we won't need to have it towed.

The garage is on Escalante's main street. The owner and the mechanic are busy unloading a trailerful of new snow tires. I wait for them in the office, a large room smelling pleasantly of axle grease and with a nice selection of calendars on the walls. When the trailer is empty, I go back outside.

"You the fella that hit the deer?" he asks.

"Yeah, but we didn't find it."

The mechanic laughs. "What can I do for you?"

"I need you to tell me that the car is safe to drive. We have to get it to a repair shop in St. George."

"St. George?" he says, raising one eyebrow, but he lets it go. He goes over to the car and fiddles with the hood catch, and to my amazement flips it open. I was afraid to do that for fear I'd never get it closed again. Besides, my looking under the hood wouldn't have helped. Nothing about a modern car engine looks familiar to me. There are no fan belts to tug, no pulleys to turn, no distributor cap to jiggle, no spark plugs to ponder. The whole thing is a mysterious mess of cables and computer parts. I don't even know where the oil filter is. But I nod my head when the mechanic, after a cursory inspection, says he doesn't see anything wrong.

"Me neither," I say.

"I can't tell what shape the engine's in unless I get right into it," he says, "but I can say that whatever might be wrong with it wasn't caused by hitting the deer."

"So you think I can drive it?"

"You drove it here, didn't you?"

"Yeah, but if my insurance company calls you, will you tell them it's fit to drive?"

He considers. "I can tell them I don't see any reason why it shouldn't be."

"Good enough," I say. I go back into the office to thank the owner and ask him how much I owe him. "Oh, twenty bucks ought to cover it," he says.

When I return to the motel with breakfast—cello-wrapped Danish, the best I could do—Merilyn is on the phone again, this time with the insurance adjuster in St. George, a man named Bob Butler (Smith, Porter, Butler: does everyone in Utah have occupational names?), who tells her that the snowstorm of the century is heading his way and we'd be crazy to drive back into it.

"I was golfing yesterday," he says, "but I'll be skiing tomorrow. You're ahead of the storm where you are. Don't backtrack. Keep on going to Albuquerque, and when you get there, give me a call." He promises to have the name and telephone number of another adjuster by then. "But if I were you, I'd just sit tight in Escalante until this blows over."

"Snowstorm?" I say as she hangs up. "Great. This'll be fun."

Merilyn looks at me a little wild-eyed. "Maybe if we leave soon we can beat it," she says. "Once the storm hits, we could be stuck here for days. We're only a week into the trip. If we're going to be stuck any-where, I'd rather be stuck in Albuquerque."

She spreads a map out on the table. It's three hundred miles to Albuquerque. Escalante is on Route 12, an All-American Road, a designation given only to the most scenic of the National Scenic Byways. It continues on in a wind-about kind of way for a hundred miles before T-ing on Route 24 at Torrey, where we would turn south toward the Four Corners. There are no towns between here and Torrey, and precious few south of it. I notice the road takes a few odd three-hundred-degree turns.

"Mountains," Merilyn says. She looks more closely at the map than I do. "Boulder Mountain," she reads. "Eleven thousand three hundred and thirty feet." She looks up at me. "In a century snowstorm."

"I guess we'd better get moving," I say.

She sighs. "I guess we'd better."

Officer Jared drives up in his truck just as we leave the motel office and hands us our copy of his police report. Merilyn asks him the best way to Albuquerque.

"Well," he says, "you have to go over Boulder Mountain." He points vaguely to the northeast. "The north side never gets any sun, and it can be pretty slick. And there's a hog's back where the canyon drops six hundred feet on one side and eight hundred feet on the other. We've lost a few up there."

A few what? We don't ask.

"Do you think we should chance it?" Merilyn fixes him with a sharp gaze, as if she's got him on the witness stand.

Jared lifts his eyes to the lowering sky. "It's not snowing too bad yet," he says, "and mostly they keep it plowed." He shrugs. "Just follow the speed signs; they're there for a reason."

Before we leave Escalante, we stop at Canyon Country Gas & Goodies. While I gas up, Merilyn buys some chocolate bars and a package of candles. Then we drive off in the direction of Boulder Mountain.

★ ★ ★

*M*OUNDED snow covers the road, but the day is fine, not too cold. We are in the mood to appreciate subtle positives. We take it easy, mindful of our crumpled Echo, reassuring ourselves at frequent intervals that the car is good. The road is good. We're good, really good.

We stop at the crest of Boulder Mountain, the highest treed plateau in North America, according to the sign. Why on earth did we imagine there *wouldn't* be snow? I aim the camera at the view and take a mini-movie: there is no other way to capture the panorama of gullies and gulches that stretches, snow-scarred, in every direction. A person could disappear here.

The road heads down the mountain in a series of loops and twirls at impossible angles; then we're climbing again, and before we realize it, we're on the Devil's Backbone, a thin spine of shoulderless road with long, sharp drops on either side.

"Look at that view!" Wayne exclaims.

"Uh-huh," I say, my eyes fixed straight ahead, my foot pumping invisible brake pedals.

"Do you want to stop and take a picture?" he says.

I shake my head. "Uh-uh."

Beyond the knife-edge, the road winds down among the trees. I breathe a little easier. Broadsiding a pine seems preferable to ending up as rubble at the bottom of a cliff.

"Looks like the worst is behind us," I say gamely.

Then the snow hits. For two hours we drive in silence through the eastern tract of the Dixie National Forest. The road has been recently plowed and sanded, though the sand is soon submerged in a trackless swath that plunges and swoops around fenceless curves, the only barrier a few tall, red-tipped extensions on skinny posts, scant warning that the road stops and thin air begins.

"They must get a lot of snow here," Wayne comments wryly.

I don't answer. I'm listening to the engine, which is labouring up the inclines. We are barely making thirty kilometres an hour. The sky has lowered until it seems to press against our foreheads. We meet a truck, then an hour later, another, just the three of us on this road: an old man who grips the wheel furiously, three young boys in cowboy hats waving, and the two of us, ashen-faced tourists in our summer wear. The others are heading for Escalante. Nobody is travelling our way.

We pass the Escalante Petrified Forest. We pass the Anasazi Indian Village near Boulder, where the mail was still delivered by mule until the 1970s. We make it through a length of road I don't tell Wayne about. It is marked on the map in pink: *Closed in Winter.*

We have no interest in the sights—Mesa Verde, the Arches—I just want to get to a city where there are mechanics, car rental companies, good hotels, and at least one fine restaurant, in that order. If that makes us seem fickle, we don't care. There's a throughway farther north, but north seems like a bad idea. We need to get out of the mountains, into the desert again. The blessed desert, where there are snowplows. At Torrey, we stop at a coffee shop and ask a local couple how best to find our way south. They point to a road devoid of towns and even the named crossroads that pass for towns here. Never trust a local, Wendy said at Cliff Dwellers Lodge. We waver until we see a car pulling into the parking lot from that direction.

"*Ja*, the road is empty," the young woman says, adjusting her miniskirt as she gets out of the car. She speaks with a distinct German accent.

"Where are you headed?" we ask.

They point the way we've just come. "To Escalante."

"Not a good idea," we say. "See those clouds?" A dark blue mass presses like a bruise against the mountainside.

"In Bavaria, we have much snow," the young man says, pulling his tuque briskly over his forehead.

"We're from Canada," Wayne says. "We know snow, too."

The girl looks worried. They whisper together, then get back in their car, a yellow PT Cruiser with summer tires. Watching them start up the mountain feels like watching someone setting off on a long walk toward the end of a very short pier.

They were right about one thing, though. The road to Blanding is clear and dry. I feel giddy with relief. We drive down the gully of one soaring red canyon after another. The stone turns golden and soft, like the flanks of a young walrus, then green like lichen, then striped and rounded like Pippi Longstocking's socks. We run out of similes. Along what must, at another time of the year, be stream beds, rows of cottonwoods straggle, then miles of sage, now and then a hut, some cattle wandering aimlessly, big yellow, red, or orange tags dangling from their lobes like party earrings, but never a car, not even a truck. We are alone on the road.

The car is holding up. We congratulate ourselves on outrunning the storm. We'll find a place to spend the night and tomorrow we'll be in Albuquerque, where we'll get the car fixed and carry on. We continue making enthusiastic assurances to each other, not mentioning how low the sun hangs in the sky, or that we have not yet seen a house, let alone a motel or a town. I call out names from the map, but they amount to nothing but sand.

We've crossed the state line back into Arizona and are about thirty miles from Chinle when the real snow hits. Big, fat flakes like feathers beaten in a fury from oversize pillows. The wonky headlight shines straight up into the onslaught, stitching the flakes into an opaque white curtain that moves down the road inches ahead of us.

"I can't see a thing." There's an edge of panic in Wayne's voice I haven't heard before. "I have no idea where the road is."

"Don't stop," I insist, applying a rule I learned in defensive driving forty years ago: if you stop, someone might crash into you from behind, though who that might be on this deserted road, I can't imagine.

I roll down the window and lean out. A snowplow must have been through here earlier in the day. A thin ridge of snow lines the edge of the asphalt.

"A little to the left," I say.

"Okay, right . . . Now straight."

We inch down the highway, me calling out instructions, Wayne adjusting the steering wheel without complaint. I silently pray that the snowplow operator hasn't veered down a desolate rancher's lane or stopped suddenly in the middle of the road. I stare at the narrow ridge of plowed snow, afraid to blink for fear we'll drive over a cliff, if there is a cliff, which seems entirely possible because we are now travelling sharply downhill. Is this a plateau we're descending? Or a mountain slope? Will there be a sharp curve at the bottom, or a gentle easing onto level ground?

Level ground, as it turns out. The gods are with us.

"Stop," I say to Wayne when we pass a cluster of lights. "Let's find out where we are."

We turn in to a small subdivision planted in the middle of nowhere. I get out, pull a scarf over my head, and pound on the door of the nearest house. I imagine being invited in, served hot tea and biscuits. Canadians love a good storm: it makes us hospitable.

I see shapes moving around inside. A curtain flutters at the window. I call out, trying to sound honest, reliable.

"Please, can you help me? I just want to know where we are."

The door opens a crack. "There's a gas station down the road," a woman's voice spits out before she slams it shut.

Wayne pumps gas while I go inside to ask about motels. As I enter the station, a man grabs the door. "Can you help me out?" he says, holding up a necklace and earrings made of cheap red beads. "Ten bucks. I made them myself."

The gas station attendant inside says there is an inn down the road, but when I go back to the car, a young First Nations girl puts her hand on my arm and says softly, "Go on to Chinle. There are lots of places there. We just come from that way. The road's fine."

In Chinle, the snow subsides. We find a Best Western and check in alongside an adolescent wrestling team and the driver of a Pepsi big rig. The restaurant attached to the hotel closes just as we get to the door, so we drive out to the only other place open, the Thunderbird Lodge Cafeteria, where sullen women dish out blocks of meat loaf and ice-cream scoops of gelid mashed potatoes and bowls of pork-and-bean soup that is actually quite delicious. We haven't eaten anything but chocolate bars all day. One of the women comes out of the kitchen holding a plate high in the air. "Who ordered frybread?" I did, apparently. It comes with, as Wayne is so fond of saying. The deep-fried puff of dough is the size of a Frisbee, not good for the arteries maybe, but after the day we've put in, awfully good for the heart.

Back at the Best Western, I call Bob Butler in St. George.

"We made it," I say. If we hadn't, he is the only person in the world who would have known enough to call out a search party. I want to hug him in gratitude, as if his vigilance alone has pulled us through the storm. He gives me the name of the insurance adjuster we're supposed to meet in Albuquerque.

"You could have hit a deer and driven through a blizzard in Canada," Bob laughs. "You better come on back and see us in golf season. It isn't always like this."

IN THE morning, we open the last two snack-pack cereal boxes and eat Frosted Flakes out of water glasses with the dregs of the coffee cream. We're on the road by first light.

"Look, there's a rainbow! Two rainbows! Double luck."

"Maybe not," Wayne says. "That's a halo: there's ice up there. See those bright spots? Sun dogs. Omens."

"Good or bad?"

"Hard to say."

Now that Albuquerque is a few hours' drive away, our mad dash through the snow seems a bit of a lark. "A mere bagatelle," Wayne says. By mid-morning, we've crossed into New Mexico. *Land of Enchantment,* according to the billboards. When we stop again for gas, an older First Nations man sidles up.

"Can you help us out?" he says, nodding to his buddies standing around the car at the next pump. "We overfilled the tank and we're short a dollar. They're going to call the cops on us." Without a word, Wayne digs in his jeans and hands him a bill.

Almost as soon as we get back on the I-40—obscured, but still the Mother Road to us—the snow begins again. It's daylight, though, and the road is clear: we can almost see Albuquerque. Everything is going to be fine.

We amuse ourselves by reading the billboards aloud:

24,000 Tons of Trash Removed from New Mexico Roads in 2005.

I Choose to Wait—Abstinence until Marriage.

Dust Storms May Exist.

"You can tell a lot about a people from their billboards," Wayne says sagely. "New Mexico is obviously a place of littering virgins with a metaphysical bent."

"And very good taste," I add, for suddenly the interstate is spanned with great soaring slashes of turquoise and terracotta. "Why doesn't every place do this?" I say, awestricken by the beauty of the overpasses. As we sail under the two-tone arches, our spirits rise.

We're within fifteen minutes of the city when the cars ahead of us abruptly stop.

"The weather isn't that bad," I say to them all.

But no one moves. After ten minutes, Wayne and I pull out a deck of cards and play gin over the gearshift. We finish four games. Wayne wins every one.

The cars start to move. We inch past a semi smashed into a truck and trailer. Half a dozen more transport trucks are jackknifed or flipped on their sides, or have snowplowed into the median. An ambulance has slid off the road, lights flashing.

I get on the cellphone to the insurance adjuster. We agree to meet at the Toyota dealership in the outskirts of Albuquerque. An hour later, as we pull into the lot, five men swarm out of the blizzard toward the car.

I crank down the window. "Is one of you Paul?"

They look at each other, momentarily stymied, as if perhaps one of them is in fact Paul and they've forgotten which. Then they remember: they are salesmen, Toyota is having a sale-a-thon, blizzard be damned. Five business cards flash through the window.

"Not yet," we say. We're pretty sure we don't need a new car, though when Paul examines the Echo, peering in at the odometer, he says sourly, "Given the mileage, I doubt it's worth fixing. It's probably a writeoff. I'll let you know tomorrow."

Our puff of elation deflates. We go inside and sit with one of the salesmen, figuring out how much a replacement Echo will cost in Albuquerque and what would be involved in taking it into Canada. A lot.

"We could junk the car and fly," I say to Wayne. "Or drive the wreck home."

"No." His voice is sharp, as if I've insisted. "I'm not going to drive it like this."

We've grown testy with each other. A writeoff won't give us enough money to buy another car. And even if it did, a car bought in New Mexico won't have a catalytic converter: we can't begin to think what that will mean at the border. And, we ask ourselves, do we really want to drive in miles per hour, moving through Canada on American terms, for the next however many years?

"Wait a minute!" It hits me like a deer in a blizzard. "Paul took down the mileage, right? 155,000. I bet he thought those were miles! But we're Canadian! They're kilometres!"

Wayne lights up, too. "And that's less than 100,000 miles."

"Right." The salesman is looking glum but Wayne and I are grinning as though we just won the lottery. I jump up and give him a hug. "Everything's definitely going to be fine."

★   ★   ★

*W*AKING in our hotel room in Albuquerque, I find myself thinking about that mule deer, especially when I look out the window and see a world completely buried in snow. The parking lot resembles a giant sheet of cotton batting with a few lumps in it; the lumps are cars. The interstate is deserted; the turquoise stripes obliterated by snow. There isn't a car on the streets. The city is as still as a forest. I picture the deer lying wounded, being slowly buried by snow, coyotes closing in. I once tracked coyotes in Massachusetts with a professional tracker who told me he'd seen a coyote pack bring down a deer that had broken its leg by stepping through deep snow into a fissure. There was a lot of blood on the snow, Paul said, but when the coyotes were finished, nothing was left of the deer but a few tufts of hair. At the time, my sympathies had been with the coyotes. Now my guilty conscience is pulling for the deer.

Thoughts of the deer stay with me during breakfast in the hotel's dining room. Everyone has been storm-stayed; we are a gathering of environmental refugees. The television in the corner is tuned to CNN: every so often the blur of voices falls silent as everyone listens. *Sixteen dead across New Mexico. In Albuquerque, snow up to three feet deep. Massive power failures. Hundreds of roofs have collapsed, including most of the city's schools. Nothing like it in living memory.*

The couple at the next table are desperate to get back to Denver for their daughter's wedding. The woman across the aisle says she spent the entire night huddled in her SUV on the interstate. In the lobby, people are sitting on the floor or on their luggage; there are no more rooms here or anywhere else in the city.

In the elevator, a husband and wife from Arkansas tell us they're going out to the airport to try to get their private plane in the air. They'd been flying to Salt Lake City, where the husband was due to start a new job, when the storm forced them down in Albuquerque.

"You want to come to Salt Lake City with us?" the man asks.

Merilyn and I consider it for a moment, then she says, reasonably, "That airport is probably closed, too."

"Well, we're gonna give her a try," he says. "You're welcome to join us."

We've experienced this kind of neighbourliness before, during the ice storm of 1998, when most of eastern Ontario and western Quebec was without power, in some cases for weeks. Strangers would knock on our door and offer to lend us a generator to pump out our basement or get the freezer or the furnace working for a few hours, whichever was most critical. Hydro crews from upstate New York and as far away as North Carolina came up to help repair the downed Canadian lines. Just as Canadian crews headed south to New Orleans after Katrina. In times of crisis, we become an altruistic species. Borders cease to matter.

In our room, I lie on one of the two double beds, thinking maybe we should offer it to someone in the lobby. Merilyn is sitting at the table writing in her notebook. She has already had several conversations with the insurance adjuster, who really doesn't want to know us until next year—which starts on Monday.

"Looks like we have the weekend to do what we want," I say. "What do we want to do?"

Merilyn shrugs. "Rest," she says. "This will be the first time we've spent more than one night in a place since we left Vancouver."

I'm reading a book by Charles Bowden called *Desierto*. Merilyn lies down beside me and I read her a passage about a Navajo man whose wife sent him out to shoot some meat to go with the tortillas she was making. The man went out, and after a while he came back, sat down in a corner of the pueblo, and said nothing. Eventually, some elders went up to him and asked him what was disturbing him. The man said he had seen a mule deer and shot it, but he had only wounded the animal. The deer had run off and he'd followed it into the hills. He tracked it to a cave, and when he went into the cave he saw an old woman sitting on the ground, crying bitterly. There was a deep wound in her side. He had come home and sat quietly thinking about what he had seen. That night, the family ate their tortillas without meat.

THE SNOW has stopped but the sidewalks are deeply piled with the kind of heavy, wet snow that causes heart attacks and hernias. A few cars fishtail by and several fellow refugees stand at the corners looking down at their pant legs. We make our way to the small plaza in the old part of the city, looking for somewhere to buy food. Whether it's the storm or because it is New Year's weekend, not much is open. Eventually we find a Walgreens near the plaza and buy a few perishables for the room. In front of the store is an old covered wagon and a cluster of prickly pear cacti, each with a thick crown of snow. There's something *wrong* about a snow-covered cactus; it's as though two parallel universes have collapsed in on each other.

The walk and the cold make us hungry. We'll have a hot lunch now and eat dinner in our room, we decide, and head down a narrow alley off the plaza toward a small, steamy Mexican cafe whose tables are comfortably strewn with tourism brochures and local newspapers. A good place to sit out a storm, I think, although it's all but empty. A shelf of books is fastened to an adobe wall beside a fireplace: Carlos Castaneda, Aldous Huxley, Aleister Crowley, Margery Allingham. I take an English-Spanish dictionary and order a Corona, and Merilyn asks for a small pot of decaf coffee. We share a plate of corn tortillas with refried beans and avocado chili. No meat.

I look up "avocado" in the dictionary. I've always thought the word had something to do with lawyers.

"Hey, listen to this," I say to Merilyn, who is reading the weather page in the *Albuquerque Journal.* "'Avocado, from the Aztec word *ahuacatl,* meaning "testicle," from its shape.' We're eating prairie oysters."

"They're calling for another major snowstorm tomorrow," she says with a frown. "This one's coming from the north."

"And did you know that 'refried' beans aren't fried twice?"

"Two more feet of snow."

"The Spanish prefix *re* doesn't mean 'again,' it means 'very.' *Frijoles refritos* means 'very fried beans.'" I think about the word "redeem." Very doomed.

"All the major highways will be closed."

"You know the country Chile?" I ask.

"Snow everywhere, except maybe south."

"Did you know that the country's name comes from the Indian word *tchilli,* which actually means 'cold'?"

"The I-25 is still open."

"Or snow. *Tchilli* can mean 'cold' or 'snow.'"

"Well," says Merilyn, "tomorrow it's going be *tchilli* in New Mexico." She *has* been listening.

"Where does the I-25 go?" I ask. I have been listening, too.

"El Paso."

"Then let's go there," I say. "Let's spend New Year's in El Paso."

"Oh, let's," Merilyn says, thawing already. "We'll leave first thing."

This is the kind of planning I like.

★　★　★

*M*ORNING on the last day of the year. I finally reach Paul.

"I was right about the kilometres. The insurance company will fix the car!" I exclaim, hanging up. "They want us to bring it in Monday."

"All right!" Wayne says. "Let's hit the road."

It has been snowing for hours. At breakfast we watch announcers on the big-screen TV in the restaurant warn the worried assembled that once again the I-40 is closed, that hundreds have spent the night in their cars, that fog and ice are making driving treacherous, that it is twenty-nine degrees Fahrenheit in Albuquerque and fifty-two in El Paso. I turn to Wayne with tears in my eyes, not from the news but from the sight of two parents tenderly feeding their small daughters. I miss the kids, but I don't want to call them. I don't want them to worry. I don't want to listen to them telling us that we should be careful.

We drive slowly around the city's uncleared streets. Wayne stops at a hardware store and buys a length of heavy plastic and some duct tape to cover the wonky headlight. The temperature has dropped sharply, freezing the slush into shards that crunch under our tires as we creep out of the city through the icy mist. There are almost no other cars on the road.

The day seems surreal. It started just after breakfast, when I spoke to a couple who were trying to get home from New Orleans to Denver. They'd decided to rent a car and drive to Phoenix to see if they could get a flight there. All weekend we've been trading stories and everyone agrees: our mad dash across the mountains in a wrecked car with the storm at our backs tops them all. I feel a strange kind of pride: we've become reckless, like Americans. And everything is turning out fine.

We point the car south. The I-25 is slushy, but nothing to worry about. Within an hour, the snow is gone and the desert surrounds us under a burning sun. We stop at the Bosque del Apache National Wildlife Refuge, where a vast wetlands adjacent to the Rio Grande is alive with cranes—sandhill, common, one or two whoopers, some snow geese, and even a few rare Ross's geese. The marsh is white with their bodies glowing in the sun. We find a secondary road and drive in closer, taking care not to disturb them.

I think of the poor birds stuck in Albuquerque, pecking through the snow for bugs and seeds. "Do you think these birds knew enough to fly ahead of the storm? Or to keep going a few miles south to where they'd find something to eat?"

"Anything that's lived here for 125 million years would have figured that much out," Wayne says.

We are leaning against the hood of the Echo, watching through our binoculars, when a truck drives up a narrow dike between two of the major wetland areas. When it comes to a halt, the driver's window goes down and a shotgun barrel appears. A shot blasts out, and a thousand cranes and geese startle into the air. One of the geese plummets into the water. A dog bounds out of the back of the truck, splashes through the shallow water and retrieves the kill. We watch in horror, our binoculars pointed indignantly toward the couple—a man and a woman, both in khaki uniforms—who lazily get out of the truck, which is near enough that we can read the words printed on the side: "Park Ranger."

The dog returns with a wild goose in its mouth. The woman pats the dog and flings the bird into the back of the truck.

"What the hell are you doing?" I yell. They're almost close enough to hear.

"Let's go," Wayne says nervously, clearly uncomfortable with the idea of confronting two poachers carrying rifles.

"Why on earth would they do that? Research?"

"More likely New Year's dinner," Wayne says.

The incident pulls a pall over our mood. That, and the realization that we can't possibly make it to El Paso before nightfall.

"How about Las Cruces?"

The City of the Crosses is the second largest in New Mexico. The origin of the name is lost: locals insist it refers to some massacre or other. A cheery thought, after witnessing the murder of the goose. The town is an army brat, of sorts, laid out in 1848 by soldiers when the surrounding area was ceded to the United States after American troops invaded Mexico. Settlers who wanted to stay on the Mexican side of the border—a Mexican version of Canada's United Empire Loyalist refugees from the Revolutionary War—created the village of Mesilla, "little tableland," on the opposite bank of the Rio Grande, a vain hope, since a few years later that was absorbed by the United States, too, in its relentless land grab in the name of Manifest Destiny.

When Mesilla was founded, the Rio Grande flowed between Mesilla and Las Cruces: travellers had to take a barge from one village to the other. But the banks of the Rio Grande are low here: the river changes course at will. In 1863, it broadened, isolating Mesilla on an island; then, in the 1870s, the area became a swamp rich in yellow fever and malaria that killed dozens of Mesillans. A hundred years ago, the river repositioned itself again to where it flows now, west of both towns.

In Las Cruces we find a Best Western overlooking a busy road. It offers two New Year's Eve events: a mariachi band with dinner or an evening with Carroll Welch and her band. We accept these as our default celebrations.

If it were up to me, I'd stay in tonight. I'm a fifth-generation Canadian, with the usual WASP braid of English, Irish, and Scots, a slender thread of French thrown in for colour. At heart, though, I am a Scot, the blood of my mother's father's people pounding most palpably in my veins. It is the lass in me that every year, in these last days between Christmas and New Year's, feels driven to clean the cupboards, straighten the underwear in my drawers, and bring my files up to date for fear of the Scottish curse that whatever is left undone by Hogmanay will haunt me throughout the year.

My idea of a perfect New Year's Eve is a glass of the Widow Clicquot by the fire, reminiscing about where we've been and where we're likely to go. Markers appeal to me. I like to make plans; Wayne likes to party.

Since the Irish in me also likes a good shindig, we wander over to Mesilla, a small adobe village that seems unchanged since the Rio Grande jumped its banks. "As wild as the wild west gets," the brochure says, though this seems like wishful thinking. The plaza is empty, the lovely old adobe church, too; only a few tourists straggle through the historic buildings that rim the square, most of them now tourist shops filled with knick-knacks and anti-Bush paraphernalia.

On one side of the plaza we come upon a restaurant, the Double Eagle, which is what the American twenty-dollar gold coin used to be called. We go in to see if we can have dinner there, but the place is fully booked—"It's New Year's Eve!" the hostess exclaims in a harried voice that says, "Where have you been?"

"Can we sit at the bar?" we ask. "We've come all the way from Canada."

"We'll find you a spot," Michael, the bartender, says. "All the servers are busy, but I'll look after you myself."

The restaurant is in an old colonial house, each of its rooms now a private dining area for a family or group of friends. Michael finds us a table in the courtyard by the fountain; it's not cleared yet, so he suggests we wait in the lounge, a pillared and mirrored affair that the bartender tells us once graced the luxurious Drake Hotel in Chicago, where Joe DiMaggio and Marilyn Monroe carved their initials into one of the hotel's ornate well-polished bars, unfortunately not this one. Above us hang chandeliers as long as a tall Texan, a thousand hand-carved crystals refracting the light. To Wayne's amazement, Michael makes him a proper Bloody Caesar, complete with Clamato juice and a slug of beef bouillon. Wayne is in tippler's heaven.

"This is the first time I've ever met anyone outside Canada who knows what a Bloody Caesar is," he says happily, "and even at home, they don't use beef bouillon anymore." He sighs with the wonder of it all.

"Another, sir?" asks Michael.

But Wayne's eye is wandering along the tequila bottles. "Is that reposado?" he says.

If we had been offered a hundred places to spend New Year's Eve, this is the one we would have chosen, this old adobe house fitted with midwestern elegance, a fountain splashing in the courtyard beside our small table in Little Tableland, *luminarias* lighting our way in the star-lit desert night, a place we've stumbled into not by design, not by good planning, but by accident.

"To luck," Wayne says, raising his pony of golden Spanish liquor.

I raise my glass of sparkling Perrier. "To our very good luck."

9 / EL CAMINO REAL

*W*E thought we would get up in the morning, pack the car (a tedious operation, as we always seem to need everything we've brought with us and so haul it into the motel room like a pair of suspicious tramps), have some breakfast, and continue down the I-25 to El Paso. But there is something about Mesilla I want to see again.

"I don't know what," I say when Merilyn asks for specifics.

"Suffering a little from tequila brain this morning?" she says. I like having a permanent designated driver, but I pay in the coinage of smug grins.

We drive back under an overpass and over an underpass, past the plaza with the giant, lit-up statue of a roadrunner, and park in one of the narrow streets of the old town. As soon as we get out of the car and walk out onto the public square, I know what it is I was after. The Old West. This is our first foray into America's outlaw culture.

Canada doesn't have an outlaw culture. In Canada, the wild west was tamed and surveyed and policed before settlers were allowed in. We didn't have a frontier, we had concessions and side roads. You don't get an outlaw culture by making concessions. Government surveyors marked out the land for farms and fences and even towns, and then the North West Mounted Police made it safe for settlers by establishing laws. And when you have grids and laws, you don't get outlaws; you get criminals.

An outlaw isn't a criminal; an outlaw is a person who inhabits a place where there is no law (or thinks he does). In frontier America, one of those places was the desert territory south and east of Santa Fe. During the Civil War, La Mesilla was the capital of the Confederate Territory of Arizona, an area that included most of present-day New Mexico, Arizona, and Utah, which is no doubt why it had a courthouse. (The "La" has since been dropped, though town boosters are lobbying to bring it back.) Even after the war, La Mesilla was an important centre until the railway was built through Las Cruces in 1881. Since then, Mesilla has existed mainly for tourists, while Las Cruces has swollen into a metropolis of almost a hundred thousand people. La Mesilla is hanging on for dear life. Except for the occasional gift shop, it hasn't even put a lot of effort into tarting itself up for tourists. We like that.

Walking along the boardwalk that circles the small bandstand in the Mesilla plaza, we pass a pink adobe building on the southeast corner called the Billy the Kid Gift Shop. The sign is a reproduction of the only known portrait of Henry McCarty, also known as Henry Antrim, William H. Bonney, and, most famously, Billy the Kid—a young, bucktoothed, inoffensive-looking fellow reputed to have killed twenty-one men, one for every year of his life. He was certainly responsible for the deaths of at least four men during the Lincoln County Cattle War, a kind of Hatfield-and-McCoy feud over grazing rights in which, because there were no lawmen yet, both sides hired professional gunslingers to protect them while they rustled each other's cattle. It may be true that Bonney killed people with a little more enthusiasm than most, but he was far from unique. He was simply the one who was caught rather than shot.

At his trial, which was held in La Mesilla in 1881, Bonney was found guilty of murdering a man named Brady and sentenced to hang. He was moved from here to Lincoln but escaped by killing his two guards and riding off, still handcuffed, into the desert. The relentless Pat Garrett rode after him and two months later found him and shot him in Fort Sumner, at the home of their mutual friend Pedro Maxwell.

Garrett was also a gunman and a murderer, but he'd been appointed deputy sheriff of Lincoln County, and Bonney had a price on his head. Except for the star, there wasn't much to distinguish the two. I think of Garrett as the original gumshoe, the character in American detective novels who, although nominally on the side of the law, resorts to methods of pursuit and capture barely distinguishable from those of the criminals he is supposed to be saving us from. In fact, the word "gumshoe" originally meant "thief," because thieves wore rubber-soled shoes in order to sneak around more effectively, which is why Americans call running shoes "sneakers." Eventually, lawmen took to wearing gumshoes so that they could sneak around after the thieves and ended up becoming gumshoes themselves. Pat Garrett was a gumshoe in cowboy boots, which would make him, I suppose, a gumboot.

Merilyn and I browse through the Billy the Kid Gift Shop, but I am more interested in the building than I am in owning the head of Wile E. Coyote on the end of a pencil. The structure itself doesn't seem to have changed much since Bonney's day: thick adobe walls, round posts holding up a low, flat roof. If this is really the courthouse in which the trial took place, it was a good choice. A bullet from a six-gun could never whistle through these walls. I remember all those television shows and westerns, in which shopkeepers wearing suspenders (you could always tell the shopkeepers by their suspenders) huddled behind their thin walls as bullets splintered patterns of daylight into the boards above their heads. Even as a kid I wondered why Hollywood didn't build thicker walls.

Between 1920 and 1950, Hollywood made five hundred movies set in Canada, every one of them filmed in California. The sets presented an imaginary Canada—vast unpopulated snowfields, lonely Mounties, scores of lakes hemmed in by sturdy pines. Perhaps those Hollywood westerns depicted a fake Wild West, too. I do remember reading that very few outlaws wore handguns in leather holsters. Handguns were hard to keep in a holster when riding a horse, impossible to aim accurately, and no good at all for distance. The favoured weapon of the outlaw was the Winchester rifle. And yet we see all these gunslingers in the movies slapping leather in dusty plazas like the one we're circling in La Mesilla.

There is a bookstore on the square, the Mesilla Book Center, one of the best we've seen in days. It was closed the night before, but now its door is wide open. That's the other reason I wanted to come back. The shelves have books from years ago, still at their original prices. I come across a first edition of Michael Ondaatje's *The Collected Works of Billy the Kid,* which I haven't read since it was published in 1970. The book is a montage of prose and poetry, an assemblage of perspectives on the life of William Bonney, fragmented and isolated, and mostly taking place in the desert between his trial here in Mesilla and his death in Fort Sumner. Hollywood may be comfortable with the notion that you can always tell the good guys from the bad guys by the colour of their hats, but Ondaatje isn't so sure:

> *There was good mixed with the bad*
> *in Billy the Kid*
> *and bad mixed with the good*
> *in Pat Garrett.*

It seems a very Canadian thing to say.

★   ★   ★

*M*ESILLA behind us, we stop for a walk in the Chihuahuan, our third desert on this trip and the largest in North America. One of the books Wayne bought in the bookstore was *A Natural State: Essays on Texas,* by Stephen Harrigan, a naturalist and an inveterate desert walker.

"Listen to this," I say to Wayne, reading as we walk. "'There are two ways to look at the desert. You can see it contriving to extinguish life or straining to support it.'"

"I guess I've always seen it as contriving to extinguish life."

"You would," I say. "It's all that work with buried dinosaur skeletons."

We top a rise and look out over a sea of low, round hills covered in creosote bush, *Larrea tridentata,* a scraggly, thigh-high evergreen shrub that the Spanish call *hediondilla,* "little stinker," because of the peculiar smell of its yellow flowers. It's January, so the air just smells dry.

"I've never seen anything like it. The plants are spaced as if somebody planted them."

"It's just that they suck up so much water that nothing else can survive within that radius," Wayne says.

Deserts seem like mountains, almost impervious to the influence of humans. But, according to Harrigan, much of this desert is manmade. Ranchers overburdened their land with livestock, and complex grasslands degenerated into simple desert scrub. Harrigan quotes an early homesteader who returned decades later to his ranch: "Where once I'd thought there was more grass than could ever be eaten off, I found no grass at all. Just the bare, rain-eroded ground . . . Somehow, the brightness seemed gone from the land."

We return to the car and drive on. Soon the desert on either side of the highway disappears, replaced with sprawling acres of cattle pens, tens of thousands of black-and-white Holsteins, flicking their tails in the sun. Dung heaps rise like small mountains. Here and there, a heifer curls contentedly on top; the rest stand in a stupor between the milking sheds. The scene reminds me of a contest I entered when I was twelve: count the cows and win a prize from Nestlé's Quik. I spent a week methodically ticking off the animals, then sent in my tally, convinced no one else would have the stick-to-it-iveness to complete the task. They must have, though, for I never heard from Nestlé.

We are heading into new territory. Not only are there cows everywhere—this part of the country produces 5 per cent of America's milk—but the lovely turquoise-and-terracotta overpasses of New Mexico are gone, replaced by dark Texas concrete and a pillar topped with a giant metal star that looks like the weapon of an ancient race of giant ninjas. There seems no change in the physical, natural landscape, but once again the vernacular of the road signs shifts. In Washington, they were whimsical: *Click-It or Ticket.* Oregon was terse: *Ice. Slides.* California was conversational: *Watch for Falling Rocks.* Texas pulls no punches: *Don't Mess with Texas. Drink Drive Go to Jail.* I can't help but note the contrast with the downright homey signs we see in Canada: *Please Drive Carefully, Children Being Children.*

At the exit for downtown El Paso, we see a red circle with a slash through it, the international image for "no," as in *No Smoking* or *No Passing.* The icon at the centre of this sign is a gun.

"Does that mean what I think it means?" I say to Wayne.

"Yep," he says. "Don't shoot and drive."

In town, the same black pistol is suspended in its slashed red circle on the sides of buses, at the entrances to buildings. We ask the clerk checking us into the Camino Real hotel what it means.

"Oh, y'all just have to leave your gun at home if you want to ride on the bus or come into the bar," she says pleasantly. I want to ask if hers is pearl-handled, but think better of it. She'd probably show it to me, and then what would I say? "Nice gun?" I'm Canadian: guns aren't part of my conversational repertoire. Even pictures of them make me uneasy. A few years ago I wrote an essay for *Canadian Geographic* magazine on the difference between how Canadian and American settlers viewed their guns. I read hundreds of letters, diaries, and recollections:

Canadians rarely mentioned their guns except in a list of tools, along with their axe, their adze, and their hoe. American guns were always in evidence, a weapon propped by the door. If the Madonna of the Trail were sculpted in Canada, I'm fairly certain she wouldn't be carrying a rifle. She'd be holding a sheaf of grain.

It's still early afternoon, so we go for a walk through the streets of El Paso. In a park decorated for Christmas, there are red ribbons on the trees and stars traced in LED lights over signs that read *Alcoholic Beverages Not Permitted* and *Feeding the Birds Is Prohibited.*

"If you want to know what people usually do in a place, look at what's not allowed," Wayne muses. I imagine a bunch of gun-toting, wine-sipping renegades defiantly tossing bread crumbs to the pigeons.

We are trying to follow a self-guided tour to the historic downtown, but we aren't sure we've found it. Signs point to *Historic Downtown, Historic Rio Grande District, Historic Heights,* as if tacking on the word "historic" makes the place seem interesting instead of deserted and slightly decrepit. The buildings we pass show architectural signs of former glory, but as often as not the upper storeys are boarded up, doors removed and stacked against the windows, the facades dark and crumbling.

El Paso was a sleepy border town before the excitement of the Civil War, when it was occupied by Union troops from California. Then the coming of the railroad—the same Atchison, Topeka and Santa Fe line that boosted Las Cruces—turned El Paso into a boom town. Bootlegging and prostitution saw it through the Prohibition days, but when the ban on booze was lifted and the Depression era hit, the city went back to being a poor cousin of Juárez, its sister city across the Rio Grande.

"My God," Wayne says. "El Paso is Windsor, and Juárez is Detroit. No wonder I find it so depressing."

It was here in El Paso, in 1947, that Jack Kerouac, dead broke, went looking for someone to pay for his gas the rest of the way to California. "We tried everything," he writes in *On the Road.* "We buzzed the travel bureau, but no one was going west that night. The travel bureau is where you go for share-the-gas rides, legal in the West. Shifty characters wait with battered suitcases. We went to the Greyhound bus station to try to persuade somebody to give us the money instead of taking a bus for the Coast. We were too bashful to approach anyone. We wandered around sadly. It was cold outside... Across the river were the jewel lights of Juárez and the sad dry land and the jewel stars of Chihuahua."

"Interesting that he says 'across the river,'" Wayne muses. "I would have said 'across the border.'"

We've been following the Rio Grande south through New Mexico, from Albuquerque to El Paso. From here it drifts east, drawing the boundary between the United States and Mexico since the treaty that ended the Mexican War in 1848.

Names are everything and nothing. What is the Rio Grande to Americans is to Mexicans the Rio Bravo del Norte: wild, restless river of the north. And what the Mexicans call the American Invasion of Mexico, Americans call the Mexican War, as if they had nothing to do with it, even though the battle was provoked in 1845 when the United States annexed the state of Texas, which had declared itself an independent republic almost a decade before.

That year, the journalist John O'Sullivan, in urging his country into war with Mexico, wrote that America should assert "the right of our manifest destiny to overspread and to possess the whole of the continent." He compared the right of the United States to all of North America "to that of the tree to the space of air and the earth suitable for the full expansion of its principle and destiny of growth." Andrew Jackson picked up the phrase "Manifest Destiny" and used it to promote not only war with Mexico but also the annexation of California and Santa Fe de Nuevo México—hundreds of thousands of square miles of land that stretched from where we stand now to where we started this journey. I can't help wondering if the war would have been as popular without the catchphrase that turned aggression into some sort of godly fate.

The Mexican War was one of dozens the United States has instigated in its relatively short history to either expand its territory or exert its influence. Wayne and I are travelling through a country that, over the past 150 years, has invaded Mexico, Cuba, Guatemala, Grenada, the Philippines, Panama, Vietnam, Cambodia, Laos, Iraq, Afghanistan, not to mention countless covert interventions by the Central Intelligence Agency. It is easy to forget that not all Americans supported these wars. In the case of the Mexican War, American devotees of Manifest Destiny and southerners hoping for new slave states to balance the ledger were in favour of the invasion, but the newly elected congressman Abraham Lincoln was against it. So were John Quincy Adams and Henry David Thoreau, who was jailed for refusing to pay taxes to support the war, thus inspiring his famous essay "Civil Disobedience," written in 1849: "The government itself, which is the mode which the people have chosen to execute their will, is equally liable to be abused and perverted before the people can act through it. Witness the present Mexican war, the work of comparatively a few individuals using the standing government as their tool."

American soldiers deserted in droves from the Mexican War. Nine thousand left the army during the fighting, among them the seven hundred Irish Catholics who formed the St. Patrick's Battalion and fought on the side of the Mexicans. When the Americans finally hoisted the Stars and Stripes over Mexico City, the soldiers of the Battalón de San Patricio were court-martialled: forty-eight were hanged, the rest were branded with a "D," for deserter. The Mexicans, who called them Los Colorados because of their ruddy, sunburned complexions and their Irish red hair, hailed the survivors as heroes and gave them land on the Pacific coast, where they founded the village of San Patricio, a lovely, quiet, fishing community where I wintered for several years.

I feel a great affection for Mexicans, in part because their country reminds me of Brazil, where I spent my childhood, in part also because Mexicans and Canadians are the thin bread on either side of the bulging meat that is America in this continental sandwich. We've both been invaded: the United States marched on Canada twice, once in the autumn of 1775 and again in 1812. Both times, the invaders assumed (as they did in Iraq) that they would be welcomed as liberators. Instead, Canadian settlers fought back, choosing British laws and institutions over those of the new republic. In fact, Canada and Cuba stand as the only two countries in the world to successfully repel an American invasion.

But the threat isn't over yet. Just last year, the *Washington Post* revealed an American plan to invade Canada, formulated in the late 1920s, approved by the United States War Department in 1930, updated in 1934 and 1935, withdrawn in 1939, and finally declassified in 1974, long before this over-consuming country began to run out of water.

"Don't worry, they won't invade us," Wayne says. "They already think they own us."

After 9/11, George W. Bush, a son of Texas, said, "Every nation in every region now has a decision to make. Either you are with us or you are with the terrorists." His father had said before him, "The world trusts us with power and the world is right. They trust us to be fair, and restrained. They trust us to be on the side of decency. They trust us to do what's right."

Do they? Do I? I trust Uncle Russ and Blanche Russell and Bay Bridge Betty. I trust Officer Jared and Paul the insurance adjuster. But America? What does it mean to trust a country?

RUDYARD KIPLING, the great British imperialist, travelled across America at the end of the nineteenth century. At one of his stops, he overhead an American say, "We kin feed all the earth, just as easily as we kin whip all the earth." The land was the key to both—to nurturing and sheltering themselves against reprisals.

Wayne and I walk down Santa Fe Street toward the Paso del Norte International Bridge. Some of the buildings are being renovated; most are barricaded by metal grilles over their windows and doors. Cars are lined up at the border, old, dented Dodges and mangled pickup trucks waiting to cross over to Juárez, and we walk along a chain-link fence until we get as close to the Rio Grande as Wayne dares. The river has been hemmed in by a ten-foot fence, lit up by floodlights, and reduced to a tiny trickle of water flowing over concrete. It looks like an open sewer running through a playground. It's hard to believe it's the same river that we've been following since Albuquerque.

"This rio doesn't look so grand anymore," Wayne says.

"'Behold now the glorious condition of this Republic,'" I say softly, quoting Kipling, "'which has no fear.'"

* * *

"*W*ELL, I should warn you, ma'am," says the man at the bar, wearing a string tie and a white Stetson, "that I'm from Texas and I agree with everything George Bush ever said."

If this were the 1940s, the woman sitting next to him, a young, nervous brunette in a silky dress, would, at this point, blow smoke in the man's face and call for the check. In this more enlightened age she merely looks bored and sips at her drink. She's evidently thinking of one or two things George Bush has said that only a dribbling moron could agree with.

"I just mean," she says, "when you think of what war has done all over the world and all . . ."

We're sitting at a corner table in the Camino Real's immense Dome Bar, a vast, pillared room, originally the hotel's lobby, with cherry stone walls, gold fixtures, and a circular bar in the centre under the largest and most beautiful stained-glass dome I have ever seen. It must be fifty feet across, arching up into the afternoon sky pouring coloured light down into the room without, however, alleviating the gloom. The hotel's brochure informs us that the dome was made by Tiffany in 1912.

"I wonder if they shipped it here in one piece," I say to Merilyn.

"It boggles the mind," she says.

Apart from us and the couple at the bar—who, it turns out, are not a couple, as the Bush enthusiast now stomps off and is almost immediately replaced by a young soldier wearing desert camouflage in six shades of beige and brown—the room is echoingly empty, and the eerie, greenish-red light from the dome, along with the soldier's uniform, makes us feel as though we're in a tropical forest. The soldier dumps a kit bag beside his bar stool. He has apparently returned from somewhere far away, as he and the woman are now engaging in protracted reunion activities that would seem to be more appropriately conducted in a room upstairs, which, when she has finished the last of her drink, is where they appear to be headed.

"Did I ever tell you the story about the soldier and my friend Susan?"

I start a lot of stories that way. Merilyn never says, "Yes, several times." It is one of the things I love about her.

"It was the early 1970s. Susan and two of her girlfriends were on a bus trip through the United States. There were three of them, so they took turns sitting two together and one alone. When it was Susan's turn to sit alone, a young man in uniform sat beside her, a soldier on his way to Vietnam. They got to talking, and after a few hours he asked her to marry him. He told her that knowing someone was waiting for him back home would help him survive the war, give him a reason to stay alive. Susan turned him down, of course, but you know her: she did it gently, almost guiltily. After a while she fell asleep, and when she woke up, the man was gone. She was sorry she hadn't said goodbye, but then she looked down at her hand. He'd slipped an engagement ring on her finger."

"That's so sad," Merilyn says. "But I guess that's what you get in a country at war."

"We're at war," I remind her. "Canada has three thousand soldiers in Afghanistan."

"At least we don't glory in it. Not yet, at any rate."

It's the middle of the afternoon, New Year's Day, and Merilyn has ordered a margarita. She's been reading about margaritas in the brochures. There's also a brochure about the artwork hanging in the lobby, one of which is a reproduction (surely) of Augustus John's portrait of James Joyce.

"Did you know the margarita was invented in Juárez?" she says. I tell her I did not. I thought it had been invented by Hemingway in Key West. "That was the daiquiri," Merilyn replies.

"Apparently," she goes on, "Pancho Morales was working as a bartender at Tommy's Place, a bar in Juárez, in 1942, when a woman came in and ordered a drink he'd never heard of."

"Probably a Bloody Caesar," I say.

"So Morales mixed her some tequila, Cointreau, lime juice, and a lot of ice, and named it after his wife. Isn't that nice?"

"Inspiring," I say. "I once invented a drink. Did I tell you? We were in the Gobi Desert, it was hot, and all we had was a bottle of gin and a case of canned peaches, for some reason, so I mixed the gin with peach syrup from the cans. We didn't have any ice. We drank it, but I don't think you'd want it to be known as a merilyn."

"No, probably not."

"What happened to Pancho?" I ask.

"He immigrated to the United States and spent the next twenty-five years working as a milkman."

We raise our glasses. "*Sic transit gloria mundi*," I say.

Another customer walks into the bar. The waitress shows him to the table next to ours. He has long hair, glasses, and a beard and is wearing a battered brown fedora, a baggy sports jacket, and cargo pants. He orders a beer, then opens a book and, without taking off his hat, proceeds to mind his own business. The book is called *Luxury Hotels*. He's a second-storey man, I surmise, a diamond thief, although he looks a bit hefty for a cat burglar. A second book lies on the table beside the beer: *Theories of Perception.* Okay, he might be harmless enough, but he could be a demonic cult leader with a taste for high living. Billy the Kid looked harmless, too. Best to let him be.

"Hi there," Merilyn calls across to him. "Are you an environmental refugee, like us?"

The man closes his book, keeping his index finger between the pages, and looks at us. "I was in Washington trying to get home to Santa Fe," he says, "but the plane couldn't land in Albuquerque because of the snow, so we were diverted to this godforsaken place. Nice hotel, scary city."

"Washington?" I say. Plenty of weird cults in Washington.

"Visiting my mother," he says.

Right. "Is this one of the luxury hotels in your book?" I ask him.

"No," he says, looking around. "It would have been when it was built, though, which was just after the 1910 Mexican Revolution. Pancho Villa is supposed to have ridden his horse right into this lobby."

"It's a good thing he didn't fire off his six-shooter," Merilyn says, and we all look up at the Tiffany dome.

"I don't think it was there then," says the stranger.

After a bit more chatting, we introduce ourselves. Our new friend's name is Mike Fischer: he's not a cult leader, after all, but a designer-builder from Santa Fe. He passes us his card: Santa Fe Adobe Design. "I build houses." He's stranded in El Paso until the Albuquerque airport reopens; then he'll have to fly from here to Albuquerque and take the airport shuttle to Santa Fe. Merilyn tells him we're driving back to Albuquerque in the morning, and he's welcome to come with us.

He looks dubious. "Are you sure?"

"Plenty of room," I say. "You could be stuck here for days."

The next morning we have our first passenger, not counting the deer. When I bring the car up from the underground garage and park in front of the hotel, Mike climbs in without commenting on the condition of the Echo's hood and headlight.

"What kind of houses do you build?" Merilyn asks him as we thread our way out of El Paso back onto the I-25.

"I use a lot of adobe," he says.

He studied architecture at the University of Washington, in his home state, but felt a growing disaffection for the international, box-style, Brutalist designs of the 1960s that grew out of Le Corbusier's obsession with poured concrete. When he moved to Santa Fe thirty years ago, he worked in construction in order to gain a hands-on appreciation for building techniques and local materials. He became intrigued by adobe. "It's a lot more forgiving than other building materials," he says. "You can shape it, and slight imperfections actually make it look better. A house made from adobe is more sculpture than architecture. And more authentic: in New Mexico, you can't get much more authentic than adobe."

It strikes me as odd, I tell him, that a desert people would adopt a building style that requires so much water. Adobe is clay mixed with water and pressed into a form to make a brick, which is then taken out of the form and baked for three days in the sun.

"Each brick," Mike says, "required a gallon of water, and a typical New Mexican pueblo would have used tens of thousands of bricks."

Although most of the ancient pueblos in the Southwest, he tells us, were made from stones and mortar, many were located near springs that provided year-round water or on arroyos that concentrated water during the brief rainy seasons. The bricks in some of these pueblos are often slumped and misshapen, as though they were used before they were completely dried, suggesting haste to build while the arroyo was still running.

"This was true of San Marcos, one of the largest pueblo villages in the Southwest," Mike says. "At one time it housed more than seven thousand people."

"Is it still around?" Merilyn asks.

"No, it was abandoned in the late 1600s, shortly after the Pueblo Revolt."

Sparked by the Spaniards' brutal suppression of native religions, the Pueblo Revolt of 1680 pushed the Spanish out of Santa Fe all the way back to the Rio Grande. The Puebloans then set about erasing every vestige of European culture they could find: they burned Christian churches (and a few friars), repurified baptized natives by washing them with yucca soap, nullified Christian marriages, renamed Spanish settlements and missions. In an excess of purity, they even destroyed Spanish crop seeds and tore up introduced plant species such as fruit trees. This final symbolic gesture might have been one too many, for eight years later the Puebloan leader Luis Tupatú sent an emissary to El Paso del Norte asking the Spanish governor to return: his people, he said, were starving.

About halfway between El Paso and Albuquerque, we stop at the Bosque del Apache again to stretch our legs and look at birds. The Apache and the Navajo eventually replaced the Puebloans, who had been in decline in the lowland deserts since the horrendous twenty-five-year drought that lasted from 1276 to about 1300. Drought meant no rainy season, and no rainy season meant no food and no adobe. The Puebloans of the highlands, along the San Juan River in Chaco Canyon, in Mesa Verde, and around Santa Fe and Taos (where there was water), managed to hang on, but by the end of the seventeenth century the Apache had the fertile bosques along the Rio Grande pretty much to themselves. These bosques, bright green strips of cottonwood, Russian olive, and tamarisk, provided summer camps for the Apache, who spent the season stocking up on fish, ducks, and geese. And not only Apaches; while we train our binoculars on a flotilla of sandhill cranes, a coyote trots out onto the causeway and gives us a long, territorial look.

"Time for lunch," I say, thinking about the coyote heading toward the cranes, but Mike takes my comment more personally.

"We're close to San Antonio," he says, looking at his watch. "We could have a burger at the Owl Cafe."

I recognize the sign for the Owl Cafe, a low, windowless building not far from the I-25. Without knowing it, Merilyn and I had parked nearby on our way down to El Paso to look at a gray flycatcher, a small tyrant the colour of sky in a Dutch painting. Mike fills us in on the cafe's history. The cafe's first owner was Conrad Hilton's father, but the place is mainly famous for having been the favoured haunt of scientists working on the Manhattan Project in nearby Los Alamos, in 1945. Apparently, they would take a break from splitting atoms to come down here to drink beer and eat José Miera's fiery green-chili cheeseburgers. They must have felt that their chemistry and Miera's were fairly closely related.

The cafe is noisy, dark, and crowded; the tables and the long bar in the first room are full, and a waitress leads us through two more dining areas before finding an empty booth. Of course we order the chili cheeseburgers. Mike and Merilyn order root beers, and I ask for a pint of draft. Merilyn wonders aloud what happened to all the people in the area who were exposed to radiation during the bomb testing.

"Maybe they mutated into little emaciated bald people with big eyes," I say. "They could have been the so-called aliens that were sent to Roswell."

Mike laughs. "What a cover-up," he says.

I was joking, but now when I look around the crowded room I'm not so sure. Why is it so dark in here? Why do all the men leave their ball caps on? What kind of fuel fires the grill?

"How do they get these burgers so hot?" I ask, chugging half my beer.

"Hot?" says Mike. "This isn't hot."

I look at him suspiciously. Is he one of them?

*   *   *

My son, when I talk to him from the pay phone outside the cafe, says it is so warm back home that he's not yet wearing his winter coat. "Ship it here," I tell him. "I'm freezing."

"Odd time to be making a trip like this," Mike muses from the back seat as we near snow-covered Albuquerque. It didn't seem odd to us. We think of ourselves as travellers, not tourists: we prefer the off-season.

But as we head back into a landscape that looks more like Nunavik than New Mexico, I wonder if maybe Mike doesn't have a point.

When we drop him off at the airport, he says if we're ever in his city we should look him up. We tell him we will.

"Let's go this afternoon," Wayne says as we drive back into Albuquerque.

"We have to rent a car anyway," I say. "And the I-25 seems to be open going north. Let's do it." Spontaneous planning: the best of both our worlds.

It is mid-morning when we pull in under the sedate porte cochère of Jess Munos Auto Body shop. No wrecks, no grease monkeys in sight. This might be a computer repair business or the front office of a genteel moving company. A friendly, clean-cut man named John takes the keys to our crumpled Echo. He is an enthusiastic local booster. When he hears we might be going to Santa Fe, he tells us not to miss the San Miguel Mission, the oldest church in North America.

"Did you earn that?" I ask, pointing to the silver buckle on his belt that says "Rodeo Champion."

"I sure did. I wouldn't wear it if I didn't. I wrestle steers."

He tells us how he once escaped an elk by running around a tree. "You can't outrun those animals. All you can do is go in circles: we turn faster than they do." I make a mental note: when in danger, run in circles.

"I'll have you on your way by the weekend," he promises.

We believe him. John calls a car rental place and within minutes, a young woman pulls up in a big Pontiac. Round-faced and jolly, Gloria quizzes us about our trip as she ferries us across town. "Where ya been?" "Whatcha doin' here?" To every reply, she snorts a little laugh. "Gotcha!" she says. "Gotcha!" The little cherries on the lapel of her black pea jacket dance against her breast with delight. She gives us a good rate on a Grand Prix, and we head north feeling buoyant.

As we near Santa Fe, the weather becomes colder, the snow on the road hardened to a slippery sheen. Although the slope is long and gentle, we've climbed to seven thousand feet above sea level. Once again, we're in full-on winter. The culture seems to have changed, too. Although the overpasses are decorated like Navajo blankets, gone are the righteous billboards exhorting the right to life and abstinence until marriage. The signs we zip past now extol the virtues of Gucci shoes and multi-million-dollar estates. Santa Fe, it seems, is high-end America.

But when we take the long way into the city, we pass clones of every hotel and motel chain in America. We could be outside Flagstaff or Sacramento or El Paso. When we get closer to the centre of town, a few private motels and inns appear. The Stage Coach. The Silver Saddle. The El Rey.

"Let's go for a mom-and-pop this time," I suggest. "Something close enough that we can walk to the main plaza."

In Santa Fe, the old town is downtown, not some historic district roped off for tourists, as it is in Albuquerque or Sacramento. Within a few blocks of the plaza, we find the Santa Fe Motel & Inn, a cluster of adobe rooms set back from the road among some trees. A lovely, soft-spoken young woman tells me the room is $99, then, after some discussion, agrees that $69 will do fine. She shows us the patio with its adobe fireplace, each wrought-iron table heaped with a tuque of snow. The room feels like sunshine: terracotta floors and turquoise walls with wooden shutters on the windows, a bathroom done in Mexican tiles, a bed-sitting room, and a small kitchen with a gaily painted wooden table and chairs. We take it for two nights, with an option on a third on the off chance that the car takes longer to be repaired than John promised.

I feel at home here. Maybe it's the snow. Maybe it's the tropical decor. Maybe it's the anti-Bush sentiment. On our way into Santa Fe, we passed a crossroads where chanting protesters were hoisting signs at each of the four corners.

Bring Our Soldiers Home. End the Occupation. Impeach for Peace. Jail Bush.

New Mexico is definitely a blue state. In the Billy the Kid Gift Shop at Mesilla, I was tempted by a car freshener that was a full-face portrait of the goofily grinning president, with the caption, "Bush's Dumb-Ass Head on a String." At the University of New Mexico Bookstore in Albuquerque, I almost bought a book called *Bad President*. Now, as we walk along Santa Fe's tony plaza, we pass a massive countdown clock in a store window. *Backwards Bush. Democracy Is Coming! 747 Days, 17 Hours, 47 Minutes and counting . . .*

It occurs to me that New Mexico is more like where we are from than any part of the United States we've visited so far. Even Seattle. Not the geography or even the climate: I'm thinking of the way it was settled. In Canada, the first European immigrants sailed into the belly of the continent along the St. Lawrence River and through the Great Lakes. From those shores, they headed north. For the most part, European settlers in the United States arrived on the eastern seaboard and pushed steadily west. But New Mexico, like Canada, was settled by priests and traders and eventually families moving north from Mexico into the heart of the continent. The frontier for them was not a line moving steadily west: wilderness surrounded them, as it did the first Canadian settlers. Surely this has some effect on the psyche. Northrop Frye theorized that it created in Canadians a garrison mentality. I've never bought that: reading settlers' diaries made it clear to me that they weren't afraid of the wilderness. They did stick together, but from a sense of community, not defensiveness. Being surrounded by the unfamiliar makes people community-minded. Just as pushing out from a settled area makes a hero of the individual.

George Bush is descended from that line of American tough-guy heroes. His response to 9/11, his invasion of Iraq: it all just seems paranoid. Maybe that's why he makes Canadians like me anxious. Maybe that's why New Mexicans stand on street corners, hoping he'll leave the White House and go home to Texas.

*   *   *

*W*E wake up to the sound of a snow shovel scraping asphalt; it is six-fifteen and the motel's owner is trying to clear the parking lot of the two feet of fresh snow that fell during the night. His assistant is blasting at the frozen ridges of ice with a propane weed burner, then whacking at them with a metal pole. There is a lot of sound and fury.

In the breakfast room, which is small but warm and smells like real coffee, we talk to a couple from Colorado who tell us that during the night the husband went out in his pyjamas to see why the dome light in his car was still on, and she went out in her nightie to watch, and their unit door swung shut behind them. Luckily, their cellphone was in the car. They called the emergency number taped to the office door, and the motel's owner drove across town in the blizzard to let them back into their room.

We spend the rest of the morning doing the tourist thing, walking around Santa Fe's attractive central square, making note of good places to come back to for dinner. Most of the people seem to be fellow tourists; a few look like locals who have come into town on errands. There are well over a hundred art galleries in Santa Fe, as well as the usual gaggle of souvenir shops. The plaza is surrounded by expensive clothing stores, some down-to-earth eateries. We spend an hour in a photography gallery, which has prints of photographs by Edward Weston, Ansel Adams, and Henri Cartier-Bresson that are so clear and sharp it's as though they were printed this morning in the back room. I stand in front of one of Weston's sensual desertscapes and can almost hear the wind scraping over the dunes.

Under the covered walkway that shades the plaza's sidewalk in front of the old Palace of the Governors, which is not yet open, groups of Navajo craftspeople sit beside blankets on which they have spread arrays of silver earrings and bracelets, turquoise necklaces and rings. Merilyn and I walk arm in arm. She stops to admire a heavy turquoise necklace proffered by a Navajo jewellery maker, and I urge her to buy it. She finds an intricately woven shawl in a below-ground-level shop, and

I urge her to buy that. I like Santa Fe, where everything is so expensive it feels special.

Waiting for the restaurants to open, we go into the Loretto Chapel, a small church just off the plaza, built in the 1870s as part of the convent for the Sisters of Loretto (Holy Faith). Five years later, when the sisters grew tired of having to climb a ladder to get to the choir loft, they made a novena to St. Joseph to send them a carpenter who would build them a proper set of stairs. On the ninth and final day of the novena, a mysterious man showed up with a donkey and a tool box and built them a miraculous spiral staircase: it twists twenty-seven feet up to the loft, a wooden helix without nails or any apparent physical support.

We sit in the quiet chapel looking at the bentwood staircase, trying to see what is so miraculous about it. It looks to us like an ordinary spiral staircase, although admittedly a handsome one. I particularly like the veneer covering its underside, no doubt in deference to the modesty of the nuns who had to climb it. We feel like a pair of heretics. If, as is bruited, the mysterious man with the donkey was St. Joseph himself, the staircase would be the work of Christ's earthly father. Some experts claim not to be able to identify the wood used in its construction. Maybe it's gopher wood, the wood Noah's Ark is supposed to have been made from, also unidentified. These are elevating thoughts, I think. No: escalating thoughts. Or perhaps lofty.

"Time to leave," Merilyn says wisely.

By now the Palace of the Governors is open, and Merilyn is keen to see the mud floor in the seventeenth-century chapel that was sealed with ox blood. A group of eight tourists, including us, are led from room to room by a docent named Linda, who has evidently spent some time on the stage. Her talks, explaining how settlers were recruited in Spain in 1598 for the mission to Santa Fe, are lively and interactive.

"You, sir," she says, pointing at me, "you look like a fine fellow. Are you a cobbler? Or a blacksmith? I'm going to make you an offer of free land, guaranteed work, and all you have to do is pledge that you will live in this Spanish colony for the rest of your life. What do you say?"

I say I think it's time to take John's advice and see the San Miguel Mission.

The mission is a few blocks south of the palace. The church was built in 1610 by the 250 Spanish colonists and 700 natives who came north from Mexico; they raised it on the ruins of an ancient kiva site sacred to the Tlaxcalan. We pay our dollar to get in and take a place on the benches, conscious of sitting on layer upon layer of sacred history.

The original mission bell, we are told, predated first contact: cast in Spain in 1356, it weighed 780 pounds—20 pounds of gold, 5 pounds of silver, and 755 pounds of copper. It had been rung to signal the start of the Pueblo Revolt in 1680. The building was partially destroyed during the anti-Spanish frenzy that followed the revolt, and the original bell disappeared. This one was brought in by mule cart in the early 1700s, when Spanish rule was restored; it now hangs on a post inside the front door, beside a rubber mallet and a chart showing where to hit the bell to achieve specific notes. I study the chart for a while, then try playing "Frère Jacques," but all the notes sound the same to me.

Being a tourist, even for a morning, is thirsty work. At noon we meet Mike Fischer at the Pink Adobe and Dragon Room Lounge, a restaurant across from the mission. The beer is local and the specialty is a Steak Dunigan—a seven-ounce New York strip loin buried under a mound of green chili and mushrooms. The room is long and narrow, with a bar along one side, and we find a table in a corner beside a tree trunk that rises from floor to ceiling; halfway up, a metal cat clings to it with metal claws. Above us hangs a wooden monkey, poised like a trapeze artist but holding a chandelier, and I think of Poe's orangutan in "The Murders in the Rue Morgue." The absence of tourists is refreshing after a day of jostling in front of blankets spread with Navajo silver earrings and storefronts stacked with grey-and-white Hopi pottery. Twenty years ago, Jan Morris worried about the "Aspen syndrome" that seemed to have come to Santa Fe, the recent arrivals who became instant locals, equipping themselves with "flouncy layered frocks with marsupial pouches, multitudinous silver jewelries and Navajo wall rugs." Many of the shops and inns we peered into seemed to be run by such people, whose real roots were in southern California or Texas, but none of them, and certainly none of their customers, are here in the Pink Adobe. Except us, of course, but we're here with Mike, who is something of a regular.

Mike has brought along a sheaf of blueprints for Crescent House, his latest, nearly completed project. He rolls the sheets out on the table and pins the corners down with beer glasses. The house, he says, is built entirely of adobe and local spruce and is shaped like a two-storey letter "C" curled around a central kiva that gives the design its focus and strength. "I call it a kiva," he says, "but whoever buys the house will probably call it a studio, or the nurse's quarters." He shrugs.

"How much will it sell for?" I ask.

"Probably about three and a half million."

"Can we see it?" Merilyn asks.

"Sure." He seems pleased. "I've got the car here, we can go up there after lunch."

We drive through Santa Fe and up into the hills overlooking the city. All the houses here are huge, sprawling, single-storey, all owned by presidents and CEOs. Mike turns onto a winding gravelled track that curves around mounds of shrubbery and along a stone wall that opens into a carport. To the left of the carport is the circular kiva; the main entrance to the house is on the right; the roof above the carport is the main floor of the house. From the entrance we climb a staircase the banisters of which are woven branches cast in bronze. At the top of the stairs we enter the largest living room I've ever seen: "Eighty feet by twenty-five," Mike says, with wide pine boards below and thick, rounded spruce logs overhead. Buff adobe walls protrude into the living space to form hallways and alcoves, a corner fireplace, a transition to the kitchen. He shows us the bedrooms, a fully equipped exercise

room, and a master bathroom so big it challenges the notion of a bathroom as a room to be used by one person at a time.

It is a kind of living architecture, organic and sculptural. It seems
not so much constructed as evolved according to Mike's whimsy and
enthusiasm. He had a marble countertop installed in the dressing
room, and when he saw that there were trilobites embedded in the
marble, he had lights put under the counter that shine up through the
fossils. The effect is stunning, but it involved remaking the entire van-
ity. When he thought the curved stairway might be daunting to some
visitors, he put in an elevator to the main floor. A huge boulder that
had turned up in the excavation beside the main door was left there,
jutting through the wall; Mike is thinking of hollowing it out and
planting a fern garden.

"All these rough surfaces," Merilyn says. "How would you ever clean
them?"

Mike gives her an amused look. "I hadn't thought of that," he says.
"I guess they'll hire someone."

The inside curve of the living room gives out onto a deck that is
also the roof of the kiva. Leaning on its railing we look out past the
lights of Santa Fe over a vast, dry plain, fading in the crepuscular light.
Mike points to a distant mountain peak: "That's in Colorado," he says.
On our left, a faint glow on the horizon is Albuquerque, sixty miles
away. And on our right, Taos. Surrounded by adobe, with a 180-degree
view commanding miles and miles, we feel like cliff dwellers ourselves.
Mike points to a house above us—Pottery House, designed by Frank
Lloyd Wright—then to an empty lot immediately below. "I own that,
too," he says. "I'm going to build another vision house on it, like this
one, only I'm going to call it Shard House. All the uprights will be in
the form of pottery shards."

Pottery shards at the foot of a cliff, below an adobe pueblo carved
into the hillside: it's like a modern Mesa Verde. Mike is not just playing
around with million-dollar clay blocks; he's recreating the ancient history of New Mexico.

*M*y brief visit to the Georgia O'Keeffe Museum in Santa Fe has not prepared me for the gorgeous landscape we drive into as we head north along the Rio Grande toward Taos. The hills move in closer, black mesas that O'Keeffe painted and Ansel Adams photographed. The two met in the summer of 1929, when, drawn by descriptions of New Mexico's wild beauty, they both journeyed to Taos. O'Keeffe was forty-two and already famous; Adams twenty-seven and completely unknown. They became friends, bonded by their love of the southwestern landscape Wayne and I are passing through—spare, subtly coloured, its lines etched hard against the sky—a landscape impossible to look at without seeing their art.

Eight years before O'Keeffe's first trip to New Mexico, her lover, Alfred Stieglitz, exhibited more than forty nudes of her: photographs of her hands, her breasts, her body. The exhibition was sharply erotic, visible proof of what Stieglitz once said, that when he photographed, he made love. The portraits caused a public sensation. Suddenly, O'Keeffe was not a painter; she was the master photographer's model.

For twenty years, although she and Stieglitz were married, O'Keeffe spent her summers alone in New Mexico. At first she rode into the hills on pack horses, then she bought an old Model A and roamed the countryside as we've thought of doing, driving off the roads into the dry desert canyons. She collected bones and painted flowers, the hills, and skulls of long-dead animals.

I'm curious about this relationship, Stieglitz and O'Keeffe. At the museum, it was not her art so much as the images of her that stirred me: portraits by various photographers that tracked her from a heavy-lidded, sultry young woman to a firm-lipped old lady, that tough, imperial gaze never varying across a century. Stieglitz was fifty-three and O'Keeffe was thirty when they fell in love; Stieglitz left his wife for her, yet they conducted separated lives, often thousands of miles apart.

I understand the appeal of a creative partnership, of throwing your lot in with someone who knows what it is to love shape and texture and shares your vision of the world, someone equally obsessed with images (in their case) or words (in ours). Even so, I understand O'Keeffe's pressing need for solitude. I am happy when Wayne goes off to join a scientific expedition to China, or Patagonia, or the North Pole. I can't wait for the private time those trips allow me, yet I rarely carve out that solitary space for myself. Why is that? I wonder as we drive into Taos. Was O'Keeffe stronger than I am? More self-absorbed? More dedicated to her art? Or was Stieglitz more overbearing? Whatever the cause, she left New York every summer to get away from his mesmerizing gaze, the unblinking eye of his camera, to remember who she was.

I think of Canada, sharing a continent with the burly, assertive United States: maybe we'd get along better if we could just find a way to spend a little time alone.

TAOS IS exactly as Simone de Beauvoir described it: "a faithful, scaled-down replica" of Santa Fe. The same plaza ringed with arcades, curio shops, and, on one side, the famous adobe hotel, La Fonda. We feel vaguely disappointed. Without a church to tether it, the plaza seems without purpose. In front of the bandstand some young people in heavy knit sweaters and tuques have set up portable tables laid out with food—muffins, bread, soup, stew—all of it salvaged from local grocery trash bins.

We decline the scavenged lunch, cross the plaza, and go into La Fonda, which houses one of the two restaurants on the square. We eat at Joseph's Table, where I order the molasses flank steak with duck-fat frites. Wayne chooses marinated pork, which arrives mysteriously as a sandwich. The waiter recommends the mousse for dessert, admitting, "I had a Belgian couple who said it's not really a mousse."

"That's not a mousse," Wayne says, "that's an elk."

The waiter starts to leave, then turns.

"Where are you from?"

"Canada," we say in unison.

"I wondered," he says thoughtfully. "The accent is unusual, and you look people in the eye. That doesn't happen all that often in my country."

ON OUR way out of La Fonda, we notice a small sign on the reception desk: *Forbidden Paintings of D.H. Lawrence.*

The next tour isn't for an hour, but a private viewing can apparently be arranged for three dollars apiece.

"I didn't know Lawrence was a painter," I say.

"Maybe he wasn't. Maybe that's why they're forbidden," Wayne says.

We know Lawrence as one of the great writers of the twentieth century, but in his own time, his public reputation was that of a pornographer and a wastrel of his considerable talent. His novels were banned and burned in England for their frank descriptions of sex. Because his wife, Frieda, who left her husband and three children to marry Lawrence, was a cousin of Manfred von Richthofen, the "Red Baron," they were not issued passports until after the First World War. In 1919 they began their years of wandering—their "savage pilgrimage," as Lawrence called it, taking them first to Italy, then to France, Ceylon, Australia, and finally New Mexico.

In 1924, the wealthy widow Mabel Dodge Luhan gave Lawrence and Frieda 160 acres about twenty miles north of Taos in return for the original manuscript of *Sons and Lovers,* a book that had provoked from Lawrence one of the most delightfully searing responses to a publisher's rejection on record: "Curse the blasted, jelly-boned swines, the slimy, the belly-wriggling invertebrates," Lawrence wrote to a friend when the novel was turned down by Heinemann, "the miserable sodding rutters, the flaming sods, the sniveling, dribbling, dithering, palsied, pulse-less lot that make up England today."

Lawrence, the literary outlaw, found New Mexico much to his liking. In an essay written in 1928, the year *Lady Chatterley's Lover* was published, Lawrence wrote that "New Mexico was the greatest experience from the outside world that I have ever had . . . A new part of the soul woke up suddenly, and the old world gave way."

We pay our three dollars and the young man leads us down a narrow hall toward a private dining room. He seems to know (and care) little about Lawrence. Sullenly, he draws a gold, floor-to-ceiling drape to reveal a wall of gaudy images, stiff red nipples and huge erect penises, a slavering bacchanalia.

The bored young man begins his spiel. "Nine oil paintings from an exhibition of thirteen that were confiscated in 1929 from the Dorothy Warren Gallery of London . . ."

"By the bad-art police," Wayne says under his breath.

The young man takes no notice of us. We try to stop him with questions, but he drones on. When he comes to Lawrence's death near Vence in 1930, I interrupt.

"It's pronounced Vence, as in 'wants.' Not as in 'fence.' It's a town in southern France."

He mumbles on. "Frieda Lawrence returned to Taos when Lawrence died and buried his ashes at Kiowa Ranch. She brought the paintings with her, and when she passed on, they were sold to Saki Karavas, who owned the La Fonda Hotel. He never would disclose what he paid for them, and though he received many generous offers over the years, he refused to sell them. Today the hotel and the paintings have been lovingly restored, preserving two Taos treasures."

After O'Keeffe's work, these paintings are an embarrassment. And yet Stieglitz wanted to exhibit them in his New York gallery, an eagerness that may be explained by the fact that he never saw them.

Why would a man so skilled in language spend his time ineptly shaping images with paint? Just before this trip, I reread *The Plumed Serpent*, Lawrence's novel about Mexico, written partly at Kiowa Ranch. I also read an early draft of the novel, which he called "Quetzalcoatl." The sexism and sex aside, the writing is superb. Even so, Lawrence insisted that painting "gave me a form of pleasure that words can never give."

I suppose his paintings were like my gardens, satisfying to me, even beautiful, though mundane and gauche to the sophisticated observer. But with luck, nature will obliterate them the minute I'm gone. It is appalling to imagine a bored young man leading people through my perennial beds to show them what a sorry gardener I'd been.

The photographs that accompany the paintings are more interesting. Lawrence appears gaunt and sickly from the tuberculosis that had yet to be diagnosed, hardly the portrait of a pornographer. Frieda is squarely German. Mabel Dodge, the staunch patron of the arts. Squinting into those faces, I find it hard to imagine the sex games this threesome got up to. Maybe that's what drew O'Keeffe to Taos. Maybe it was an inner landscape she was hoping to explore.

"It must have been like the Sixties," I say to Wayne. "Funny how we forget to account for context."

On the way home, we pass a huge electronic billboard that blinks: *Caution, Inclimat Weather Expected.* On the radio, the announcer reports that it is thirty-nine degrees Fahrenheit in Santa Fe and sixty-eight degrees Fahrenheit in Central Park. Last night's wet, heavy snow triggered an avalanche in Colorado that pushed two cars off the road, temporarily burying the passengers.

"I hope our breakfast companions get home safely," I say.

"Us, too," says Wayne. "Inclimat weather or no."

10 / **JEFFERSON, TEXAS**

"*W*E found some unexpected parts that need replacing," the mechanic at Jess Munos's repair shop tells us when we call from Santa Fe on Friday. I wonder, not aloud, how a Class A car mechanic can find unexpected parts in a car but let it pass. We're enjoying New Mexico. He promises the Echo will be ready by noon Monday. "But call first," he says, before hanging up. Unexpected parts are no doubt hard to come by.

On Monday we drive the Buick back to Albuquerque, and Gloria from the rental agency gives us a lift to Jess Munos's. When we arrive, the Echo is in one of the repair bays being washed. It looks brand new, which shouldn't be surprising, since half of it is. We get the keys from John, and while Merilyn pays the bill, which all but maxes out our American Express card, I bring the car around to the front of the shop and load our belongings into the trunk, the back seat, and anywhere else I can find.

"Where's my manuscript?" Merilyn asks anxiously. She'd sleep with it under her pillow if she could.

"It's here, behind your seat," I say. Right where she can reach out to touch it from time to time. I know she likes to keep it close. I wonder if she's ever going to ask me to read it.

We seem to have acquired a few items. Merilyn says there is a science to packing. The things we are likely to need first, for example, should go in last. The computers should not go in the trunk. A novelist friend told me a horrifying story about the time when, after a month's writing retreat, she packed her laptop in the trunk, on top of her suitcases, because she thought she would need it first if inspiration struck, and when she got home, she discovered that the magnets in the speakers under her rear window had erased her entire hard drive. It sounds like an urban myth, but it is at least as hair-raising to me as the murdered hitchhiker or the baby in the microwave. Since then, I've put the computers in the back seat, under the books and wine bottles, where they are safe. Mine has a small dent on the lid, but at least it still has its mind.

Having said our farewells to Albuquerque, we are back on the I-25, making our way south, the sun in our eyes, the Rio Grande running like a fellow racer beside us. We turn east at the Bosque del Apache and drive past the Owl Cafe with a friendly nod. After two weeks in New Mexico, we feel almost like locals. But soon we are into the Chihuahuan Desert, moving along a thin strip of asphalt bordered closely by cactus, and once again nothing feels familiar. We perk up in our seats, smiling: it's the strangeness a traveller yearns for.

We are crossing the infamous Jornada del Muerto, the Journey of the Dead Man, a ninety-mile-wide stretch of the Chihuahuan Desert between El Paso and Santa Fe. A *jornada*, the Spanish word for journey, is the distance a person can travel in a single day. Travelling to El Paso through the Chihuahuan was shorter than the Camino Real, which followed the twists and turns of the Rio Grande, but also a lot drier. In the desert, a *jornada* is effectively the distance from one reliable source of water to the next, but in the Jornada del Muerto, there is no reliable water at all. The "dead man" was a German trader who, in 1666, was arrested for witchcraft; he escaped from his pueblo prison near Albuquerque and rode off down the shortcut toward Mexico. His desiccated remains were found weeks later, beside those of his horse.

The section of the Chihuahuan we're driving through receives a few brief but torrential showers in the summer months, then not a drop of rain the rest of the year. When it rains, the earth grows a skin of black grama grass, and the creosote bushes flower. Now, in January, hardy shrubs like rabbitbrush, inkweed, and mesquite stud the landscape, quivering forlornly over patches of Apache plume, chocolate flower, and desert willow. Prickly pear cactus colonize the roadsides, their flat, round pads (actually branches) held up like admonishing hands, warning us to stay on the roads, not to venture any deeper into the dead man's journey.

Today, the Jornada del Muerto is home to the White Sands Missile Range, the 54,000-acre expanse of New Mexico where the boys from Los Alamos National Laboratory worked when they weren't eating chili burgers at the Owl Cafe. We are in fact very close to the Trinity Site, the spot where they erected the one-hundred-foot tower upon which Fat Man, the world's first atomic bomb, was detonated on June 16, 1945.

We've all seen the movie: six miles away, men in crisp army uniforms stand in the stark desert looking north, hands shielding their eyes, scruffy journalists zigzagging among them, Samuel Allison calling the sixty-second countdown, J. Robert Oppenheimer looking intense and exhausted. Most of the spectators are in the control room, a kind of bunker half buried in sand, but some are outside, smoking and laughing nervously. The project's commander, Brigadier General Leslie Groves, the director of the Office of Scientific Research and Development, Vannevar Bush (no relation), and the president of Harvard University, James B. Conant, view the explosion from a shallow trench. *Why aren't they wearing safety suits?* we cry out. Only the poor sods sent to examine the site after the explosion wore safety suits and gas masks, although of course those weren't much help. Gas wasn't the problem. The test generated more than thirty roentgens an hour of radiation, about the same as was later released in the Chernobyl disaster: radioactive dust falling on cattle fifty miles away burned holes in their hides. Even then, the powers that were didn't get it. Radiation affected the cattle, they said, but it wouldn't hurt humans "because cows don't take showers."

From the road, we think we can see the hillside where the scientists watched the detonation. Some distance away is what looks like a silver balloon, marking the Trinity Site.

"Do you want to drive in?" I ask Merilyn.

"Not particularly," she says. "It's the phenomenon that interests me, not the fact of the explosion. Did they decide to explode the bomb here because deserts already look dead? Didn't they realize it was teeming with living things? How smart were these guys?"

We stop at a small, deserted-looking gift shop on Route 380 advertising pieces of "trinitite" for sale, and Merilyn gets out to buy a chunk. Trinitite is sand fused to glass by the Fat Man detonation, which was estimated to have created temperatures in the tens of thousands of degrees Celsius. This green, glassy crust coated the entire 1,200-foot crater created by the blast. I'm a little leery of having bits of it in the car. It might be radioactive.

"What did the store's owner look like?" I ask Merilyn when she returns to the car.

"The shop is closed," she says.

"Cancer, probably," I say. Merilyn gives me her look.

The blast, equivalent to the explosion of twenty thousand tons of dynamite—the same size as the bomb later dropped on Hiroshima—killed vegetation and animals, insects, birds, micro-invertebrates, fungoids, and, for all I know, protozoa for miles around. Nothing as hot as Trinity had ever existed on Earth before, and some scientists seriously warned that the blast would ignite the entire atmosphere, turning the planet into a fiery, lifeless ball. As it turned out, although the fireball rose ten thousand feet into the air, the atmosphere remained unignited. But how could the ground under the blast not be radioactive?

I'm not the only one to be antsy about the White Sands range. In 2000, when a forest fire swooped down on the valley and burned half of Los Alamos, including many of the buildings of the Los Alamos National Laboratory, local citizens fled in panic from the smoke, fearing that it was a radioactive cloud. "Now we know what Hiroshima was like," one of the refugees said. Seriously.

Oppenheimer believed in the curative powers of faith, that the bomb would set the world free. Instead, nuclear energy has made us suspicious and paranoid. H.G. Wells predicted the splitting of the atom in his 1914 novel *The World Set Free*. In it, nuclear energy is used first to replace every coal-burning power plant in North America, and within a few years, no automobile anywhere is still burning fossil fuel. In real life, atomic energy was used first to kill 200,000 people in six minutes, and sixty-five years later, most of our electricity still comes from burning coal or oil. Our cars are built the same way they were when H.G. Wells delivered his manuscript to his publisher in his Model T Ford. The world has not been set free; its chains have been tightened.

*   *   *

$\mathcal{M}$ALPAIS, a great streak of black basalt some fifty metres thick, rises out of the White Sands Desert and continues for some forty-five miles, cutting through the Valley of Fire. It is a welcome relief from the flat monotony of sand, and we stop for a closer look.

"It's as though it cooled just this morning," Wayne says.

"It was fifteen hundred years ago."

"That's this morning, in volcano time," he insists.

Nature has had a hard time colonizing this buckled, twisted stream of hardened lava. Where we are, the black stone is still shiny.

Only cactus and Adam's needle, a relative of the Joshua tree, grow in the cracks where the cooling lava split. Wayne finds a place behind a cactus to pee, then hops back to my side of the lava bed, brushing at something on his thigh.

"Yikes!" he yells. He must have brushed up against the cacti that doggedly push their roots into the black surface dust. Carefully, we pick the needles out of his jeans and the palm of his hand.

I take the wheel while he nurses his wounds. The towns we pass through look desolate. Neither of us feels the urge to stop and look around, though we do pull over for the Official Scenic Historic Markers, which tell stories of the region on one side, with Points of Interest indicated on the reverse, mostly ghost towns and monuments to the long gone. We stop for birds, too. A cactus wren. A loggerhead shrike. A string of western meadowlarks sitting like finials on a row of fence posts. The last jail that Billy the Kid broke out of is closed for the season. (It looks more like a garage than a jail.) We take a picture at the Smokey the Bear sign overlooking Lincoln National Forest, where the real Smokey was found as a cub clinging to a tree after a forest fire. Rangers raised him to become their mascot and, eventually, the icon of forest fire prevention.

"And taught him to hold a shovel," Wayne says, putting the camera away.

The town of Lincoln used to be called Las Placitas del Rio Bonito. It was home to the first water since the Rio Grande and thus marked the end of a ninety-mile *jornada*. How desperate those travellers on horseback or in the back of a wagon must have been by the time they got this far. We feel vaguely guilty for crossing in a matter of hours what must have taken them day after arid day. I have the urge to apologize again, this time to all those mothers with their parched, squalling babes.

We eat sandwiches and drink bottled water in the car on a windblown stretch of grassy desert.

"Let's go into Roswell for coffee and dessert," I suggest.

"Dessert at the end of the desert." Wayne can't help it. It's a tic, like Tourette's, these uncontrollable bursts of wordplay. "After sandwiches in the sand."

We know we're getting close to Roswell by the billboards. The Golden Arches *i'm lovin' it* sign shows Ronald McDonald swooping down in a spaceship, trailing "Un-Official Crash Site" in his slipstream. A gnarly green hand holds up the note "Open 24 Hrs."

The main street of the town is wide enough for a landing strip. Most of the shops have embraced aliens with a passion. We walk past the Cover Up Cafe, the Not of This World coffee shop, the Alien Zone, which advertises a Cosmic Jukebox. Shop windows feature miniature dioramas of balloon-skulled, slant-eyed creatures firing lasers across cut-out plywood mountains and, my favourite, a little Airstream trailer with an alien lounging outside in a salvaged sofa chair, a tiny beer can balanced on one arm.

Roswell has been synonymous with aliens and UFOs since the summer of 1947, when Mac Brazel, a foreman on the Foster home-stead about twenty miles north of Roswell, found some odd debris—"a large area of bright wreckage made up of rubber strips, tinfoil, a rather tough paper and sticks," he reported to the newspapers. It was odd enough that Brazel told the sheriff and the sheriff called the Roswell Army Air Field, which sent over a major to pick up the wreckage. On July 8, 1947, the RAAF apparently issued a press release (no one has been able to find it) stating that the 509th Bomb Wing had recovered a crashed "flying disc." Later that day, another press release hastened to clarify that it wasn't a flying saucer, it was a wrecked weather balloon.

Into the gap between those two stories have crawled legions of ufologists, most famously Stanton T. Friedman, who, thirty years after the fact, interviewed the major who did the original cleanup. This time, the story goes, the major told the truth: the Foster homestead was the crash site of an alien spaceship. Witnesses came forward. There were, it turned out, eleven crash sites. Some of the aliens had survived. In

1989, a mortician reported that he'd done autopsies on the aliens who died. Finally, in the 1990s, in an attempt to quell the speculation, government inquiries were held and official reports issued. The recovered material, they determined, was fallout from a secret government program called Project Mogul, which launched high-altitude balloons in an attempt to detect sound waves generated by Soviet atomic bomb tests and ballistic missiles. And the aliens? They were hoaxes perpetrated by the media or cases of faulty memory related to the recovery of anthropomorphic crash-test dummies used in military programs like Project High Dive, the high-altitude parachute tests in the 1950s. No matter. National polls at the time showed a majority of Americans believed that aliens had visited their country and, more specifically, had landed at Roswell, and the government was covering up.

I remember Roswell from *The X-Files*, the television series featuring the alien-hunting Mulder and Scully and the motto "The Truth Is Out There." In the second episode, called "Deep Throat," Mulder and Scully end up at the Ellens Air Force Base, where ufologists believe some of the Roswell wreckage was taken.

"They're here, aren't they?" asks Mulder with barely repressed glee.

"Mr. Mulder," replies the enigmatic Deep Throat, "they've been here for a long, long time."

Some 80 per cent of the world's population believe there is life on other planets, in other galaxies, but Americans have made a culture of so-called aliens. I wonder if that's because they are particularly intrigued by the idea of humanoids evolving on another planet. Or do they just like being scared? Or is it because, being a frontier nation, they are pathologically frustrated at no longer having a frontier? Extraterrestrials would be proof that there is another habitable planet out there, a place they could "discover" and colonize when they've completely exhausted this one. A final frontier, as Captain Picard of *Star Trek* puts it: a place "to boldly go where no one has gone before."

That, it strikes me, is the essence of the American myth: they believe themselves a nation that consistently confronts and survives the impossible. Historically, the impossible was nature: rushing rivers to be forded, rugged mountains to be scaled, endless deserts to be crossed. It has always been landscape—real estate—that Americans have been after. Their fixation with territory is so intense that in Texas a person can legally shoot someone dead for simply stepping onto their property.

The only real estate yet to be claimed is whatever may be "out there." In the same way that the NASA space program wasn't a pissing contest with the Russians so much as a yearning for new territory, aliens aren't proof of a conspiracy so much as evidence of another New World, where there are unmined mountains to climb and clear rivers to cross.

There are rumours that Hollywood has a new *X-Files* movie in the works. They're calling it *I Want to Believe*. Americans already do.

*   *   *

*W*E are a bit nervous about crossing through Texas, the land of George Bush and Waco and *Dallas*. We sort of sneak into it on a back road, hoping no one will notice. This is not unlike the way the state was first settled; in the early 1820s, wagonloads of American settlers filed quietly into the region when it still belonged to Mexico, hoping to strengthen America's claim to make it part of the Union. By 1830, Americans outnumbered Mexicans three to one, and in 1836, Texas declared its independence from Mexico. By then its population was more than 50,000, mostly Southern farmers who had brought their slaves with them: there were 3,000 slaves in Texas when it was annexed by the United States in 1845, and by the end of the Mexican War, in 1848, it was clear that Texas would be a slave state. When the Civil War started a dozen years later, the population of Texas was 600,000, of whom 180,000 were slaves. Its chief agricultural product was cotton.

We are driving through evidence of the Lone Star State's status as a cotton state: on either side of the highway are flat, red fields covered with drifts of white balls. At first we think in horror, *Snow*. But no: it's cotton. We stop. All along the roadside, gathered in hollows, snagged on the stubble of their own stalks, are millions of cotton balls.

I have never seen a cotton field before, but I'm pretty certain there are cotton fields in my family history. Just over a decade ago, I discovered that my father was African-American. He came from a family of refugee slaves who worked their way up from Kentucky into Indiana and Michigan in the 1800s, marrying whites and slowly turning from black to mulatto before arriving in Canada in 1880, light-skinned enough that my father was able to pass for white. My father insisted he knew nothing about this line of our ancestry—to him, having white skin meant he was white. But I have the documents, including a copy of his parents' marriage licence, on which someone had written "Colored" in the box asking for nationality. In the 1920s, at least, "Colored" wasn't only a race, it was a country. A country my father refused to inhabit.

I stoop and gather handfuls of prickly, grey-white cotton balls, revelling in the feel of them in my hands, their lightness, their insubstantiality, their firmness and immense weight, and begin stuffing them in the car. More and more of them, running back and forth between the roadside and the car, until every crevice around the driver's seat is filled and overflowing, and I stop. I am not just collecting souvenirs, I realize; I am picking cotton.

* * *

"*M*ORNIN'! How're y'all doin' today?" a big man says as we enter the Lynch Line bookstore in Albany, Texas.

Despite a worrisome fondness for firearms and white pickup trucks, Texans are an extraordinarily sociable lot, although this garrulity is not reflected in their architecture. Here in Albany we were stopped by the enormous, nineteenth-century county courthouse, sitting squat at the centre of the town square. We'd decided against the interstate and even the red highways, choosing instead a thin yellow line that cuts a horizontal stripe across the upper half of the state. In town after town we'd seen the same arrangement; gone are the green Spanish adobe plazas, so compatible with socializing; instead, Texas is built around imposing, limestone structures dedicated to governance—courthouse, jail, tax office, police station, county archives in the basement, land registry and tax office on the second floor. No bandstands, no meandering footpaths, no shrubbery, just straight concrete sidewalks leading up to the imposing palace's four central doors.

"Good morning," Wayne says. He spotted the bookstore in the row of shops fringing the square and made a beeline. It isn't just a bookstore: the Lynch Line also sells "Texana," bits of Texas history and memorabilia. Confederate Army swords and badges, shaving mugs, various household items, postcards, and daguerreotypes. I finger a bowl of marbles, thinking of our granddaughters.

"That your car out front?" says the big man. "Y'all're a long way from home!"

He introduces himself as Clifford Caldwell, the store's owner. His wife, Shirley, is sitting at an antique desk behind an antique cash register. They're both historians, having worked with the Texas Historical Commission, and each has written a book about early Southern history: Clifford's, self-published, was called *Dead Right: The Lincoln County War.*

"I was in Canada once," he says. "They took my car apart at the border. They figured if I was a Texan, then I must be carrying a gun."

"You do carry a gun," Shirley says, smiling.

"'Course I do!" Clifford booms. "But I know enough to leave it at home."

"We should go," Wayne says quietly to me. He looks pale and shaken.

"Why?" I ask. "What's wrong?"

"Let's just go."

I pay for the marbles while Wayne waits outside on the sidewalk. When I join him, he points mutely to the store's front door. Etched into the glass is the image of a noose hanging from a telephone pole.

"I just realized why this place is called Lynch Line," he says.

IN MINERAL Wells, Wayne, who has been checking shop windows for etchings since leaving Albany, spots a sign in the window of a coffee bar called HiJo's advertising free Internet access. He is teaching an online course in creative writing, which means that every Tuesday and Wednesday, like addicts desperate for a fix, we madly search for places to climb onto the World Wide Web.

While he works at his laptop, I ask a woman at the next table about the towering, abandoned-looking building across the street.

"The Baker!" she exclaims. She looks to be in her sixties, a bottle blonde with painted-on eyebrows, but with a lively twinkle in her eyes. She reminds me of Gloria Swanson in *Sunset Boulevard*. It takes me a moment to realize she's referring to the building. "There used to be three big hotels like that here, because of the hot springs, you see. The Baker, the Damron, and the Crazy Water. I live in the Crazy Water."

I tell her it's my dream to live in a hotel.

"Oh, it's not a hotel anymore," she says. "It's for old folks like me. You're Canadian, aren't you?" I wonder how she can tell, but before I can ask, she explains. "I was born in Alberta, moved to Vancouver when I was one. I'm ninety-three now." She laughs. "No, I'm not, I'm eighty-three. I don't know why I do that."

We both laugh and look through the HiJo's window at the Baker. It was a latecomer to this spa town. Construction started in 1926 with a budget of over a million dollars. Fourteen storeys doesn't seem high today, but at the time it put the Baker on the international list of skyscrapers. It had 452 rooms and two complete spas and was the second hotel in the United States to boast a swimming pool, the first that was Olympic-sized. Despite opening less than a month after the stock market crash of 1929, it did a roaring business for forty years. Judy Garland stayed there, as did Clark Gable, the Three Stooges, Roy Rogers, Marlene Dietrich, Dorothy Lamour, and Jack Dempsey. Lyndon Johnson and Ronald Reagan were guests. "Bonnie and Clyde stayed there, too," Gloria says, "but they registered under assumed names." She laughs.

"Maybe they came for the lunch. There's a menu still stuck to the wall inside the door: three courses for seventy-five cents. Imagine that, a three-course lunch." She shakes her head.

"But I *like* living at the Crazy Water," she says after a pause, as though to convince herself. "When I was a girl in Vancouver, my favourite radio program was a dance-band show, *Live from the Lobby of the Crazy Water Hotel*. I never in a million years thought I'd end up living there."

"How did you?" I ask her.

"My son had dogs, and I'm allergic," she says. "So it was me or the dogs." Her face settles into sadness, and she takes a sip of coffee, leaving a bright red imprint of her lips on the cup. "He thinks the world of those dogs," she says.

ALTHOUGH WE'RE on the Texas Forts Trail, we see no forts. Occasionally, a sign promises *Historical Marker Ahead 1 Mile,* but nothing materializes except sometimes an arrow pointing to a cemetery. We miss New Mexico's loquacious plaques with their stories and maps.

Mostly what we see beyond the windshield is fields. Dust blows across the asphalt, soil on the move. Tumbleweed, too. Mistletoe hangs from the leafless mesquite branches. The only wildlife in evidence is roadkill—coyotes, deer, skunks, rabbits, a possum—and turkey vultures. Lots of turkey vultures.

"They smell the natural gas," Wayne says. "Pipeline companies use them to find leaks."

Somewhere around Tatum, the radio quits. The cigarette lighter, where we plug in the recharger for the computer, has also gone dead, and the left turn-signal light is clicking in double time.

At Weatherford, just outside Fort Worth, we stop at a Toyota dealership. The service bay is empty, immaculate. It looks as though the place was just built and hasn't opened yet. As soon as we pull in, however, a cluster of mechanics surrounds the car like sharks around a bucket of chum. The flickering turn signal is a loose connection; the silent radio and dead lighter socket are a burnt fuse. A lanky boy who looks as if he could be Lyle Lovett's son fixes both.

"Where y'all headed?" he asks.

We tell him we're going to get on the interstate that skirts Fort Worth and Dallas, then pick up Highway 80 on the other side.

"Just you wait, we'll pull y'all up a map."

By the time we get to the service desk, the four young men are huddled around the computer, as they had been around the car, trying to decide where we should go next. Lindale, says one. Caddo Lake, suggests another. Marshall, for sure.

"Naw," Lyle Lovett's son says decisively. "Jefferson. Girlfriend and me went there for the weekend a while back. Nice little town. Y'all *have* to go to Jefferson, Texas." He prints us out a map.

We thank the men and ask how much we owe for the repairs. When I reach for my wallet, Lyle, Jr., holds up his hand.

"Nope. No charge. Y'all have a good trip and drive safe now."

WEATHERFORD'S CLAIM to fame—and in the Internet age, every town, county, state, and person has to have one (Wayne tells me a Texas town voted in a beer-drinking goat as mayor in order to attract tourists, and it worked)—is that Abe Lincoln lived his last days there.

"I bet you thought he died after he was shot at Ford's Theatre. He was watching a play called *Our American Cousin,* did you know that?" I say to Wayne, who doesn't respond. "But this says he was spirited away, his death staged so that he could escape the burdens of public office and a marriage gone bad. Apparently he was reincarnated in Texas as Alexander 'Billy Bob' Hamilton, who used to wander the streets of Weatherford quoting the Gettysburg Address and apologizing for the Civil War."

"I wonder who we'll find in Jefferson," Wayne says.

On the interstate, we drive under concrete overpasses and pass a sprawl of cookie-cutter houses that could be Mississauga or Calgary or Bayridge back home. Once past Dallas, we pick up US 80, a four-lane highway that takes us into the night, following the Sabine River, though we can't see it. We agree to stop at the first mom-and-pop we pass.

We pass none. In the main-street towns, huge churches are lit up, their parking lots full on a Wednesday night, billboards flashing, inviting more into the fold.

We pass a small cottage with a sign: *Lattes $199. Support our troops.*

"Expensive coffee," Wayne says.

"It's an expensive war," I reply.

The truth is, we've seen few flags and even fewer yellow ribbons or bumper stickers promoting the war in Iraq. I think of our trip to Princeton two years ago, when all the truck stops and restaurants, even the cars themselves, were festooned with the Stars and Stripes. The bumpers here are oddly bare, not even the usual "My wife, sure; my dog, maybe; my gun, never."

By the time we get to Jefferson, the town is dark, but we know we've come to the right place. The main street is straight out of the mid-1800s, one beautifully restored building after another, framing a red-brick road.

We stop at the Jefferson Hotel. The door is locked; the parlour we glimpse through the window looks like a stage set for an Ibsen play. I knock. I am jabbing some obvious combinations into the security lock when a man with long hair, wearing a leather vest, comes up behind us. He is the spitting image of Lee Marvin.

"They lock that door at five o'clock," he says. "D'y'all have a key?"

"No, we're looking for a room," we say in unison, like Hansel and Gretel, lost and hungry in the forest.

"Well, there's another hotel down the street. If that's full," he says enigmatically, "come back to my place and we'll set you up with some karaoke."

Karaoke?

Fortunately, the Excelsior House, the hotel down the street, has a room, a large luxurious room with a four-poster canopied bed and a glassed-in sunroom with a red-tiled floor and white wicker furniture. The sunroom gives onto an interior courtyard where we can hear the splash and laugh of a fountain. We take it for two nights. I don't say a word about the price.

"Do you know what time the president is addressing the nation?" I ask the woman who checks us in. She's wearing a smart suit, expensive pumps, eighteen-karat jewellery. She can't be the night clerk, I think. We must have roused the manager.

"No, I don't," she says with complete indifference. "I'm reading a cookbook and watching a cooking show." She shifts her eyes from page to screen, as if demonstrating a complicated manoeuvre.

Although we could have made it into Louisiana, we've decided to stay in Texas because it is George W. Bush's home state. Being here tonight will be like being in Cuba for the semifinals of the World Baseball Classic. We imagine sitting among Americans, all eyes on the president as he outlines his plan to send another twenty thousand troops to Iraq. Will everyone cheer? I imagine cautioning Wayne to wipe the scorn off his face. I want to know what Americans think about their leader.

We stop at Lee Marvin's Internet cafe, thinking we can watch the address on his television while Wayne teaches. But no. "Our server is down," Marvin says apologetically. The television in the corner is resolutely tuned to a sitcom. "I have no interest in the president's address," he says, then goes on to add that Jefferson is the most haunted town in Texas. "Spiritualists came here to verify that fact, and counted 150 ghosts in the downstairs of this establishment alone. Right where you're standing. The Excelsior, too," he adds for good measure. "Steven Spielberg stayed there once, and halfway through the night he got up and drove to Marshall, he was so spooked. What room y'all in?"

"Diamond Bessie's," Wayne says.

"He was in the Jay Gould Room. The one y'all're in, that's more haunted than all the rest of 'em put together."

We leave him to his sitcom before he remembers about the karaoke, and continue down Austin Street. The only other place open is Auntie Skinner's Riverboat Club, named, I presume, for the old Dixieland song "Auntie Skinner's Chicken Dinners." It really is a club: the waitress says we have to join if we want to be served alcohol.

"How much?" Wayne asks.

"It's free."

I ask her if we get a membership card.

"No, you don't get anything, but without it, you don't get a drink."

"Without what?" Wayne asks.

"Without you joining the club," she says. "It's like that pretty much everywhere in East Texas now. Y'all want to sit at the bar?"

The television above the bar is tuned to a basketball game that no one is watching. We take a table at the back, where Wayne can plug in his laptop.

"What time does the president come on?" I ask the waitress.

"Oh, I wouldn't know about that," she says.

"We thought everyone would be watching."

She screws up her pretty face and looks around. There is a birthday party under way at one long table; the others are occupied by people who look like locals, dressed in jeans, plaid shirts, and workboots. The men, too. No one is glued to a television screen.

"Honestly," she says, leaning close, "I don't think anybody in here would be much interested, if you know what I mean."

After dinner we retire to our room and channel surf, looking for George W. We listen to the leader of the House and the leader of the Senate both bemoaning the lack of consultation, switch to a string of speeches in the Senate, find a Republican from Minnesota saying he'll never support increasing troops in Iraq, then a well-meaning Democrat reading his email into the record. Then suddenly there he is, with his too-narrow eyes and disappearing upper lip. The president looks scared. He is wearing a pale blue tie, as if he tried to look like a banker but the fabric faded in the glare of the television lights. Gone is the windbreaker of 9/11. This is the fourth year of the war: three thousand died last year alone.

"The situation in Iraq is unacceptable to the American people," he says. That much, at least, is true.

We are lying in bed in George's home state, apparently the only two people in town interested in what George W. Bush has to say. Not even two: Wayne has fallen asleep. I feel as if the little homunculus on the screen is talking to me and me alone. I reach over to turn out the light.

"Give it a rest, George," I say, clicking the remote. "Nobody's listening."

*　*　*

WACO, Texas, is in the morning papers. There's an army base in Waco, and troops interviewed there fully support George Bush's "surge"—sending twenty thousand more soldiers to Iraq. To me, the town is better known as the scene of two horrific events: the massacre of eighty-three Branch Davidians in 1993 and the brutal lynching of a black boy, Jesse Washington, in 1916. I guess I'm still feeling spooked by Albany. I've never been anywhere where racism is even acknowledged, let alone celebrated, where lynch mobs are such a proud part of the local heritage that reminders of them are etched in glass. What other Klan memorabilia is hidden away in trunks and closets along the Lynch Line, waiting for the call to be brought back to use? My father's unwillingness to inhabit his own skin is making more sense. Wouldn't it be easier to do what he did: pretend I'm as white as everyone thinks I am? It's what I did in Albany. It's what I'm doing in Jefferson.

Admittedly, Jefferson seems at first to be only nominally part of Texas. It sits at the tip of a long bayou that connects it to Louisiana: there is more of New Orleans in Jefferson than there is of Houston. The Excelsior has been in continuous operation since it opened in the

1850s. In fact, so little has changed in the hotel over the years that it is easy to imagine that the Civil War is still being fought or is only recently over and the news that the North won hasn't come up the bayou yet. Jefferson is a decidedly white town; the only blacks in evidence are either carrying rakes or pushing trolleys heaped with hotel laundry.

Each of the rooms in the hotel is named after someone famous who stayed in it. There's the Lady Bird Johnson Room, the Grant Presidential Room, the Jay Gould Room that so spooked Steven Spielberg, named for the railway baron who stayed here in 1870. Oscar Wilde rested here, as did George and Laura Bush, though no room bears their names. There is a Blalock Room, in honour, I assume, of Hank Blalock, designated hitter for the Texas Rangers. Ours is called the Diamond Bessie Suite, for a woman who was apparently murdered while staying here.

"They say her ghost still walks about," the woman at the desk says matter-of-factly, handing us a skeleton key after our dinner at Auntie Skinner's. "Her murderer was never found."

"My father would never sleep in a murdered woman's room," I say to Merilyn as we undress.

"You are not your father," she replies. Which is true, although I am not entirely unsuperstitious. I toss spilled salt over my left shoulder. I don't cross cutlery on a table or name the Scottish play in a theatre. I like baseball, which is rife with superstitions. In matters of religion, I am like the filmmaker Luis Buñuel, who when asked about his beliefs replied, "I'm an atheist, thank God."

Diamond Bessie's bed is so high off the floor we need a footstool to get into it, but we sleep soundly in its rarefied atmosphere. During the night I climb down to go to the bathroom and on my way back pass a floor-length mirror in the dark, nearly frightening myself to death. In the morning, we both wake up.

Across the courtyard from our suite is the Plantation breakfast room, its shutters open to the morning light. Coffee in our sunroom first, we decide, certain there must be a little bell pull somewhere that will make a fresh pot appear magically at our door in seconds. But we can't find it, so I get dressed and go out on my first mission of the day.

In the 1850s, when the Excelsior was built, Jefferson was a growing concern, on its way to becoming the sixth-largest city in Texas; only the port of Galveston saw more trade. The population peaked in 1872 at just over seven thousand. Many of those were carpetbaggers and Union soldiers sent to Texas to "reconstruct" the rebels after the Civil War. Today, its population has dwindled to a few thousand, and although the town is quaint, its quiet streets lined with live oak, cottonwoods drooping over the bayou, it does not appear to be thriving. Then again, it's mid-winter.

Lee Marvin's establishment is called the Big Cypress Coffee House. Sidewalk-to-ceiling windows, eight tiny tables piled with newspapers, tin ashtrays, and plastic cups; except for these and the Coke machine by the door, it looks very French. The Louisiana influence, no doubt. Marvin is standing behind a handsome oak counter at the back, his arms crossed. He looks as if he's about to tell me that the place isn't open yet, but since it obviously is, he seems at a loss for words. I go up to the counter and order two decafs.

"I don't do decaf," he says, as though it's a matter of principle with him. He busies himself shuffling things about on the countertop: cigarette pack, matches, chipped cups, some dubious-looking biscotti, tip jar. His hands are trembling.

"What *do* you do?" I ask.

He considers the question. "I can fix you a double espresso latte Americano," he says.

"How about just a regular coffee," I say. "To go." I can take caffeinated coffee in the morning, but Merilyn can't. It makes her sick.

"Sure," he says, and disappears, under a banner that reads *Happy New Year!* down a hallway to the back where, judging by the noise of the machine he turns on, he makes me a double espresso latte Americano.

"Do you take cream?" he calls out over the machine.

"Yes."

"I ran out of cream last night," he responds jubilantly. "My friend likes White Russians. I can't keep cream in the place. Milk okay?"

"Milk is fine."

When enough time has passed for me to sit at one of the tables and read a lengthy newspaper account of the recent passing of Gerald Ford (I'd forgotten that Ford served on the Warren Commission, investigating Kennedy's assassination in Dallas), Marvin reappears with a paper cup of coffee and two jugs of milk, all three of which he holds triumphantly toward me. "Go nuts, young man," he says and nods to the sugar and stir sticks on a sideboard, below an array of rather bizarre costume jewellery. "My girlfriend's work," he says. I wonder if she's the friend with the weakness for White Russians.

I don't want to go back to the hotel without a decaf for Merilyn, so I wander farther up Austin Street, guiltily sipping my latte. Everything else is still closed, so reluctantly I return to the hotel and find Merilyn in the sunroom, happily pouring herself another decaf from a pot she procured from the hotel kitchen.

MERILYN AND I stroll across the courtyard to the Plantation room, where the tables are laid with white cloths and heavy silver. Breakfast is served by a beautiful young black woman who confesses that she doesn't know why they don't make hash browns and she doesn't like hominy grits very much. She keeps her eyes studiously averted from ours as she talks. I try the grits anyway. When she comes back, I tell her they taste like wallpaper paste, and she admits a shy smile.

Afterwards, I visit the used-book store across the street from the hotel. Books on the Bayou is the kind of used-book store I like: crammed with books, books piled on chairs and boxes, books drooping from inadequately supported shelves, books scattered on floors and tables and windowsills, books seemingly suspended from the ceiling.

Behind the counter by the front window sits a small man with a big head, a white beard, and oversized horn-rimmed glasses. He looks a bit like George Burns playing the Wizard of Oz. I nod and sidle past him into the mayhem, but the books themselves are disappointing, mostly beat-up copies of bestsellers. On every available wall surface there are framed photographs of the owner, Fred McKenzie, in various phases of his apparently peripatetic life.

One of the photos gives me pause: it shows Fred and an unidentified woman on a tandem bicycle, with a wire basket carrier full of a dozen copies of Fred's book: a two-volume history of Hickory Hill. Fred is an author. There are more copies of the book near the front door, and I pick up volume one, a hefty tome, and look through it. Hickory Hill is a tiny town, now called Avinger, just up the road from Jefferson. Population 464. How can anyone write two thick volumes about such a small place? Why not write about Jefferson? I am about to ask Fred when my eye is caught by another of Fred's books: *The Abe Rothschild Story*. It is an account of the case against Abe Rothschild for the murder of one Diamond Bessie. This one I buy.

"We're staying at the Excelsior," I say to Fred as I make my purchase. "In the Diamond Bessie Suite."

"That so?" Fred says. "Diamond Bessie never stayed in that hotel," he adds.

"She didn't?" I am half relieved and half indignant.

"No, she and her husband stayed in the Brooks House. It's long gone."

"But her ghost . . ."

Fred gives me the look.

I recross the street to Marvin's cafe, order a double espresso latte Americano, sit at a table, and read Fred's book. On Friday, January 19, 1877, a couple arrived at the Jefferson train station and registered at the Brooks House as "A. Monroe and wife, Cincinnati, Ohio." Mrs. Monroe wore so much jewellery that local citizens referred to her as Diamond Bessie. That night they were heard quarrelling in their room, and on

Saturday, Monroe bought a pistol at a Jefferson gun shop, unremarkable in a Texan but a little suspicious for a Cincinnati man. Later that day the couple went for a walk in the country. On Sunday, Monroe took the train back to Cincinnati alone, wearing, it was reported, his wife's rings. On February 5, the body of a woman resembling Diamond Bessie was found less than a mile from Jefferson; she had been shot in the left temple. The circumstantial evidence was overwhelming.

Investigators discovered that A. Monroe was in fact Abe Rothschild, the ne'er-do-well son of the Rothschild diamond family from Ohio, and that Diamond Bessie was Bessie Moore, a one-time prostitute who had been Rothschild's mistress for several years. Rothschild was charged with murder and spent three years in the Jefferson jail awaiting trial. He was tried three times and finally acquitted. The corpse found was not sufficiently decomposed to have lain outside for two weeks, "exposed to Texas weather," as the coroner put it. It was a particularly cold winter, and the body was found lying in two feet of snow, but it wasn't frozen. Rothschild's case must have been among the first in American legal history to be decided solely on forensic evidence, flimsy though it was, but that didn't change the general feeling around town: that nothing good ever came to Jefferson by railroad.

*　★　★　★*

*M*Y gut tells me Jefferson is a small town. I don't care what the population sign says. The size of a town is determined by the speed with which news travels.

While Wayne wanders the town, I peruse the parlour of the Excelsior, where the hotel's history is on display: old menus, invitations to balls, registers opened to significant signatures. I pause over Jay Gould's, a jaunty blue jay penned in place of his first name. In the comments column, his cursive curse slants across the line: "The End of Jefferson!"

Gould came to Jefferson after the Civil War intent on buying land to build a railroad, but the people who lived here liked the riverboat trade. It made the town what it was: the only inland port in Texas. They refused to sell. Despite Gould's prediction, even without the railroad, the place continued to thrive with the hordes heading west, fleeing the ruin that was the post-bellum South.

What killed Jefferson was the Yankees. In 1873, traffic on the Big Cypress Bayou (the river is still called a bayou, in the Louisiana tradition) came to an abrupt stop when the U.S. Army Corps of Engineers removed a log raft from the Red River above Shreveport, Louisiana. The raft had kept water levels in the Big Cypress high enough that boats could travel from Jefferson to Caddo Lake, entering the Red River south of it. When the raft was blasted free, the riverbanks collapsed, rendering the Big Cypress all but impassable. The railroad was built after that, though not with Gould money, and the main trunk line bypassed Jefferson on its way from Texarkana to Marshall. A small branch line eventually reached Jefferson, but the town never made the economic shift from steam to rail. Jefferson became, quite literally, a backwater—beautiful and genteel, a sleepy Louisiana time capsule tucked in the eastern hip of Texas.

I love backwaters. I love history. I love buildings that wear their stories on their facades.

I am very happy in Jefferson.

"Who owns the hotel?" I ask the woman behind the desk. I'm thinking of all the lovely old hotels Wayne and I have stayed in, most of them, during our short twenty years together, moving from private hands into the maw of the chains.

"The Garden Club," she answers, with a slight toss of her head, a gesture that for some reason reminds me of *Archie*'s Veronica.

"Excuse me?"

"The Jessie Allen Wise Garden Club owns the Excelsior—and half of Jefferson."

In the 1950s, she tells me, a group of women, wives of affluent Jeffersonians, formed the club as an excuse to get together. They hadn't been meeting long when they heard that Excelsior House was about to go up for auction. They decided to pool their resources and buy it, as a rescue project. Each member of the club took charge of a room, restoring it to its original elegance. "George Haggard's wife did your room," she says, straightening the sign-in register with a certain proprietary air. Suddenly, I understand the revolving door of well-dressed women of a certain age standing behind the desk.

I've barely walked a block when a white van pulls up beside me and a yellow-haired woman pokes out her head, calling, "You the one wants to know about the Garden Club?"

See what I mean about small towns?

"Git in," she orders, and I do. "I have some errands to run but I shouldn't be but just a minute."

Mary Kiestler is the current president of the Jessie Allen Wise Garden Club. It runs a quilt exhibition, a Mardi Gras, and a spring heritage-house pilgrimage every year. Mary tells me she retired here a few years ago from Fort Worth, moving into the house her husband helped his father build when he was twelve, using materials from an old schoolhouse that was being torn down.

"I don't garden," she laughs, "but I hate to see our history disappear like that."

This Garden Club is about a different kind of growing. Determined to stop the decline of Jefferson and to restore it to its former glory, the women have bought and sold other buildings through the years to save them from the wrecker's ball. With delicious irony, they had Jay Gould's private Pullman car, *Atalanta*, brought back to Jefferson and mounted under an awning, next to a house with turquoise beauty-salon chairs lined up on the verandah. They bought the historic Jewish synagogue and are converting it into an old-time playhouse. Today, there are sixteen Jefferson buildings listed in the National Register of Historic Places. I doubt these women have time for gardenias: they're too busy being real estate tycoons, architectural restorers, and town saviours.

"I could live here," I say to Wayne when we meet to go for a walk.

Wayne and I do this a lot: look at a place for its move-to potential, even though we are perfectly happy living in eastern Ontario. It's a way of gauging the feeling of a town, I suppose. And this one feels good. It's small enough that there aren't sidewalks in front of the houses: the lawns just feather out toward the road. In place of gaudy signposts, the red-brick streets are inset with brass wedges that say, ever-so-genteelly, *Stop* and *Keep Right*. We watch a pair of mockingbirds eating supper at a blue-berried shrub and follow a drift of white-throated sparrows through the cypresses to the bayou. At one time, Mary told me, there were canary cages hanging under the front verandah of the Excelsior; it was called the Canary Hotel then. The only singing I've heard so far, though, was from the black girl washing the windows on the balcony above our sunroom, rolling, joyful hymns that I savoured as we ate our grits and eggs and orange-blossom muffins.

I expect Wayne to say he loves it here, too, but he says nothing. He doesn't have to. His face is a mask of unease at this sudden plunge into America's Deep South.

11 / SELMALABAMA

*M*ID-MORNING, I get ready to leave Jefferson, but with reluctance.

"I wish I'd looked at the real estate listings," I say as we put our things back into the car. We're wearing shorts and T-shirts. The sun, at last, is almost hot. The only thing we have to do now is find a laundromat.

"Why didn't you?" Wayne asks.

"I guess I didn't want to be tempted." Lee Marvin told us he'd come for a day, stayed for a week, and ended up buying the coffee shop. Lord only knows what would happen if we took our suitcases back into the Diamond Bessie Suite.

But seeing Wayne's disquiet is making me look at Jefferson with new eyes. At the local laundromat, all the women are black. All the house-keeping and wait staff I saw at the hotel were black. In the restaurants, the busboys and cooks, but not the bartenders or waitresses, were black.

Is this evidence of a colour line? Too small a sample to tell, per-haps, but something in the way the maid kept her eyes lowered and punctuated every item with "Yes, ma'am" as the thin white woman listed her jobs for the day made me think she was exhibiting more than simple southern courtesy.

The women at the laundromat don't seem to be doing their own wash. Their loads are huge batches of white sheets and towels and mattress covers. I put our few things in the washer and walk across the street for a doughnut.

An Asian woman and her son appear to be operating the place. "Cake or regular?" she says.

"Cake," I reply, pointing to a chocolate glazed with crushed peanuts. I feel suddenly nostalgic for Tim Hortons. Hippocrates observed that whenever people from one country travel to another, they are often beset with a debilitating lassitude. From this, the father of modern medicine concluded that people absorb topographic influences from their place of birth and that separation from them can be injurious to health. He called this lassitude "nostalgia," from the Greek *nostos,* to return, and *algos,* to suffer. I'm not actually suffering; it's just that doughnuts, for me, have more to do with Canada than with the Deep South.

Back at the laundromat, the women have moved outside to gossip with a man who has just quit smoking.

"I can breathe!" he exclaims with the fervour of the converted. "In just two days, I can breathe good again."

The laundromat is large and clean and empty. Nothing much to do but read the notices on the bulletin board at the back. An offering of recycled lumber, a hunter green matching sofa and chair. A small poster advertising a Dream Walk on Martin Luther King, Jr.'s birthday, three days from now.

There are candy machines and beside them, as if placed there as a deterrent, a weigh scale. I put in a quarter and stand very still, as the machine directs. The numbers creep upward until I step off in horror. I have gained ten pounds: all those hash browns. The machine grinds on, spitting out my lucky lottery numbers for the day—30, 16, 64—and finally my fortune: "Things will be better tomorrow."

I move our clothes to a dryer and, from the rack of religious pamphlets, pluck a book of Christian prayers for all occasions. I thumb through it as we head out of town. There are no prayers for fat travellers about to have a bad day. No prayers for travellers at all.

*   *   *

*W*E take Highway 2 to avoid the interstate, leaving Texas as we entered it, and cross into Louisiana near Caddo Lake, an eerie stretch of water that spans the border of Louisiana and northeastern Texas. Together with Big Cypress Bayou, Caddo Lake and its surrounding wetlands cover some thirty thousand acres of prime bird habitat. This morning, it is a study in grey: silvery bald cypress trunks rise from mercury-slick waters; moss like heron's wings waves desultorily, though I can see no breeze. Maybe there are birds in the branches. I'm glad we're not here in summer, when the place must buzz with Jet Skis and fishermen. Looking out over the still waters, it's not inconceivable we're the first people on earth—or the last.

I'm wondering what birds might be tucked into the recesses among the trees when suddenly a huge black-and-white-and-red bird dips across the road.

"An ivory-billed!" I call out, braking hard. The ivory-billed woodpecker has not been seen for fifty years—the last confirmed sighting was in Louisiana in 1944—but last year a canoeist reported a sighting in Arkansas, not that far north of here. Part of me, the same part that is not entirely an atheist, wants to believe that it isn't impossible that I could be the one to positively identify the last remaining ivory-billed on earth. We are in dense mangrove swamp country, more water than land, Spanish moss hanging from skeletal trees rising from murk and disappearing into mist. Definitely ivory-billed territory.

"Why couldn't it be an ivory-billed?" I say to Merilyn, backing up the car and scanning the trees. In Cuba, I heard a recording of the ivory-billed's call, which sounds like an alien distress signal coming from some distant part of the galaxy.

By the time we get out of the car, the bird, whatever it was, is long gone.

"Pileated," Merilyn writes in her notebook.

We stop for gas at a small convenience store in the middle of the mist-grey forest. Rain, or possibly overflow from the swamp, has turned the yard in front of the store into a Rorschach of ruts. A single pump stands in the middle like a small lighthouse, the hose trailing on the ground. From the shelter of the store's doorway, a black man in grey coveralls watches me, smoking a cigarette. When he makes no move toward the pump, I assume it's self-serve, so I get out and pick up the hose. There is no nozzle at the end of it. The man nods and waves us on.

The feeling here is of a once-verdant land now overgrown and swamped, the world immediately after the Flood. We are only a few miles from Greenwood, the boyhood home of John Bentley Mays, the Canadian writer and art critic who spent the first eighteen years of his life in Louisiana. In his memoir *Power in the Blood,* he writes of Greenwood in the 1940s, when his father was a merchant and cotton plantation owner, as a kind of earthly paradise. The house he grew up in after his father's death in 1947 was surrounded by "traditional Southern plantings: shade-giving pecans and low figs and taller china- berry trees and mimosas, flowering redbuds and fruit trees, nandina bushes with bright red berries, and abounding roses." By the time his Aunt Vandalia died, however, in 1990, the grounds had grown to ruin, overtaken by weeds and poisonous snakes and Virginia creeper, like the woods around Snow White; and now, driving through simi- lar towns and the dark woods between them, it is as though the decay that began in Aunt Vandalia's garden has crept out to engulf all of Louisiana, perhaps the whole South.

★　★　★

*M*OORINGSPORT. Plain Dealing. Whynot. The names of the towns on the map spread over my knees are forthright. Noth- ing at all like the wild optimism of those who settled the area where we live. Newbliss. Prospect. Sweets Corners. (Delta, Harlem, and Charleston are also within a half-hour's drive of our house in Ontario: Canadians, in assigning place names, indulge in either nostalgia for where they've come from or unbridled ambition for where they find themselves.)

The speed limit in Louisiana drops to a lackadaisical fifty-five. The *Don't Mess with Texas* signs have been replaced with *Don't Trash Louisiana,* but everybody seems to anyway. The roadsides are white with fast-food throwaways or, as they are called here, to-go boxes.

Louisiana is a revelation, not only because of the bilingual sign that welcomes us: *Bienvenue en Louisiane.* After a few miles of moss-draped swamps, we emerge into forested hills: the northern part of the state is—or used to be—a swath of pineries. This is where the South came for the lumber to rebuild after the Civil War. In 1895, Louisiana's stock of standing timber was surpassed only by that of the Pacific Coast and Idaho. Virgin stands of longleaf, shortleaf, and loblolly pine, cypress, and hardwood covered some 25,000 square miles. By the beginning of the First World War, this sliver of a state led all others in lumber production.

Today, lumbering isn't even listed as a major industry, though obviously Louisiana is still cutting down trees. Palisades of tall conifers flank the road, a screen that almost, but not quite, hides the rough, grey slash of total clear-cut behind. Here and there regrowth has begun, a fur of green, too dense and random to be a replanted forest. Louisianians seem to prefer to leave Nature to look after herself, prolific old dame that she is.

I draw our yellow highlighter line through the town of Trees, which consists of two churches and a boarded-up catfish shop, clear-cut trailing off in all directions, oil donkeys nodding here and there among the stumps. Later, we pass through Forest, which is marked by the same denuded landscape, though the town is more prosperous, a huge lumberyard parked under the water tower, where the town's name is freshly stencilled, apparently without irony.

We take a back road through farm country to pick up US 80 again. At a crossroads deep in the countryside, we come upon three people sprawled in the roadside litter: an old man, a boy, and a toothless woman. They have margarine containers between their legs and are scrabbling in the dead leaves under a twisted and soaring ancient tree.

"Stop! Wayne! Please!"

I roll down my window.

"Hi there," I call out.

"How y'all doin?" the woman drawls, leaning back. This is the standard Louisiana greeting. Not hello, but an immediate inquiry into the state of your well-being.

"Good, good," I say, oddly touched that she's asked. It seems an antidote to the dire prediction of the weigh scale in the laundromat. "What are you picking?"

"P'cans," she says, opening the vowel wide and lifting the end of the word the way people here do, not in a California Valley girl upspeak sort of way, but in a singsong, a wavy vocal line that invites you to ask for the rest of the story.

"Can I see? What do they look like?" Apart from our salvaged California almonds, the only nut I've ever picked is a walnut, which comes encased in a big, hard, fuzzy fruit the size and shape of a lime-green tennis ball.

The woman opens her dark fist to the nuts that lie smooth and mottled in her pale palm. They look like big runner beans, nothing at all like the mahogany-coloured nuts we buy at Christmas in our northern grocery stores. She sifts through the leaf litter and picks up another, as if to prove their provenance.

"What do you do with them?" I ask. I'm thinking pecan salad, pecan soup, pecan pie.

"Ah sells 'em."

I try again. "Do you have to shell them?"

"No ma'am, ah jist sells 'em."

ALL ALONG the road we pass signs that declare *We Buy Pecans*. I finally get my chance at the Piggly Wiggly where we stop for gas. (I also purchase a can of Jack Daniel's Tennessee Sour Mash Whiskey & Cola for Wayne and a double-wrapped half-loaf of bread for our lunch.) I scoop the nuts from a bushel basket, $2.49 a pound. They are sweet and crisp, better than any pecan I've ever tasted. But not as satisfying, I think, as what I might have had from that old woman, had I the courage to ask.

I am keen to buy local produce, to see what grows in the gardens here. The tables of the South, in my mind, groan under a bounty of exotic fare—hominy grits, gumbo, okra, collard greens, mirliton, crawfish, gator, frogs' legs, raccoon, squirrel, shoofly pie—but other than catfish stands and nuts, we see little unusual agricultural produce. In fact, everything about Louisiana seems familiar. The houses here are just like those at home, ordered, it seems, from the same generic North American catalogue of house plans. The roads are surfaced and striped and signed just the same. People dress like we do, eat like we do. Only the accents are different. If you drive through, never talking to a soul, you could be driving through just about anywhere, except for the parish signs. Louisiana is the only state of the Union divided into parishes instead of counties, just as Quebec is the only province in Canada to hang onto its parishes, too.

Anthills erupt like nipples along the shoulders of the road. The trees are mostly oaks now, nothing exotic about that, but they are festooned with balls of mistletoe. Near Shongaloo, I stop to take a picture of narcissi blooming along the roadside. The grass has the fresh, green sheen of spring. We are driving with the windows down—in January.

"That's nothing like home," I say.

Hippocrates was wrong, I think: we expect difference when we travel. Crave it, in fact. Wayne and I are vaguely disappointed that the birds here are all the usual species that populate our woods—meadowlarks, cardinals, blue jays, kingfishers, yellow-shafted flickers, red-tailed hawks, turkey vultures.

"Similar landscapes breed similar flora and fauna," Wayne shrugs. "Similar people, too."

Maybe it's true. When I think of Louisiana, I think of *Steel Magnolias*, by Robert Harling, whose home town was Natchitoches, about an hour south of Shreveport. The movie, with its complex cast of female characters, was shot in and around Natchitoches, but the original stage play took place entirely in Truvy's beauty shop. I grew up in small-town southwestern Ontario, not small-town northwestern Louisiana, but I knew those gossiping, fluffy, tough-as-steel-spikes women. I've been to those funerals where you can't stop laughing at the jokes that break your heart.

Since that movie, I've thought of Louisiana as frank and female, the kind of place where friends are loyal and family is forever, and you can rely on someone to say to you with sharp kindness, "Honey, time marches on and eventually you realize it is marchin' across your face."

★　★　★

W HEN we approach the Mississippi River on Highway 2, Merilyn is driving and I'm navigating, an ominous combination. Merilyn wants to cross the river in daylight, so we are speeding. On the map, just before the river, Highway 2 joins up with the I-20. I remember crossing the Colorado River on the I-40 and not being able to see anything, so I am happy to note that there is a little town called Delta that appears to be on the west bank, off the interstate; maybe there's another way across, a lower bridge, or even a ferry. Merilyn is dubious. I tell her that a pilot has to trust her navigator. She tells me that I am quoting the movie *Titanic*.

By this time, we're at the spot where the highway veers right to merge with the interstate, and I see another, smaller road meandering on, presumably into Delta. At the last minute I say, "Go straight, go straight," and, flummoxed, she does. Cars whir by above us on the interstate as we pick our way gingerly along the rutted track leading toward a stand of dark trees that I take to be the riverbank. Delta turns out to be a collection of trailers clustered around a bar, which is also a trailer, and the dark trees flank a muddy irrigation ditch that even I cannot convince myself is the Mississippi River. By now "dubious" is not quite the right word to describe Merilyn's state of mind. Ignoring the recommendation of her navigator, she does a neat, three-point turn in the bar's sodden parking lot and drives back the way we came.

"Emerson writes somewhere," I say archly, "that crossing the Mississippi at night is one of the seminal experiences in American life."

"You're making that up," Merilyn says.

"No, I'm not. He crossed it farther north, though," I say. "Wisconsin or somewhere, in winter. He was rowed across the ice in a skiff."

"At *night?*"

We're on the bridge, though it's now too dark to sense anything below us but a black presence, as of a living thing in the glistening darkness. A troll beneath the bridge. Old Man River, rolling along. "What is the Mississippi," Kerouac asked, "a washed clod in the rainy night... a voyaging past endless vales and trees and levees, down along, down along..."

I roll down the window, lean my head out into the wind, but all I hear is interstate. Appropriate, I suppose, since we are exactly halfway between Louisiana and Mississippi, about as interstate as you can get. I feel like an ant crawling across the belly of a dark, slithering reptile.

On the Mississippi side of the river, we are immediately struck by the glare of lights from the casinos in Vicksburg. In 1863, Vicksburg was the scene of one of two decisive battles of the Civil War. The Union army, under General Ulysses S. Grant, laid siege to the town until its commander surrendered, on July 4, 1863. One day earlier, the Union had defeated General Robert E. Lee at Gettysburg, Pennsylvania, and the fall of Vicksburg gave the North control of the Mississippi. The citizens of Vicksburg refused to celebrate the Fourth of July until 1942.

Grant became involved in Vicksburg again in 1874, when as president he had to send in troops to quell the Vicksburg Massacre. That year, blacks were given the vote for the first time, and they had the audacity to elect ten black officials, including the county sheriff. White citizens went on a rampage, murdering more than three hundred blacks. After the massacre, armed white vigilantes formed a group called the Red Shirts, which organized a campaign to discourage blacks from voting ever again. The black sheriff, who was run out of town during the rioting, returned and was shot by his white deputy. Though banned, Red Shirt groups spread to North and South Carolina, where they called themselves "rifle clubs."

It's suppertime, and we briefly contemplate the prospect of eating in one of the casinos that line the top of the bluff like storm-tossed riverboats, then decide to try our luck in town instead. It is Sunday night. The main street is lined with little shops and cafes, everything closed up tight. We reach the end of the business section and are about to turn back when Merilyn says, "Let's go one more block."

It looks dark to me, beyond the reach of the downtown street lamps. But we have a tendency to give up too soon, to turn back just before the right road or the perfect hotel. So I keep going, and sure enough, at the end of the street we find a restaurant full of people. Rusty's Riverfront Grill. The restaurant is hopping. There's even a parking space right in front. We join a lineup of eight ahead of us, two groups of four, but a waitress greets us, takes my first name, and says we can sit at the bar until a table comes free. Have we crossed into some travellers' Valhalla, I wonder, or do we just look old and travel-worn? The bartender shows us the menu, recommends the Gulf grouper, and brings us drinks. She is a young black woman, and there are several black customers at the tables. The atmosphere is cheerful and friendly, but I can't help wondering how many of these diners and servers are descended from members of the rifle clubs and their victims. Whose great-grandfathers hanged whose outside the churches and the polling booths? After all, doesn't the inscription on the memorial to the Confederate dead in Oxford, Mississippi, still exhort modern Southern whites to "unite in this justification of their fathers' faith"? What justification?

"Escape from history is impossible," wrote John Bentley Mays after his visit to Mississippi in search of his Southern roots, "hence immoral to imagine."

★　★　★

"*M*Y, isn't it a beautiful day!" the tall black man booms as he enters the lobby of the motel. We'd driven out of Vicksburg after dinner, looking for a cheap place to stay after our Jefferson extravaganza, and have ended up at this very nice Budget Inn outside Jackson, Mississippi. The Wi-Fi doesn't extend to our room, but we are happily set up in the little lobby at one of the breakfast tables, coffee and muffins at our side, our computers flipped open, Wayne checking in on his students, me electronically calling home.

"Good mornin', y'all," he says, spotting us. He's built like a football player, but it turns out he's a plumber from San Antonio, Texas. "We're just driving back from Georgia. It's warmer there than it's ever been. Our son called and says he's comin' to visit, but we put the dog in the kennel and said, No, we'll come to you, that way you can do the cookin'!"

He turns to the clerk behind the reception desk. "Y'all know what's goin' on in Jackson today? We're tired of driving."

While she shakes her head, I Google.

"There's a parade," I say. "Wayne! There's a parade!"

I love parades. They make me cry.

"It starts at Freedom Corner, where Medgar Evers Boulevard meets Martin Luther King, Jr. Drive." The names thrust me into a time warp: I'm fourteen, weeping in front of the television, my father telling me to get cleaned up for dinner. In 1963, Medgar Evers boycotted stores and helped desegregate the University of Mississippi, then died from a bullet in his back as he carried a stack of T-shirts with the slogan "Jim Crow Must Go." Two southern juries deadlocked trying to bring a verdict against the fertilizer salesman who shot him; he wasn't convicted until 1994. In 1968, Martin Luther King, Jr. was shot face-on, standing on a motel balcony in Memphis, Tennessee, after giving a speech. "I've been to the mountaintop," he'd told the crowd that night, "and I've seen the promised land. I may not get there with you. But I want you to know tonight, that we, as a people, will get to the promised land!"

"All right, then!" the man exclaims. He gets directions from the clerk, and when she's shown us both the way on her desktop map, he asks, "Where y'all from?"

She's Pakistani, maybe Indian. She smiles shyly. "Huntsville, Texas."

"My son lives in Huntsville, Canada," I say.

"Well, then," the man laughs, opening his arms to include the whole room. "We're all of us connected!"

FREEDOM CORNER is blocked off. We inch down side streets clogged with men on horseback, young people with shiny band instruments, girls in sequined bathing suits and knee-high white tasselled boots. We park behind a beauty parlour with a sign advertising *Best Cold Braids in the World* and make our way back to where the parade is forming. A trio of bongo drummers keeps up a steady beat as the high school bands and majorettes pass, trucks and cars bursting with politicians who toss handfuls of candies and crayons into the crowd. Hand-lettered signs taped to the trucks' windows say *Happy B-Day, Dr. K.* On the side of one truck, above a photograph of King, two plush monkeys, one brown, one white, grip the edge of an open window as if they're doing chin-ups.

The music is exhilarating. In high school, I was in a marching band. I twirled a fake wooden rifle as I marched ahead of the musicians. For two hours every Wednesday we perfected our moves, stepping high, eyes right, presenting our instruments in stiff jerks, like British soldiers with bayonets. But we never marched like these kids: they boogie down the street, jiving with their trumpets. Girls in sparkly bathing suits shake their boodies, doing dance routines that would make my mother blush.

There are hundreds of people standing at this corner, hundreds more in the parade, the biggest Martin Luther King, Jr. Day parade in the United States. The joy is palpable. Parents bend to their kids, helping them scoop up the treats the politicians throw from their cars. Everyone seems to know each other; they seem to know us. They smile and wave and step out of the way with a grin when I try to take a mini-movie of one of the dance routines.

It's only as we turn to leave that I realize: for the past two hours, mine has been the only white face in the crowd.

*   *   *

WE cross the Alabama River at night, as we seem to have crossed most of America's great rivers. Our room in the elegant St. James Hotel, in Selma, Alabama, has a balcony overlooking the expanse of slow, muddy water, so that is where we sit the next morning in the warm sunshine, reading and drinking coffee sent up from the kitchen. Selma, we've learned, is hardly ever mentioned without identifying the state it's in. Even in Selma, it's not Selma, it's Selma, Alabama. In fact, the comma is usually dropped, so it comes out all in a rush: Selmalabama.

The St. James Hotel is a Spanish colonial building, a square of rooms surrounding a covered courtyard that contains a waterfall and a sprinkling of tables and chairs. Apart from Veronica, the desk clerk, we are its only inhabitants. We have the run of the place. When I tire of reading, I wander the halls, explore the large, empty conference rooms, go through unlocked doors into deserted chambers filled with ancient linen presses and tarnished champagne buckets and through those onto a wide, open patio where the winter sun plays off the river running a few feet below the wrought-iron railing. To my left is a block of dilapidated buildings; almost every building on this street is falling down or about to. Veronica tells us there was a fine-dining restaurant next door to the hotel, on the top floor, but the roof collapsed just two nights ago. It and most of the other buildings are boarded up, but some still have ground-floor shops in them. The window of an antique store on Water Avenue is a diorama of stuffed animals and wildfowl of about the same vintage as the dodo: dusty woodcocks amid tufts of dead grass, faded mallards dangling from rusted wires, ragged raccoons perched on punky logs. Touring the hotel, I am struck by the sense that we are now passing through a land of collapse and decay. Not Eliot's wasteland, perhaps—that was the desert—but something just as primal: the domain of the Fisher King.

To our right, above the hotel's silhouette, the Edmund Pettus Bridge arcs over the Alabama River like a diamond ring on a wrinkled brown finger.

Of the many changes in postwar culture in the American South that John Bentley Mays writes about—faceless suburbs engulfing once-cozy small towns, filled mostly with strangers; new, largely evangelical religions disrupting the calm of the traditional churches; the decline of the middle class in the social establishment—none, he says, "proved more alarming than the eruption of the civil rights movement." To many in the South, "it was 1865 all over again"; an essentially northern phenomenon visited upon the segregationist order into which the South had settled following its calamitous defeat in the Civil War.

But it wasn't really 1865 all over again; it was 1974. White-skinned Southerners understood Martin Luther King, Jr. They knew what King wanted and they knew how to keep him from getting it—the same way their red-shirted forebears had dealt with the problem in the 1870s, though perhaps with less violence. (As governor of Alabama in the 1960s, George Wallace prevented black citizens from voting by, among other things, requiring them to pass fraudulent "literacy tests.") What Southern whites didn't understand, what truly shattered their world view, was how white politicians and churchmen—some of them, like President Lyndon Johnson, Southerners themselves—could side with King and his followers.

In 1964, only 10 per cent of the South's 14 million blacks passed George Wallace's "literacy tests" and were allowed to register to vote. In Selma, which was 57 per cent black, only 1 per cent of the black population was permitted to register. According to the Fifteenth Amendment, preventing any American citizen from voting for any reason is a federal offence. The underlying principle of democracy isn't majority rule, it's that everyone gets to have an equal say. But "Southern states controlled all the mechanisms for enforcing federal laws," writes black historian Tavis Smiley. "So it's not a matter of conjecture on my part that those states ignored the Supreme Court and the U.S. Constitution. They did."

In Selma, black students who tried to register automatically failed their courses; black employees were told that if they registered they would lose their jobs; black homeowners would find their mortgages suddenly called in by the banks.

On Sunday, March 7, 1965, six hundred black people gathered at Tabernacle Baptist Church, on Broad Street, Selma's main thoroughfare, to begin a march to Montgomery, the state capital, sixty-four miles away along Highway 80, then known as Jefferson Davis Memorial Highway. They were marching to protest the denial of their right to vote but also in response to the death of Jimmie Lee Jackson, a black man beaten to death by police while trying to register.

George Wallace declared the march illegal. White store owners on Broad Street stoned the marchers as they passed, and state troopers and local police met them at the Pettus Bridge with tear gas, billy clubs, and bullwhips. Images of women and children left wounded and lying in the street on "Bloody Sunday" were broadcast across North

America on television and in newspapers—Merilyn remembers watching footage of the attacks, but in our house, the television must have been off that day. Sixty-five people were admitted into the two Selma hospitals that accepted blacks. When a follow-up march was called for March 21, this time led by Martin Luther King, Jr. and with protection from the United States Army, more than eight thousand people showed up, including some sympathetic whites. By the time the marchers reached Montgomery on the twenty-fifth, they were 25,000 strong. King had turned a negative into a positive: just as the defeat of Vicksburg had been the turning point in the Civil War, the victory at Selma, Alabama, was the turning point in the civil rights movement.

When we ask Veronica where we should eat breakfast, she sends us to a diner on Selma Avenue called the Downtowner. We walk up Broad, passing more derelict buildings, but fewer of them closed, and turn right on Selma until we reach the Downtowner. The white waitress, wearing a bright, jailbird-orange T-shirt with "Y'all behave!" scripted across the back, waves us toward the booths by the window.

"Y'all sit anywhere you like," she calls cheerfully. "Don't matter, I'll find you."

The centre tables have been joined together to accommodate a group of ten large, older white men, who seem to have settled in for the day, while other men pop in and out as their schedules permit. The talk is loud and in a Southern drawl we find hard to decipher: I guess at truck models and hunting paraphernalia, but I could be wrong. As we eat our eggs and chunky, deep-fried hash browns, a tall, thin white man in overalls comes in and hands around a box of metal objects for the group's inspection; porch-swing brackets, it turns out, but there are no takers. Another produces a box of blueberry and peach preserves. This is met with more enthusiasm. "My wife Hannah will *love* you for this," one of the permanent men says. Then a black man comes through the door, and the conversation is suspended while he orders a cup of coffee to go. The waitress serves him silently; he pays for the coffee and leaves without looking into the room.

"How are the hash browns?" I ask Merilyn, wanting to hear the sound of her voice.

"I wonder how many of these guys were throwing stones in 1965," she says quietly.

Quite often we think exactly the same thing.

★　★　★

"My binoculars—where are they?" Wayne asks, bursting into our room at the St. James, where I am reading about the March to Montgomery. "I've just seen an amazing yellow bird with a wide red tail."

History and natural history. Collusion and collision. One way or another, they're always vying with each other for our attention.

Back on the terrace, we spot two of the birds. Wayne identifies them as northern flickers, or yellowhammers, the state bird of Alabama. Alabamans are called Yellowhammers, the way folks from Indiana are called Hoosiers. Apparently, during the Civil War, when the battalion from Alabama joined the Confederate army, they had smart new grey uniforms with yellow flashes on their epaulets.

We've decided to stay in Selma. Tomorrow afternoon, there's a re-enactment of the march to the Pettus Bridge, and tonight, at the local performing arts theatre, there is something billed as *Selma Looking Back, Moving Forward.* We talked about moving on. Maybe there'll be some celebrations in Georgia, too, I suggested.

"Not like this," Wayne said, his voice hushed.

Wayne is not given to awe. His mind is quick, but dark. In Jackson, he stood at the fringe of the parade as if his joints had been wired too tightly together. Last night, after dinner at a Mexican restaurant where the clientele was both white and black, he balked at taking a shortcut through an alley to what looked like a park.

"What are you afraid of?" I asked, knowing the answer. Confrontation. Authority. A bullet in his back.

"Your kind is selected against," he warned wryly. "Guys like me survive. We avoid dark alleys."

"Lamarckian!" I accused.

"Maybe you're right," he admitted, and we walked down the alley to the park, which turned out to be a parking lot. I'm still not sure who got the last laugh.

"You know," he says now as we have our coffee on the terrace, watching the yellowhammers flit among the shrubs on the riverbank, "there's nothing to be afraid of. It's as safe here as anywhere."

WE ARRIVE at the performing arts theatre early. The full title of the evening's entertainment is *Selma Looking Back, Moving Forward: Commemorating Dr. Martin Luther King.* We should have known something was up by the "Jr." missing from his name. No true Yellowhammer ever makes that mistake.

A fresh-faced young white man with blond hair and a wide, gummy grin steps up to greet us in the lobby. He is wearing a Freedom Foundation T-shirt.

"Welcome," he says, thrusting his hand at my chest.

"What's the Freedom Foundation?" I ask, thinking of Freedom Corner, of King's dream.

"We're from Denver, Colorado. We're here to work for reconciliation and renewal. We do counselling, for families and couples, communities."

"Reconciliation along racial lines, you mean?"

"Yes." The ebullient facade shifts. His face is earnest now. "There is still a lot of healing to be done here."

"And you've come from Colorado to do it?"

The sparkle returns. "Yes, we have!"

The auditorium has been beautifully restored. On the stage, a bare-bones rock band is flanked by rows of teenagers wearing blue jeans and Freedom Foundation T-shirts. Of the sixty or so young people in the choir, only three are black, but they are in the front row. They look slightly dazed, as if they've been pulled in off the street at the last minute to provide a little local colour. The audience is sparse, more than half white. I'm horrified that I've started to see the world this way, two-toned.

Two singers come forward to start the evening, a young black woman with a voice like Aretha Franklin, and a thin, anxious-looking white girl who sings in a high-pitched whine and slaps her blue-jeaned thigh not quite with the beat. They try to belt out old Sixties tunes, all the "Baby!"s changed to "Lord!"s. Someone clicks on a ghetto blaster and a young black girl in a diaphanous white robe does an Isadora Duncan routine to "The Impossible Dream." A white boy named Robert reads a piece about Dr. Martin Luther King, Jr.'s "I have a dream" speech, repeating one paragraph of the original, which is genuinely moving. Then the guest speaker, Cheyenne Webb, comes on to tell us how the civil rights martyr changed her life. I struggle to feel something, but she keeps getting in the way, referring again and again to Reverend Mark, the white Billy Graham clone sitting in the front row.

"You spoke like King, you reminded me of King. You are," she says, "the reincarnation of King."

I WAKE the next morning still angry. What we were lured into last night was not the commemoration of a great man but a tent meeting, a group of fundamentalist Christians trying to convert a town in which there is already a church on every corner. I can't help wondering why they picked this place. Because it looks good on the letterhead to have a Freedom Foundation with a ministry in Selma, Alabama?

We go out for a bird walk and see trees full of cardinals and cedar waxwings and one Carolina wren. We ask Veronica at the desk to recommend a breakfast spot, then get caught up reading a plaque devoted to the Reverend James Reeb, the white minister who answered a call by Dr. King to come help in Selma. After eating at a black cafe, he took a wrong turn and ended up near a white club, the Silver Moon, where he was beaten. He later died from a fractured skull.

We spend part of the day at the National Voting Rights Museum. Sam, who greets us, explains that the museum is a people's project, the story of all the "regular folks" who made the movement what it was. One entire wall—the "I Was There" wall—is feathered with Post-it note messages from people who were at the Bloody Sunday march, at the Selma to Montgomery march, at all the other marches without names.

I was seven months pregnant on the bridge on Bloody Sunday. A trooper who saw that I was pregnant deliberately tried to run me down with his horse.

I was beaten on the bridge.

I was a State Trooper in 1965.

I have no words to express. It's all on the inside of my heart and it hurts.

The next room is panelled with FBI and police photographs chronicling the marchers, defiant as they first approach the bridge, grim as they walk to Montgomery flanked by National Guardsmen charged with clearing the bridges of bombs, the woods of snipers. (They found nothing, but at least they kept the spitters, rock throwers, and insult hurlers at a distance.) In the centre are the plaster footprints and shoes of those who made the walk. In another room, the plain sweater, cloth shoes, and rolled nylons of Marie Foster, who walked the entire fifty miles, never once accepting a rest ride. Everywhere, photos of King and excerpts from his speeches. A white girl vacuums a corner where a KKK exhibit is a work-in-progress. In the tiny gift shop, reproduction signs are for sale—*White Only* and *Colored*—and cotton bags: "Hands That Pick Cotton Can Pick Presidents."

"We should get one."

"No," Wayne says flatly in a tone that tells me not to press it.

The museum is housed in the former meeting place of the White Citizens Committee, formed by the owners of businesses and factories, bank managers and bosses who decided together that if a black man tried to register for the vote, his services would no longer be needed, his house was no longer available to rent.

I ask Sam, "How did they justify it? What did they tell themselves?"

A white woman standing nearby snorts. "The same things they said to themselves about women when they refused them the vote."

"A lot of people thought, we get the vote, everything will change," Sam says. "It wasn't like that. It's still not like that." He tells us about Sheriff Clark, who is now in a nursing home. Sam visited him a few months ago. "'I was just doing my job,' that's what he told me," Sam says. "'I could have arrested a lot more and I didn't.'"

Sam reports the conversation without judgment. "Everyone is part of this story," he says. "We want all of it here."

"They should have a portrait of York here," Wayne says as we leave. "William Clark's slave in 1805. He was the first black man to vote in America. Then again," he adds, "there probably *is* no portrait of York."

All day we've been trying to find out about tomorrow's parade to the bridge. Veronica laughs every time I ask. She stands with her back slightly arched, as if ready at any minute to lift her face to the sun, which she does when she laughs, which is very often. At one point, I ask if she has Saturday's paper; maybe there was a mention of the time and gathering place there.

"Oh, we don't have no Sat'day paper," she laughs. "Sunday we have. By Sat'day ever'body already knows what's goin' on."

Everybody but us.

I ask the housekeeper when she comes to change the bed linen. I can't shake the feeling that maybe the reason no one will tell us when the parade starts is that we're not wanted there.

"Are others welcome at the parade?" I ask tentatively.

"Why, sure."

"I mean, it's your celebration. Re-enactment, I mean."

"Oh," she says, as if she's never thought of it like that before.

"I was just a white girl up in Canada, but it meant a lot to me."

"It did, it did," she nods. "It changed everything."

She pauses to pass a hand over the bedspread, which does not need smoothing. There is no smile in her eyes, no warmth in her voice.

"Y'all come," she says finally. "Everybody's welcome. We've had enough of that other."

★ ★ ★

WALTER Hill, the guest speaker at Tabernacle Baptist Church, is a thin, intense black man from nearby Mosses, Alabama. According to the program handed to me as I entered the church, he is a native of Chicago who moved to this state when he was twelve, "received his baccalaureate degree from Miles College, and is now matriculating at Alabama State University in Educational Policy and Leadership." There are about thirty people in the congregation, including a half-dozen of the white do-gooders from Denver we saw at the revival meeting last night. We sit as far from them as we can get. There is an all-male choir at the front of the church. A succession of speakers has mounted the low dais in front of the choir to address us, each of them veterans of the 1965 march. The presiding pastor, Roosevelt Goldsby, has announced the theme of the day's service: "Remembering the Man and the Legend," the man, of course, being Dr. Martin Luther King, Jr. When Mr. Ronald Peoples has read the scripture, Samuel C. Lett has led us in prayer, and Mrs. Doris Cox has explained the significance to the voters' rights movement of Tabernacle First Baptist, where both of the historic marches began and where in March 1965 hundreds of black protesters gathered despite the local bylaw prohibiting more than three blacks to assemble to talk about civil rights, Dr. Verdell Lett Dawson introduces Walter Hill and Hill's topic, "Pharaoh, Let My People Go."

This is the first church service I've attended since my father died, and my first Baptist service ever, although my grandfather and grandmother both had "Baptist" on their wedding licence. Having been raised Anglican, with all the pomp and liturgy that entailed, I like the informality of the Baptist meeting. It isn't abasement to an absentee God: no one kneels in a Baptist church. It isn't self-congratulatory adherence to an abstract concept of superiority. There is a strong sense of community, of openness, of shared interests and concerns, natural, I suppose, among a people who know they have been more sinned against than sinning. "The pressing duty before the Negro ministry," wrote black journalist James Weldon Johnson in 1917, in an editorial in the *New York Sun*, "is to take the power of the Negro Church and make it an instrument for bettering the conditions of the race ... It is time," he continued, "to put the Negro Church into close touch with the practical questions that affect the welfare of the Negro people as citizens."

Walter Hill doesn't seem old enough to have been born in 1965, but he is a powerful speaker. Imagine a Southern Baptist version of the sermon that begins James Joyce's *A Portrait of the Artist as a Young Man*. Brother Hill isn't wearing robes or a surplice, he's wearing a plain black suit with a white shirt and tie, as are all the men in the church except me. And he is not telling us that we should be humble and penitent; he is telling us that we should be vigilant, that there are problems in the black community that need to be addressed if the struggle for freedom is to be carried on into the next generation.

"The Egyptian Pharaoh held the Israelites captive in Egypt and put them to work as slaves, turning the barren flood plains of the Nile River into plantations to feed the rich landowners, building the great pyramids to house the remains of the kings of the land. Moses said to him, 'Pharaoh, let my people go,' and when the Egyptian Pharaoh refused, Moses led the Children of Israel himself out of that place of bondage, out of that land of prejudice and segregation, toward the Promised Land."

There are murmurs of assent among the congregation. No one is missing the parallels.

"The Egyptian Pharaoh is supposed to have drowned in the Red Sea, whose waters parted to allow the passage of the Israelites but closed again to prevent their pursuit by Pharaoh and his soldiers. And so the Children of Israel reached the Promised Land.

"But there are new pharaohs today, pharaohs to be fought against with as much determination as the Israelites fought against the Egyptian Pharaoh. Today's pharaohs are keeping our people in bondage just as surely as that earlier pharaoh kept the Children of Israel in slavery. Who are these modern-day pharaohs?"

"You tell us, Brother Hill."

"The Pharaoh of Drugs!"

"Yes!"

"The Pharaoh of Dropouts!"

"Oh, yes!"

"And the Pharaoh of I-Don't-Care!"

"Praise the Lord!"

Modern black youth, Brother Hill tells the congregation, are undoing many of the gains made by the civil rights movement of the 1960s—through drug abuse and drug warfare, lack of education, and indifference. It isn't a sermon, it's a talk, and I find myself listening attentively. The clock is turning backwards, he says. It's time to stop fighting among and against ourselves and give new life to Dr. Martin Luther King, Jr.'s vision of a Promised Land.

When Brother Hill is finished, the male choir sings its last spiritual, and most of the congregation, including the bevy of young Denverites, threads its way out of the church to line up for the march. But a few of us, maybe a dozen, including Merilyn and me, hang back. When the doors open, we can hear the high school marching band warming up in the rain, Sam moving up and down the line, organizing the march. Those of us still in the church are invited to join a woman at the front, who explains that in March of 1965, before setting out from this church on the walk to Montgomery, King led the people of Tabernacle First Baptist in singing "We Shall Overcome." And we are going to sing it now, before the Dream March, because although we have come a long way since 1965, there is still a long road ahead. We stand in a circle and join hands. I am between Merilyn and an elderly white-haired man who looks at me and smiles. There are tears in his eyes. I smile back and take his hand, and together, haltingly at first but with increasing conviction, we sing.

WE JOIN the line in the rain behind the high school band, resplendent in their royal blue gold-braided uniforms under transparent plastic raincoats. Sam patrols up and down the sidewalk. He wants everything to go right, although there doesn't seem to be much of a plan other than to walk from here down Broad Street to the bridge. "Follow the band," he tells us, and when it starts up, we do. Merilyn and I have no umbrella, but a man beside us holds his over the three of us. He says he's come all the way from Chicago for this march; his parents were in the first two, and he is here in their memory. He doesn't ask us why we're here, and I wonder what I would say if he did: that I'm here to atone for my father's repudiation of his African-American blood? To assuage my guilt at never having lifted a finger in defence of civil liberty?

We have a police escort; white cops stand at each intersection along Broad Street, keeping a lane clear for us. Store owners, some black and some white, come out onto the sidewalk to cheer us along. Drivers honk their horns. Sam shouts at them: "All right, all right!" We wave and they wave back. We are part of a knot of walkers as we pass the Mom & Pop Easy Travel, Ray's Jewelry Repair, Rexall Drugs, Meemaw's Treasures, and Cahara Furn, which sells "Robes and gowns, Christian books, gifts, Christian supplies." On the sidewalk outside the store is a sandwich board with the information that Edgar Cayce worked in these premises from 1912 to 1923. "Many psychic readings were given in the back room," it says. I wonder if he foresaw this.

The band is playing a spirited march, the majorettes high-stepping, their white knee-high boots splashing down on the rain-soaked pavement. We stroll along behind them, keeping our distance from the Denverites, not one of whom put a nickel in the collection plate.

A young woman in a long, flowing African-print coat falls into step beside us. She's a lawyer, she tells us, just come from the county jail where her client, a young black man, was charged with parole violation for being drunk.

"He wasn't drunk," she says, "he has diabetes. He was sick. He was trying to get to the hospital. The damned police officer just assumed he was drunk and brought him in. The judge wouldn't even let me speak in my client's defence. Told me to shut the hell up. When I refused, she had me arrested."

We'd seen her in the church. When the route of the march was announced, she stood up and said, "To the jail! We should be going to the jail! Do you think Dr. King would let a whole meeting pass and never mention that a young black man was being unjustly held? Are we just going through the motions here, remembering something way back when?"

"I thought things had changed some," Merilyn says to her.

"Oh, they changed all right," she says bitterly. "The judge was a black woman."

At the bridge, the band swings left onto Water Street and stands marking time while the walkers mill around, unsure of where to go. Sam says a few words about the 1965 march, then another man takes the microphone and introduces the lawyer we've been talking to.

"When that woman was arrested for contempt of court, they searched her," the man says, "and they found a concealed weapon. You know what it was? Her voice. That's what they wrote down. Concealed weapon: voice."

He passes the mike to the lawyer, who begins to tell the story of her young client. The band moves off; people disperse to their homes. Her voice becomes more and more desperate. "No one says anything because we have a black mayor and a black chief of police. But I don't care whether your skin is black or red or white or green. Injustice is injustice."

Merilyn and I stay and listen, and in the end she is speaking only to us. I don't think she recognizes us. She tells us again about the black judge and the overzealous cop.

"And do you know what that cop's name was?" she asks us.

We shake our heads.

"I could hardly believe it," she says, shaking her head, too. "He was a white man, and his name was Jim Crow."

12 / ATHENS, GEORGIA

MONTGOMERY, Alabama, is bigger than Selma, but in at least one respect it is no different from Selma or Jackson or El Paso or dozens of other cities we've seen across America—it is empty at its core.

In Jackson, when we left Freedom Corner, we headed downtown, thinking we'd find a good restaurant, maybe a bookstore. We asked a policeman how to find the city centre.

"Take Bailey. That'll get y'all there."

We drove down Bailey, which followed some railroad tracks and a line of low warehouses. Then we turned on Pearl toward a tall building that had had all its windows blown out. We eventually found the state capitol building, the ubiquitous imposing courthouse, the library, but the wide streets around them were empty of cars, the sidewalks deserted, many shop windows, too. No restaurants. Definitely no bookstores.

"Go down Galatin," one man offered, so we tried that, circling back on our trail.

"Do you know how we can get downtown?" Wayne asked the

passenger in the car next to ours at a red light. Wayne never asks for directions. This had to mean we were well and truly lost.

"Thetaway," said the fellow, pointing the way we'd come.

After an hour, we still had not found anything that fit our definition of downtown: shops, cafes, theatres, bookstores, a little street life. All we saw were empty, windblown streets, boarded-up buildings, and traffic lights changing incessantly for no one.

"There must be a heart to this city," I insisted. "We're just not looking in the right place."

Back on the highway, we passed mall after mall, their parking lots full of cars. When we left Mississippi and crossed into Alabama, we drove through one town after another, their centres gutted and vacant, here and there a shop set up in a building of faded glory, a truck with a mobile yard sale, a rack of clothes installed under the awning of a disembowelled gas station. And always, somewhere on the outskirts, a glaring strip of oversized box stores.

In Selma, the downtown streets were four lanes wide. Lovely antebellum buildings stood boarded up, plate glass windows cracked and taped. Signs for bail bonds and quick cash for income tax refunds outnumbered stores with necessary goods for sale. When I asked Veronica, at the hotel, where she shopped, she jerked her head north.

"Out the highway," she said.

Selma has a population of 33,000. There are no city buses.

"So you have to have a car?" I asked.

"Yes ma'am," Veronica replied. "Or hire yo'self a taxicab."

If the government oppresses you, you can march to Montgomery, but what do you do when Walmart has you in chains?

Jane Jacobs, in her book *The Death and Life of Great American Cities,* calls it "the sacking of cities." Americans have become their own Visigoths.

Steinbeck noticed the decaying city cores almost fifty years ago. In *Travels with Charley,* he offered "a generality concerning the growth of American cities, seemingly true of all of them I know. When a city begins to grow and spread outward, from the edges, the centre which was once its glory is in a sense abandoned to time. Then the buildings grow dark and a kind of decay sets in; poorer people move in as the rents fall, and small fringe businesses take the place of once flowering establishments. The district is still too good to tear down and too outmoded to be desirable."

The collapse did not begin with box stores or the automobile or the suburbs. It began, I suspect, with those courthouses I've been noticing along the way. That odd clustering of government buildings at the heart of a town is the signature of the City Beautiful movement, spawned in the United States at the end of the nineteenth century. Civic buildings were designed not as places for people but as monuments—to power, to wealth, to civic security. They were arranged along boulevards or bordered by parks, anything to set them off from the rest of the city, to produce a grand and imposing effect. Often, what urban planners called slums—what Jane Jacobs calls densely populated, tightly knit downtown communities—were bulldozed to make room for them.

"Invariably the ordinary city around them ran down instead of being uplifted," writes Jacobs. "People stayed away from them to a remarkable degree."

The courthouse with its narrow skirt of grass may look like a New England common or a Spanish plaza, but the intent and the philosophy are the opposite of community: this construction divides a city into them and us.

Jacobs wrote her great urban planning treatise in 1961, the same year Steinbeck went on the road with his dog, Charley. Seven years later, she left the United States and settled in Toronto, a move prompted by her desire to protect her draft-age sons from the Vietnam War. We like to think of her as our own, standing with us in our more-or-less constant criticism of America, but I wonder if we're any better than Americans at making desirable places where we can live together in close quarters. Most Canadian towns still have some life at the centre, but the drain has begun; you can see it in the blank stares of the empty storefronts. Box stores and outlet malls are popping up along our highways, too. Already there are over three hundred Walmarts in Canada; the busiest in the world is in the Square One Shopping Centre in Mississauga, Ontario. In proportion to our population, we don't have all that far to go to catch up to the United States, where there are almost four thousand stores (Walmart is the world's largest public corporation by revenue, America's largest grocery retailer, and its largest private employer).

Jacobs didn't believe it was just the big retailers and the handy automobile that were ruining cities. She laid the blame on the planners, who traditionally refused to recognize cities as complex, integrated organisms.

"Human beings are, of course, a part of nature, as much so as grizzly bears or bees or whales or sorghum cane," she argued. "The cities of human beings are as natural . . . as are the colonies of prairie dogs or the beds of oysters."

What kills cities, it seems to me, is this insistence on hiving off their parts: bedrooms in the suburbs, civic buildings in the centre, shops "out the highway." The modern North American city is being dismembered, its functions separated, parcelled out. No wonder the centre cannot hold. These things, taken together, are what gives a city heart.

★　★　★

WE cross the border from Alabama into Georgia on the I-85, aware that we are travelling against the desperate tide of Southern history. By the time Thomas Jefferson began the long construction project that would be Monticello, in 1768, much of the agricultural land throughout the Old South was already exhausted. A century of intensive farming in Virginia, first of tobacco and then of cotton, on land that had not been rich to begin with, and without the relief of any system of crop rotation, had depleted the soil to such an extent that many plantation owners simply pulled up stakes and moved west to the neighbouring state of Georgia, the flat, disheartened land we are driving through now.

In the 1840s, when Georgia land had become good for little but peanuts, families moved to Alabama, then Mississippi, then Louisiana. Intensive farming didn't take long to ruin that land, too. "By 1860," writes Roger G. Kennedy in *Mr. Jefferson's Lost Cause,* "the alkaline uplands of Mississippi and Alabama were showing their bones." So it was on to Texas.

From the time of the Louisiana Purchase in 1803 until the Civil War, it was not uncommon on these roads to see entire families moving to their new plantation lands in the West, the whites in their covered, horse-drawn carriages, preceded by wagonloads of their household goods and long phalanxes of their slaves—their human goods—trudging through the dust ahead of them. Most Southern families made this one-way migration at least twice in a generation, steadily moving further west.

It wasn't as though Southern agronomists didn't know about crop rotation and soil depletion. The point was that allowing arable land to lie fallow every two or three years cost money. Plantation owners still had to feed and house their slaves, whether the fields were producing cotton or not. And land in the West was so cheap that it was less expensive to buy new acreage, and clear and break it, than it was to properly tend land in the East.

It gives me a grim sort of satisfaction to think of this possible land of my forebears as sere and diminished by white ineptitude; I feel as an Israelite might have felt looking back on Egypt after the plagues had swept through it, plagues that the Egyptians had brought upon themselves.

WE ARE headed for Athens, Georgia. Back home, friends told us they had been to the University of Georgia in Athens for a conference and were struck by how often they had come across the name Grady while walking around town. "The place is full of Gradys," they told us. "White Gradys, black Gradys. If your father's family came from the South, then Athens is the place to look." It struck me as a promising coincidence that the village where Merilyn and I live in eastern Ontario is named Athens, too.

I'm not actively researching the Grady family history. A few years ago, however, I did discover a Thomasina Grady, a black woman with a white slave owner's surname, who moved from somewhere in Georgia to somewhere in Kentucky and from there crossed the Ohio River into Indiana in 1835. She and her husband and children and grandchildren—one of them my great-grandfather, Andrew Jackson Grady—weathered the Civil War on a farm near Spencer, Indiana. Somewhere in Georgia might easily have been Athens, given that there were plantation-owning Gradys in the area. I don't know what I'll do, exactly, in Athens. Maybe someone who looks like me will come up and shake my hand. At the very least, I might feel, for the first time in my life, what it's like to set foot on ancestral soil.

I know there is a Grady Memorial Hospital in Atlanta. I remember reading that the actor Whitman Mayo, who played Grady in the TV sitcom *Sanford & Son,* died there in 2001. And there is a Grady College of Journalism at the University of Georgia, in Athens. Both the hospital and the college were named after the journalist Henry Woodfin Grady, who was born in Athens in 1850, much too late to have been an ancestor of mine. But Henry Woodfin Grady's father was William S. Grady. Henry and William are both common names on my father's family tree, and William S. Grady was a slave owner. I don't know whether slaves who took their masters' surnames tended to perpetuate their Christian names as well. I think it unlikely, but the coincidence draws me toward Athens.

William S. Grady was killed during the Civil War at the siege of Petersburg, Virginia, in 1864, and Henry was raised by his mother until he graduated from the University of Georgia and married into a wealthy cotton family from nearby Rome. Like me, he became a journalist. He started the *Rome Commercial* and the *Rome Daily,* both of which went bankrupt within a year. In 1872, he bought a half-interest in the *Atlanta Herald,* which folded in 1876. Still undaunted, he borrowed twenty thousand dollars and purchased the *Atlanta Constitution* and this time succeeded in turning the newspaper into the most popular weekly in the United States. He specialized in "newsletters," a term he may have coined, and pioneered the practice of actually interviewing the subjects of his stories. He used his paper as a platform from which he extolled "the New South," a term, if not a notion, he also invented.

The New South, he believed, would be a post-bellum paradise of diversified agriculture, prosperous industry, and a conciliatory attitude toward the North. He was known as "the orator of the peace-makers" in the North but viewed as something of a traitor below the Mason-Dixon Line. A famous speech delivered in New York in 1886 began: "There was a South of slavery and secessionism; that South is dead. There is a South of union and freedom; that South, thank God, is living." Northerners in the audience, including J.P. Morgan and Charles Tiffany, applauded; Southerners, reading the speech the next day in the *Constitution,* scoffed.

It's hard to know what they objected to most: Grady's promise to coerce Southern farmers away from cotton, or his assurance that a Southern industrial economy would be fuelled by emancipated "will-ing" black labourers who would be "fairly treated" by their former masters. His dream, expounded in speech after speech throughout the 1880s, was to unite all Southern whites into one political party, funded by a financial and industrial culture that would rise after King Cotton was deposed. He pursued this goal with such passion that his speeches, as one biographer described them, sounded like "a cannonball in full flight," and wore him out to such an extent that, in 1889, while on a lecture tour in the North, he came down with pneumonia and died. He was thirty-nine.

My father was forever taken up with grand, impractical schemes. He would turn his father's small plastering business in Windsor into a major construction firm; he would move us to Boston to manage a chemical plant owned by the brother of Joe DiMaggio, the baseball player, or maybe to Florida, where he would play first trombone for Guy Lombardo's Royal Canadians. He never actually did any of those things, but as years passed, as he went on delivering milk for Silverwood Dairy without advancing to run the company, selling used cars in North Bay and still not owning his own dealership, or serving in the air force and never rising above the rank of corporal, I imagine the dreams sustaining him, keeping him going. And eventually killing him, for I also remember my father as a tight bundle of suppressed fury, not defeated or appalled by the unchanging number of rungs on the ladder above his head so much as baffled by it, as a fly is baffled by an invisible windowpane. In 1969, at the age of forty-four, after a fit of towering rage brought on by an imagined slight from a superior officer, he suffered a heart attack so massive it would have killed him had he been living in a less technologically advanced age.

Impractical schemes, sudden untimely death: perhaps Henry Woodfin Grady and my father were related, after all.

*   *   *

*M*OVING through the plantation lands south of Atlanta, I can't help but think of the women: the mothers, wives, and daughters in the antebellum houses and in the slave shacks behind, and the women, too, who travelled this landscape before me, especially the well-bred women travellers of the early nineteenth century who crossed the Atlantic to take a first-hand look, as I am doing, at the American South.

"Have you ever heard of Frances Kemble?" I ask Wayne. We are driving through agricultural land. Now and then we pass a stately house, but more often, these farms seem no different from farms we've driven past in Europe or back home.

"No. Who was she?"

"She travelled through here in the late 1820s. I wonder what she would have seen."

Frances Kemble was an actress. She toured the eastern seaboard with her father, a famous British actor. In Philadelphia, she left the stage to marry Pierce Butler, grandson of one of America's founding fathers, the man who insisted that the Constitution contain a provision to ensure the capture and return of fugitive slaves.

"Runaways like my great-great-great-grandmother Thomasina," Wayne says.

"I don't think Frances knew how her husband made his money."

It wasn't until after the wedding that Frances discovered she owed her comfort to cotton and rice plantations in Georgia. And she didn't fully realize what that meant until, after her second daughter was born, she travelled with Butler to the South.

Nothing in England had prepared her for what she saw: twenty people or more living in cabins the size of a bedroom, all of them sleeping on moss collected in the forest and covered with "filthy, pestilential-looking blankets." During the day, only the very young were left in the cabins; toddlers carried newborns to their mothers in the fields to nurse. The infirmary was the worst. "Poor wretches lay prostrate on the floor, without bed, mattress, or pillow, buried in tattered and filthy blankets, which, huddled round them as they strewed about, left hardly space to move upon the floor."

Frances did what she could to improve conditions for her husband's 450 slaves. She had new cabins built with proper bedsteads, bought them mattresses and blankets. But what she wanted was for Butler to free his slaves. He gave her a choice: accept his way of life or lose her daughters. She fled north, leaving the plantation and Pierce, who won custody of the girls.

She didn't keep quiet about what she'd seen. She made a fair copy of her journal and passed it to her friends. Over the years it made the rounds of anti-slavery circles in the North until finally, a quarter century later, *Journal of a Residence on a Georgian Plantation 1838–1839* was published.

"I have sometimes been haunted with the idea," Kemble wrote, "that it was an imperative duty, knowing what I know, and having seen what I have seen, to do all that lies in my power to show the dangers and the evils of this frightful institution."

What would we have done, Wayne and I, had we seen black men and women bent over in the fields? Would we have been appalled? I'd like to think so. It takes a visitor to object to what locals take for granted as a fixture in the landscape. Travellers may know less about where they are, but they see more.

Wayne has a shelf of slave narratives in his study at home. I wonder how they got written, when teaching a slave to read or write was punishable by fines and outright imprisonment. Another Frances— Frances Wright—broke that rule. When she and her sister Camilla travelled to the United States from England in 1818 on a tour of the new country, they were so offended by slavery that they decided to stay and try to effect change.

"The sight of slavery is revolting everywhere, but to inhale the impure breath of its pestilence in the free winds of America is odious beyond all that the imagination can conceive." She understood the obstacles that stood in the way of emancipation; what she could not abide was that Americans contented themselves with deploring the evil instead of "setting their shoulders to the wheel and actively working out its remedy."

The sisters bought a tract of land where the Mississippi River enters Tennessee and brought forty slaves to the estate. Their idea was to build a school and educate the children exactly as white children were schooled, thus preparing them for emancipation and at the same time producing proof that the colour of a person's skin had nothing to do with the workings of the mind.

Frances Trollope, a novelist and the mother of the writer Anthony Trollope, visited Frances Wright's colony in 1828. The two Franceses had met on board ship while travelling from England to America. Trollope was intrigued by the idea of a wilderness slave school and had promised to visit.

"One glance sufficed to convince me that every idea I had formed of the place was as far as possible from the truth," she writes in her travel memoir *Domestic Manners of the Americans*. "Desolation was the only feeling—the only word that presented itself... I decided upon leaving the place with as little delay as possible."

In her travelogue, Trollope pulls no punches. Americans, she opines, are at once vulgar and prudish, live in ugly, makeshift buildings, and travel on roads that are all but impassable. The merchants are dishonest, the scholars stupid, the women flat-chested. More than anything, she rails against American hypocrisy. "Look at them at home; you will see them with one hand hoisting the cap of liberty, and with the other flogging their slaves. You will see them one hour lecturing their mob on the indefeasible rights of man, and the next driving from their homes the children of the soil, whom they have bound themselves to protect by the most solemn treaties."

Mrs. Trollope found it hard to stomach lectures on democracy and freedom from a country founded on slavery and genocide and forged in the crucible of constant aggression. Not that Canadians were much better. Residential schools, the expulsion of the Acadians, the internment of the Japanese: we both have skeletons in our historical closets.

Trollope's travels through the South produced more than a caustic memoir. Less than a decade after her aborted visit to Frances Wright's colony, she published *The Life and Adventures of Jonathan Jefferson*

Whitlaw, which many consider the first anti-slavery novel. The book deeply influenced Harriet Beecher Stowe, who wrote the most famous anti-slavery novel, *Uncle Tom's Cabin,* based on the slave narrative of Reverend Josiah Henson, who travelled the Underground Railway to Canada.

Uncle Tom's Cabin opens with Tom being sold at a slave auction. Josiah Henson, in his autobiography, recalls the actual event in Maryland upon which Stowe's fictional account is based: "The knowledge that all ties of the past were to be sundered; the frantic terror at the idea of being sent 'down south'; the almost certainty that one member of a family will be torn from another; the anxious scanning of purchasers' faces; the agony of parting, often forever, with husband, wife, child—these must be seen and felt to be fully understood. Young as I was then, the iron entered into my soul."

In March 1857, five years after Stowe's novel was published, the largest sale of human beings ever held in the history in the United States took place on a racetrack in Savannah: all 450 slaves belonging to Pierce Butler were sold to pay his gambling debts. According to the *New York Tribune,* buyers strolled among the slaves, "pulling their mouths open to see their teeth, pinching their limbs to find how muscular they were, walking them up and down to detect any signs of lameness, making them stoop and bend in different ways that they might be certain there was no concealed rupture or wound."

The highest price paid for one family—a mother and her five grown children—was $6,180. More often than not, families were split up and sold off one by one. The highest price for an individual was $1,750, the lowest, $250. Net proceeds were $303,850, making Pierce Butler once again a wealthy man.

"They say it rained non-stop all during the two days of the sale," I tell Wayne, my voice almost a whisper. Raindrops slide down the windshield, obscuring the landscape. "People said it was as though heaven itself was crying. The locals called the sale 'the weeping time.'"

There's nothing more to be said. Wayne and I stare out the window, seeing nothing.

★   ★   ★

*W*E leave the interstate at Madison and take a red road to Athens. The town is as quaint and tidy as our friends described it. White-painted porches vie for space along hilly streets. It is Sunday and the town's record offices are closed. A "fraternity event" is being held in the Taylor-Grady House, a huge, white-pillared, Greek-revival mansion on the outskirts of town. Built in 1844 by Robert Taylor, who moved to Athens from Savannah in the 1790s, the mansion was the centrepiece of Taylor's seventeen-thousand-acre estate. Upon Taylor's death in 1863, William S. Grady bought the house, but he succumbed to a Yankee bullet before setting foot in it. His wife and son moved there in 1864; Henry Woodfin Grady later described it as "an old Southern home, with its lofty pillars and its white pigeons fluttering down through the golden air."

We stand outside the iron gate and peer over the expansive lawn, crisp and dry now in the January sun but no doubt lovely in summer, to the massively porticoed entrance of the house. I don't see any pigeons about, or golden air. Young men in tuxedoes stand around on the Doric-columned porch, smoking. I wonder if my ancestors were once inside, serving mint juleps, or out here watching through these same wrought-iron gates.

The university is equally disappointing. We drive onto the campus, passing the three pillars representing Wisdom, Justice, and Moderation and park between the library and the student union. The library contains twelve thousand letters by Margaret Mitchell, author of *Gone With the Wind,* and 960 copies of the various editions of Erskine Caldwell's *Tobacco Road* and *God's Little Acre.* So much for moderation.

Following a series of signs pointing to the College of Journalism, we thread our way along empty corridors, past a few students reclining on low benches and one or two closed concession booths, and come to a locked door marked *Journalism*. Not even the name Grady, beside which Merilyn could photograph me. By way of compensation, we go into the university bookstore. All we can see is long racks of red sweatshirts, T-shirts, and jackets, and shelves of baseball caps and beer steins with the University of Georgia crest printed on them. Not a book in sight. So much for wisdom.

That leaves justice.

In 1820, when six out of every ten people living in Georgia were slaves, an Athens gentleman named William Henry Jackson became particularly fond of a venerable white oak that had been growing on his property for as long as he could remember. It was a beautiful tree, perfectly formed, solid and stately as a Georgian day. Colonel Jackson worried about what would happen to his tree if anything should happen to him. Would a cabinetmaker cut it down for lumber? Would the town remove it to make way for a new street or a fire hall? To prevent such an eventuality, the colonel hit upon an ingenious idea. He deeded the land on which the tree grew, to a radius of eight feet from its base, to the tree, and then he deeded the tree to itself. "I, William Henry Jackson," reads the duly notarized document, "do hereby convey unto the said oak tree, entire possession of itself."

The self-possessed tree still stands in Athens on a small patch of tended turf at the corner of Finley and Dearing Streets. It is, in fact, not the original tree that owned itself, since that tree was struck by lightning on October 7, 1942, and burned to the ground. This tree, grown from an acorn produced by the old tree, was replanted by the Junior Ladies Garden Club the following spring. It is known as the son of the tree that owned itself.

Merilyn and I stand side by side, looking at the tree, our shoulders touching. Protected from traffic, vandalism, and dogs by a low, looping chain fence, it is indeed a fine specimen. White oak is a handsome tree. But I can't help thinking that, in a state where thousands of black slaves did not legally own their own children, here was a white oak that owned a prime parcel of Georgia real estate. At a time when thousands of human beings were the property of a handful of white masters, here was a tree that owned itself.

"Let's get out of here," I say to Merilyn.

★ ★ ★

ORNING brings an email from Wayne's brother, who reports that an ice storm is pelting a swath from Texas to New York.

"Not again!" I exclaim. It seems as though we've been running with a gale at our backs for weeks.

Last night we lugged ourselves off the interstate at Lugoff, South Carolina, and checked into a cheap chain motel: $29.95, my lowest price yet. I dig yesterday's newspaper out of the wastebasket, a gift from a former tenant, and smooth the pages across the bed. In our media-deprived travellers' haze, we've missed all kinds of news—riots in El Salvador, a mine collapse in the Congo, car bombings in Baghdad. And there it is, a triple whammy of severe winter storms. In California, night after night of freezing temperatures. Seventy-five per cent of the Central Valley's citrus crop destroyed. Another storm is sloping up from the Rio Grande toward New England. The third is rising now from Texas up through the Carolinas. Hundreds of thousands of people are without power. The governor of Oklahoma has declared a state of emergency. The governor of Missouri called in the National Guard. A dozen people in Texas are dead.

"What's going on with the weather?"

"It isn't weather, it's climate," Wayne says laconically. "We used to call it global warming, but the weather isn't just going to get warmer, it's going to be more unpredictable. And more extreme."

Just what we need: more extreme. September storms are standard in this part of the world, as hurricanes blow up the Atlantic coast. There's a history of March storms, too. The eastern United States logged its storm of the century in March 1993: Georgia got six inches of snow, tornadoes broke out all over the South, and more than three hundred were killed as the tempest raged from Central America to Canada. It's only January, but this year seems determined to set new records, too.

"Maybe driving up the Shenandoah isn't such a good idea," I say tentatively.

We had planned to travel north from Athens, up to Asheville, North Carolina, where we'd get on the Blue Ridge Parkway, which would take us up the Shenandoah Valley, a verdant stretch that angles northeast through West Virginia and the Commonwealth of Virginia, the Blue Ridge Mountains on one side, the Appalachians on the other. Champlain claimed the valley for France on his map in 1632. The Confederates used it as a back door to get at Washington and Philadelphia. I thought Wayne would appreciate the new wines as well as the history of the region, and I'm keen to hear the music—Virginia bluegrass and those famous Appalachian dirges and laments. Before we left on this trip, I watched Maggie Greenwald's movie *Songcatcher,* about another one of those intrepid turn-of-the-century women, a musicologist who walked into the wilds to record the hill music of America. Maybe it's just as well that foul weather bars the way; I'd like to keep intact my image of a banjo-plucking mammy crooning on every ramshackle porch.

"We need to talk," I say to Wayne. I love a plan as much as anybody, but I'm not willing to risk my life for it. "We need to get out of the way of this storm."

★   ★   ★

"*W*E need to talk." Words to chill a man's heart. They are usually code for "Everything you thought you knew is about to change." Nothing good comes after hearing those four words.

"What's a little rain?" I say. "Nothing we can't handle."

"It's not a little rain," Merilyn says. "It's a lot of freezing rain."

"We'll be in a valley. 'Oh, Shenandoah, I long to hear you.'"

"The storm is in the Appalachians. Cold air sinks. It will be freezing in the valley."

"Well, then, we'll stick to the mountains. Warm air rises."

"But the rain will freeze there first," Merilyn says. I can hear the frustration in her voice. She thinks I am being unreasonable.

I must still be reacting to Athens. How is it, I wonder, that in depressing, dilapidated, defeated Selma, I felt an unexpected kinship with the people I met, whereas I couldn't wait to put tidy, genteel Athens behind me? Am I just being perverse?

"You're just being perverse," Merilyn says. "Whenever there's a storm, you want to drive into it."

"It's not a storm," I say. "It's nature. We can't run from nature. 'Away, I'm bound away, 'cross the wide Missouri.' Wait, how did the Missouri get in there?"

"Wayne, be serious. Please."

"Okay, look," I say, losing patience. "We've already made this decision. The Shenandoah Valley has the I-81. Look at the map. The I-81 runs right up and hits the Canadian border at Gananoque. We could be home in two days. We don't need any alternative plans."

★   ★   ★

"*M*AYBE not," I say, but Wayne is no longer listening. He has picked up his book and is on the bed, barricaded behind *Death of a Writer.*

"Don't tempt me," I mutter, turning back to the map. The I-95 heads north in the lee of the Appalachians, but it runs through another megalopolis: Richmond; Washington, D.C.; and Baltimore— wall-to-wall urban sprawl. East of the interstate, though, there's a red highway that hugs the coast: Route 17. It'll be slower, but I reason that the weather has to be warmer close to the water. I boot up my computer and check the forecast for Myrtle Beach, Wilmington, Jacksonville, and Plymouth.

"There's still a severe weather warning for the Shenandoah, but there's a road up the coast, along the Outer Banks," I say, keeping my voice even. "It won't be exactly hot, but at least the temperature is supposed to stay above freezing. Doesn't it make more sense to go that way?"

"Whatever you say."

This is what drives me crazy. In Wayne's world, it's either his way or my way. I want us to talk about it and make it *our* way. He just wants to head off into the storm, like Daniel Boone.

That's when it comes to me. Women are from Canada. Men are from the States.

TRAVELLING, SUDDENLY, seems like too much work. I'm tired of planning, accommodating. The cold and wet make me want to curl up by a fire, draw a warm shawl around my shoulders, speak to no one for a week. Maybe *that's* the difference between these two countries: the United States is relatively warm; Canada, more often than not, is cold. When you're warm, you reach out; when you're cold, you huddle into yourself. Perhaps our national characters—America, the assertive extrovert; Canada, the cautious introvert—are nothing more than a human response to weather.

Wayne and I are barely speaking as we head east into Camden, South Carolina, following the recommendation of the grandmotherly woman who greeted us at the Welcome Center just inside the South Carolina border. Her assistant, a young black woman, suggested Boykin, a village owned by a family that restored the whole place.

"Maybe we could get a hotel there," Wayne suggested.

"Honey," she laughed, "y'all put your foot down in that town, your toes'll hang out."

Camden is definitely bigger. It is apparently the oldest inland city in the state. The town was part of a plan by George II of England to settle the interior. During the American Revolution, it was a major British supply post and the site of the worst American defeat of the revolution.

"It's also the steeplechase capital of the world."

"The board game?" Wayne says, trying to make up.

"I don't think so," I say grudgingly. "But maybe."

Main Street is an American invention; Camden has a Broad Street, proof of its British roots. We notice how many banks there are, mostly private institutions with names like First Palmetto, Planters, Wachovia.

"'Watch over ya?' Are they kidding? Who would trust a bank called Wachovia?"

Banks and churches. Churches and banks. There's one or both on every corner, it seems: the Starbucks outlets of the East. If it's true that you can tell a lot about a town by its architecture, then Camden is full of very rich sinners.

We do a quick drive-through and press on. Something has changed in us. We seem to have lost interest. Curiosity is a peculiar animal: poke it a bit and it's a lively thing, but it can just as easily hide its head and doze. We look flatly out the windows. The only difference I can see between this place and where we come from is that the gas stations have boiled-peanut stands in the middle of the aisle, beside the potato chips and chocolate bars. They look like popcorn kiosks. Patrons help themselves, scooping hot, dripping peanuts into paper bags.

Wayne is on automatic pilot, his foot heavy on the gas pedal, when we pass the roadside stand.

"Oh, let's stop," I say. "We can't go through South Carolina without at least tasting a boiled peanut." What kind of travellers are we, anyway?

Wayne backs up to the *Fried, Roasted, and Boiled P-Nuts* sign, hand-painted in bold red letters. Cloth bags of peanuts hang from the awning; baskets and sacks of nuts are piled along the counter. Half of the stand has a big sign saying *Fried Peanuts;* the other urges *Hot Boiled Peanuts.*

I must look confused.

"We love our peanuts boiled here," the young woman behind the counter suggests, opening her vowels up wide. She's wearing a siren-red sweatshirt from the University of Georgia, Athens.

"Can I try one?"

"Sure thing," she says and dips a solitary peanut out of the steaming vat. It's white, like a fat maggot, a steamy slug. "It's a bit messy," she says apologetically.

The peanut tastes like any boiled bean, a little mushy, but sharply salted from the boiling brine.

We buy a bag each, plus some apples. If we get storm-stayed, we won't starve.

A van of Mexicans passes us, young men wearing T-shirts and feed-store ball caps. Catholics travelling north to convert the Baptists? Environmental refugees from the California citrus freeze, heading east to pick peanuts? We'll never know.

We stop outside a Hampton Inn. I open my computer and, yes, there's a wireless signal.

"Do you mind if we use your Wi-Fi?" I ask the woman behind the desk.

"Why sure, c'mon in. Here's the password. Y'all can sit in the breakfast room, if you like."

Wayne settles at one of the small round tables and sets to work. I get him a muffin and a coffee, then sit mesmerized by the flat-screen television that takes up one wall of the room. It has been almost five months since I've watched TV, and I stare at it like a toddler, struck dumb.

The screen is tuned to the weather channel. It's snowing in Dallas. Roads are closed, travellers stranded. The high-pitched drama in the announcer's voice reminds me of Albuquerque. There's a weather advisory for Shreveport, Jackson—all the places we've just left. Lubbock, Texas, is shut down altogether. The cold and wet are pluming north and east. Freezing rain predicted for Charlotte and Raleigh. The Shenandoah Valley is coloured bright pink on the weatherman's map. Who, I wonder, chose such a cheap and cheerful colour to denote treacherous weather? Only the Atlantic seaboard is still a benign blue line that defines the eastern edge of the continent.

The Doomsday Clock, the announcer tells us, has been moved one minute closer to midnight, in recognition of the threat climate change poses to the survival of humankind. Soon we'll all be environmental refugees.

"Looks like we made the right decision, for now anyway," I say to Wayne. "We'd better stick to that thin blue line."

IT'S LONG past the time when we should have stopped for the night. We're both hungry and cranky. Darkness has descended when we finally reach Washington, North Carolina. We look for a nice mom-and-pop motel, but they all seem uniformly rundown, paint peeling, windows like cellblock slits, the parking lots deserted or spotted with wrecks. We give up and go to a Days Inn, where the young woman at the desk gives us a room right beside the only other guest in the place, a fellow with a medium-sized moving van.

It is eight o'clock at night. Normally, we'd be looking in the phone book for a decent restaurant or nibbling on duck pâté and smoked salmon as we play gin or read amicably in our room. But tonight we order pizza and turn on the television, indications of how low our spirits have sunk. We're no longer travellers, we're a dumpy middle-aged couple wanting only comfort food and a mindless evening watching *American Idol.*

"You look like a distinguished gentleman," the pizza delivery man says when Wayne answers the door. Wayne eyes him suspiciously.

"I mean it as a compliment," the man says, smiling broadly. He's about Wayne's age, has a greying beard, and is wearing a thin black jacket that is soaked at the shoulders. Water drips from the peak of his baseball cap, but he doesn't seem to notice. He nods at me, lying rumpled on the bed. His smile is infectious.

I sit up. "Looks pretty bad out there," I say.

"Nothing that won't blow over," he says brightly. "Sun's supposed to shine tomorrow."

Wayne takes the pizza and sets it on the bed, then peels off a couple of bills. They all look the same here in the States, but I can see the numbers. He hands the money to the man and closes the door.

"That was a big tip," I say, no disapproval in my voice. The man delivered more than pizza: he brought a bit of South Carolina into the room.

Wayne is searching through our kitchen things. When he finds the red plates, he lifts a slice of pizza onto one and offers it to me, like a gentleman.

"He earned it," he says, a smile softening his face. "There's a storm out there."

13 / THE OUTER BANKS

MELISSA, the night clerk, promised us there would be decaf in the breakfast room in the morning, but there isn't. I press the new man at the desk into making a pot. When the carafe is three-quarters full, I say, "Do you mind if I stop it now? I like my coffee strong."

"I don't know," he says, waddling over with a worried look. His toupée is a peculiar shade of brown. "You might burn yourself."

"I'll be careful," I say, sliding the carafe aside and slipping a cup under the drip. He looks dubious. I'm Canadian, I want to say, I'm not going to sue you, but after all these weeks such easy distinctions no longer seem fair. I nod my thanks and take two polystyrene cups and the carafe to our table in the lobby's breakfast nook.

I've forgotten my notebook. When I go back to the room, the swipe card doesn't work. The manager is summoned, but his card doesn't work either. It is agreed: no cards work. Whatever happened to keys? I stand huddled in the rain, imagining us stuck here for days while they look for some computer nerd to come and open our room. I contemplate the cost of a broken window.

At last, a congenial cleaner produces a gizmo from his trolley that somehow opens the door. "No close," he warns me sternly, shaking his finger in my face.

I nod vigorously. No close. Not on your life.

It is all too much, too early, especially today, when travel has lost its lustre and I just want to be in my own kitchen with my own coffee pot, my own favourite brimming mug, not this plastic at my lips.

We eat the comes-with breakfast in the motel lobby: plastic tubes filled with garish Froot Loops and other puffed and sugared grains, cook-your-own waffles that smell of neoprene smothered with fake maple syrup, uniform slabs of white bread that move desultorily through the conveyor-belt toaster, plastic packets of sickly jam and butter and peanut butter. It all tastes the same.

"Let's not do that again," I say as we get back into the car.

"It's quick," Wayne says.

"But deadly."

"Okay, tomorrow we'll find you some great hash browns."

We're aiming for the coast, where the names of the towns—Kill Devil Hills, Nags Head—suit our mood. I look out through the rain-smeared window at houses flanked by palms and tall shrubs flowering pink and white against bare branches—hibiscus? magnolia? The slight rousing of my curiosity lifts my spirits a little, too.

The landscape is as flat as settled earth can get—ocean-bottom flat. We've left Route 17 for US 264, which takes us out onto a protuberance of North Carolina that extends farther into the Atlantic than Miami. Only Long Island, Rhode Island, and a bulge of Maine are farther east on the continental United States. On the map, the coastline here looks nibbled by mice.

"Mattamuskeet National Wildlife Refuge," I say, reading a huge billboard. Wayne's mother used to do this: read every sign she passed—*McMann's Dry Goods. Pedestrian Crosswalk. No Turns Between 3 and 6 pm*—a running commentary that used to drive him crazy. It still does. I try to keep my roadside reading to myself, except for times like this, when we could use a break, a diversion, a way back into our travelling selves.

"Birds," I say, leaning forward to squint up at a fan of white waterfowl flapping low overhead. "Swans! Could this be that swan wintering ground Rachel Carson wrote about?"

Wayne pulls over to the side of the road.

Rachel Carson was the first to sound the environmental alarm with *Silent Spring* in 1962, but I've always felt a kinship with her, too, as a fellow fan of the novels of Gene Stratton-Porter, the author of *Freckles* and *A Girl of the Limberlost,* books that led both of us as children into nature. Carson started out writing pamphlets for the United States Fish and Wildlife Service. In 1947, she produced one on the Mattamuskeet, at the time one of the wildest places on the Atlantic coast, with dense woods of pine, cypress, and gum and wide expanses of marsh grass crawling with alligators and trembling with birds, hundreds of thousands of them. It has been a wildlife refuge for more than seventy years: fifty thousand acres that take in Mattamuskeet Lake, a long, shallow indentation less than three feet deep. In the fall, ducks, geese, and swans swoop down the skyways from above the Arctic Circle to winter here on this mild nub of wild land sticking out into the Atlantic.

I have a bleak thought. We're not only travelling against the flow of American settlement, we're travelling north against the wisdom of the world's waterfowl, too.

We drive down a side road, and sure enough, tens of thousands of shorebirds are milling on the lakeside, warbling to each other, suddenly breaking into flight, as if they've had enough, they're going home—but no, they circle round and glide back to where the others continue to scrabble and squawk.

"Tundra swans," Wayne says.

"Whistling swans," I say, still feeling querulous. I seem to remember that the windpipe of a whistling swan has an extra loop, which causes it to emit a high note, something like an oboe or a clarinet. I listen intently while Wayne searches for identifying marks, on the birds and in the bird book.

"Same bird, two different names," he says, looking pleased. "We're both right."

According to the sign, as many as thirty-five thousand tundra/whistling swans congregate here, down significantly from the hundred thousand that Carson estimated in 1947. With a wingspan of close to seven feet, whistling swans are the second-largest waterfowl in North America. There are smaller birds, too: snow geese, osprey, bald eagles, some twenty-two species of ducks. We identify blue-winged teals, mallards, black ducks. Alligators still swim lazily in the canal, thankfully out of sight. Canada geese circle overhead, honking at us to carry on.

Go home, the sound says to me. *Go on home.*

* * *

WALTER Raleigh dedicated his unfinished epic, "The Ocean to Cynthia," to Elizabeth I. In it, he styled himself the Ocean and Elizabeth as Cynthia, the Moon. It was a nice conceit, erotic but not *lèse-majesté*. Raleigh was the vast, unpredictable, moody sea, but he was ultimately controlled by Elizabeth's unanswerable lunar sway. They may have been lovers—the poem hints at it—but no one will ever know. She claimed not, but her excuse was an abnormal vagina—queens talked like that then, apparently—an unusual and inhibiting disposition of bones and flesh, rather than disinclination. She was, however, pleased with Raleigh's tribute. She liked the idea of an unsullied English monarch ruling the oceans.

We are crossing onto Roanoke Island, where Raleigh sent a boatload of explorers, in 1585. The island is in North Carolina now, part of the Outer Banks, but Raleigh called this land Virginia, another homage to his virgin queen. Carolina was for Charles, who would come later.

After a year of reconnoitring, the group, led by John White, returned to England to prepare a larger party of settlers, a hundred men, women, and children, to build a permanent colony in the New World. They arrived on Roanoke Island in 1587 and proceeded to build houses and fortifications, plant crops, and generally prepare for winter. The first European born on American soil was born here, a girl named Virginia Dare. White returned to England, promising to come back in the spring.

For various reasons—not least the attempted invasion of England by the Spanish Armada in 1588—White didn't make it back for three years, by which time the colonists had vanished. He found the letters "CRO" carved into a tree, indicating that they might have gone to the native village of Croatoan to join the friendly chief Manteo, but White was unable to travel the fifty miles to the village to check. He returned to England.

None of the original settlers were ever heard of again. They may have been killed by unfriendly natives, they may have assimilated into Manteo's clan, or they may have tried to make their way north to Chesapeake Bay. It *is* known that a hurricane swept through the area in 1589, which may account for the missing buildings, but the fate of America's first European settlers is also America's first mystery.

Roanoke seems, to us at least, a remarkably good choice for a colony site. Thin but fertile soil, an excellent climate, a strategic location that commands the narrow run of ocean that separates the Outer Banks from the mainland. The town of Manteo still has a comfortable feel to it. It's the first place we've been where there is universal free Wi-Fi. There is also a good bookstore, where I buy a copy of *The Lost Colonists,* by David Beers Quinn, and Muriel Rukeyser's biography of Thomas Heriot, the mathematician Raleigh sent to Roanoke, on the theory that every successful colony needs a great mathematician, to make maps, calculate tides and full moons, and generally astrologize and geomance.

I am in my element: I wrote my master's thesis on Walter Raleigh, and although I never finished it, I've never lost my fascination with the man or his time.

The parking lot at Fort Raleigh—a reconstruction of the palisade constructed by the missing settlers—is big enough to accommodate a dozen tour buses, but this is January and the island is as deserted as it was when White returned. There is a slight drizzle. The light in the surrounding woods is grey and shadowless. We try the door to the small stockade and find it locked for the season, on its porch a faded map under a sheet of Plexiglas. The signage tells little about Raleigh's lost settlers and a lot about the Freedmen's Colony that replaced it during the Civil War.

In the first year of that war, Roanoke Island was captured by the Union army in an attempt to block the South's ability to ship cotton to Europe. Without its primary export, the Confederate army would starve, they reasoned, and a hungry army makes mistakes. Under Union control, the island became an unexpected haven for runaway slaves from North Carolina and Virginia. By 1862, there were 1,000 blacks living around the fort, 3,500 at the colony's peak, all of whom depended on the government for support. Some of the men formed the First and Second North Carolina Colored Volunteers and fought against the South at the battles of Olustee, New Market Heights, Jackson's Creek, and Petersburg—it might have been one of their bullets that killed William S. Grady. But when the war ended, the government broke up the Freedmen's Colony, and although some families petitioned to stay on the island without support, most of them returned to the mainland to work for their former owners, "going back to semi-slavery for the present," wrote one of the missionary-teachers on the island, "but hoping for better times in the future."

Their actual buildings and gravesites were neglected and lost until 2001, when anthropologists used satellite imagery to locate traces of foundations and cemeteries among the trees. Following the map's directions, we drive along Airport Road to the new aquarium, where, nestled between two modern buildings, we find a small, treed triangle with three grave markers carefully set in concrete. One says: *Rachel Dough, born Jan 15, 1815, died July 20, 1895, 'For I know my Redeemer liveth.'*

In "Report of Transportation Furnished to Freedmen, January 1866," an Amie Doe is listed as having been shipped off the island to Plymouth, Virginia. I had a cousin in Windsor whose last name was Doe. It's a slender thread, I know, but sometimes the finest tapestries are made with the thinnest of threads.

★ ★ ★

*M*Y mind turns constantly to home. Wayne, too, has a bad case of the Channels, he tells me over lunch at the Full Moon Cafe in Manteo. Small and intimate, it reminds us a little of our favourite cafe back home, where we courted in our early days together and still often contrive to share a meal.

"Channel fever," he explains, though I know what it means; he's told me before. But that's what couples do for each other: listen to their stories. "When British ships entered the English Channel, the crews could think of nothing but getting back to their families. Along the way, if the vessel had to stop at an English port for some reason, they'd jump ship and head off on foot; they were that anxious to get home."

I've been away from our house for almost half a year. I'm keen to be back, but I'm a little worried, too. I've been spoiled—no cooking or cleaning, and now I haven't made my own bed for more than a month. How will I manage a household again? I don't look forward to all the work, or the cold, though I yearn to be home. Maybe we should move. Go to Jefferson. Or Selma. Or Manteo.

Wayne leaves for the bookstore. I stay at the Full Moon, nursing my coffee. The only other patrons are three women who look to be in their seventies. All through lunch they've been chatting about kids and grandkids and clothes. Now, their talk turns to politics.

"Did you catch Larry King last night?"

"No, what did he say?"

I miss a few sentences, then pick up the thread when I hear Condoleezza Rice's name.

"Well, she sure knows how to wave getting off a plane, I'll give her that."

"You know what they call her, don't you?"

Their heads bend together. I have to strain to hear.

"Bush's little black puppet."

They move from dissing Rice to dissing Bush, glancing at me now and then to see if I'm taking it in, and if I am, how I respond. I give them a wan smile, trying for disapproving approval. They giggle.

I find Wayne in the Manteo Booksellers. He's jubilant.

"The best bookstore I've seen in a month." Maybe that's all we really need: a book fix. I buy a few novels: John Updike's *Terrorist, The Lay of the Land* by Richard Ford, Margaret Atwood's *The Penelopiad.* At the checkout, I give Wayne a present, a ball cap with "Can't Live Without Books" embroidered across the front.

We're getting back into the groove. I ask Wayne if we couldn't please find a real mom-and-pop motel for tonight.

"Our last night."

"Omigod! It is, isn't it?"

"Right," he says. "No more chains."

Tomorrow we'll be in Princeton, with friends, a short day's drive from home. The trip is barrelling toward its conclusion. Suddenly, I want to slow it down. See every sight. Talk to every local. Eat real food. A fish fry. Carolina barbecue. And in the morning, for once I want real hash browns.

At one time, the Outer Banks, this skinny, two-hundred-mile band of islands protecting Pamlico and Albemarle Sounds from the Atlantic Ocean, was nothing but a ridge of high, shifting dunes. Nags Head (Americans have given up on apostrophes, too, it seems) was inhabited by pirates like Blackbeard, who lured merchant ships aground by tying lanterns to nags' heads. There are so many shipwrecks along this stretch that it's known as the graveyard of the Atlantic. Feral horses, they say, gallop across the dunes, descendants of the Spanish mustangs that swam ashore from wrecks. This is where humans first took flight: in 1903, the Wright brothers lifted off from Kill Devil Hills near Kitty Hawk in the world's first powered heavier-than-air vehicle.

We see none of this. No horses. No wild inventors. No dunes. Even the Atlantic is reduced to flashes of dismal grey between holiday houses that run chockablock along the shore. On either side of the road, fast-food joints and chain hotels wave billboards in our faces. We might as well be driving through any resort town in the coastal United States.

Then suddenly, a gap in the faux Cape Cod construction and there it is, the motel of our dreams, a low red building settled cozily into the sand with a white porch giving onto the shore. The room is panelled in knotty pine, with bedspreads our mothers might have bought.

The woman at the desk is chatting with a friend about her daughter. "She's graduating this year," the friend says. "The first person in our family to finish high school."

"Is that a fact?" the motel owner says. "If you want, I could do her hair."

We find a restaurant that isn't a chain. This is our last night in the South, and though we are on the sea and should be eating fish, we order barbecue, succulent pulled pork in a vinegary, peppery sauce. It is unbelievably delicious and deeply satisfying. I remember something I once read about the South, that the sole duty of a man was "to holler right, vote straight, and eat as much barbecue as any other man in the country."

After dinner, we walk along the beach under a brooding sky, kicking through the sand past a rhythm of wooden stairways that reach out to the moon-silvered sea, our senses heightened by the understanding that we will likely never be in this particular place again.

★   ★   ★

$\mathcal{W}$E drive the next morning farther up the Outer Banks, past Kitty Hawk, then follow Highway 158 onto the North Carolina mainland. We're still on a spit of land jutting down into Albemarle Sound, the road running straight up the middle, so there is no good view of water. We pass through the towns of Mamie, Powells Point, and Jarvisburg without feeling the urge to stop: they are not really towns but "populated places," with populations in the low hundreds. The highway becomes the Camden Causeway and crosses a wide arm of Albemarle Sound at Elizabeth City before turning abruptly north again to skirt the Great Dismal Swamp.

John White's original plan had been to return to his colonists on Roanoke Island and establish a new settlement on Chesapeake Bay, where, he thought, the soil would be richer and the Chesapeake Indians friendlier. So when he finally made it back in 1590 and found the palisade deserted, he thought the settlers might have moved north, possibly up the Elizabeth River, which we are now following. What really became of them is anyone's guess.

Mine is that they disappeared into the Great Dismal Swamp.

The swamp, all 111,000 acres of it, is to our left, a vast expanse of sedges, bald cypress, tupelo, and pine. It is the migratory home of more than two hundred species of birds and is said to shelter black bears, bobcats, raccoons, and seventy species of reptiles and amphibians. For a long time, from the seventeenth century until emancipation, it also sheltered a colony of runaway slaves.

The American definition of "slave" can be traced back to this part of the country. In 1675, Nathaniel Bacon, a white colonist, led an uprising against the Crown that was put down quickly by the colonial forces—twenty-three men were eventually hanged—but not before "Bacon's Army," as it was called, burned Jamestown and looted many nearby plantation estates. One of Bacon's demands was the total eradication of the local native population, for reasons of national security, and one of the odd results of the rebellion was that after the uprising, the colonial government passed legislation defining what it meant by "slave." It identified three kinds: an indentured Christian servant from England, who was freed after serving four or five years; an "Indian" (i.e., native North American) servant, who served twelve years; and an African slave, who served for life. Plantation owners quickly realized that African slaves were cheaper, since they would never have to be paid for their work.

With the passage of this law, which constituted a life sentence for blacks, many African slaves fled into the Great Dismal Swamp, where they mixed with the Tuscarora Indians, as well as with white pirates and vagabonds who had also set up camps in the swamp, forming a large, tight mestizo community. It isn't hard to imagine that descendants of the Roanoke Island settlers may have been there already, providing a base upon which this rebel group could grow and prosper.

As we cross the border into Virginia, I keep craning my neck for a glimpse of the flat, grey grasslands of the distant swamp. Closer to the road, an endless strip of body shops, used-car lots, and every now and then mysterious low structures made of weathered plywood and old tarpaulins obstruct my view.

When we stop for gas, I venture into a sagging, one-storey building with a sign on the roof that says *Liquors*. Inside, between darkly gleaming rows of Jack Daniel's and Jim Beam, is a neat stack of Virginia wine, "product of the Shenandoah Valley." I take two bottles up to the cash.

"What are those plywood shacks I keep seeing out there?" I ask the stubble-faced man behind the counter. "With the tarps."

The man gives me a squinty look. "You don't want to go near those," he says. "There's dawgs in 'em."

"Dogs?" I say. "Are they mean?"

"No, but their owners might be."

"What kind of dogs are they?"

"Virginia coonhounds," he says. "Gentlest animals there is, 'less you're a coon."

IN 1856, following the success of *Uncle Tom's Cabin,* Harriet Beecher Stowe published her second novel, *Dred: A Tale of the Great Dismal Swamp.* In it, Nina Gordon inherits the family plantation, which through soil depletion and runoff has become all but worthless. The plantation is run by her slave, Harry, who of course turns out to be her half-brother.

The title character is another slave, Dred, who has succumbed to the mental disease of "drapetomania," the unreasonable yearning of a slave for freedom, and is living in the Great Dismal Swamp, where he preaches his abolitionist doctrine. Dred, it seems, was based on Dred Scott, the most controversial slave of the time. Scott was born in 1799 in Virginia, the property of Peter Blow, who moved to Missouri in 1830 and sold Scott to John Emerson. When Emerson died in 1843, Scott filed suit for his freedom, claiming that since Missouri was a free state, he ought to have been freed in 1830. The case went all the way to the Supreme Court, which ruled in 1857 that Scott actually had no case, since "according to the Declaration of Independence, any person descended from black Africans, whether slave or free, is not a citizen of the United States."

Runaways and freedmen—including the swamp dwellers, Harriet Beecher Stowe's Dred, and my great-grandfather—were not and could not become American citizens. It took an amendment to the Constitution to overturn the Dred Scott decision; my great-grandfather was eighteen before he was allowed to become a citizen of the country in which he was born. Until the Fourteenth Amendment in 1868, he and his family were citizens of nowhere. Their nationality was "Colored." They lived in what James Baldwin called "another country."

Here in Virginia, we are in the very mother state of that country. The first slave ship to land in America sailed into Chesapeake Bay, up the James River to Jamestown, in 1615. George Washington was the son of a slave owner. Thomas Jefferson owned 187 slaves. Slavery persisted in Virginia almost until living memory. The novelist William Styron, a Virginian, could recall his grandmother telling him about the days after the Civil War, when her slaves were taken from her. While I was in Alabama and Georgia, I was in such emotional turmoil that I was tempted to compare myself to a Jew visiting Auschwitz, but Styron corrects me: "Slavery," he wrote, "was not remotely like the Jewish Holocaust—of brief duration and intensely focused destruction." Slavery persisted for 250 years and represents what Styron called "the collective anguish from which white Americans have always averted their eyes."

That sense of longing for redemption in the heart of American literature, and therefore of the American psyche, must spring, at least in part, from this collective anguish, for it is clear to me now that black Americans may have forgiven white America for slavery, but they have not forgotten, and neither have white Americans recovered from having imposed it. "The drama," Styron wrote, "has never ended." Slavery is still "a world that may be dead but has not really been laid to rest."

★ ★ ★

*M*ARYLAND stretches ahead of us, Chesapeake Bay under our feet. We're driving across the Chesapeake Bay Bridge-Tunnel, a twenty-three-mile double ribbon of highway that curves elegantly across Chesapeake Bay like a partially straightened strand of DNA.

My father used to sail this bay every September with his best friend, Jim, a Virginian he got to know in Brazil. They'd take a jar of peanut butter and a loaf of bread and sail off together in Jim's boat. My father would never have stood for such a meal served by my mother, but he ate it ten days straight on the boat and told us about it, laughing. We could hardly imagine him out there on the James River, leaning into the breeze, dining on peanut butter sandwiches instead of roast beef. That couldn't possibly be our father. I understand now. That's what America offered him: the chance to be something he never knew he could be.

We've seen it throughout this trip: Lewis and Clark on the Columbia, Powell on the Colorado, Huck Finn and Jim on the Mississippi. No wonder my father loved the United States. It was where he was touched by that powerful American baptism: an ordinary man transformed as he is carried by a great river to the sea.

THE BRIDGE slides us onto the Delmarva Peninsula, named for the states that share it—Delaware, Maryland, Virginia. The Delmarva is a plump uvula of land that dangles down into the Atlantic, creating Delaware Bay on one side, Chesapeake Bay on the other. We're in Virginia for a few miles, then we're in Maryland, which claims the western half of the peninsula, known as the Eastern Shore, which, from the perspective of the state, I suppose it is, since it wraps the east side of Chesapeake Bay.

The Delmarva Peninsula doesn't have a shoreline so much as a lacy edge penetrated by rivers with names like Sassafras, Wicomico, and Choptank. The land itself is flat and sandy, as if it has only just risen above the level of the sea. Not all of the state is like this. Closer to the bay, bald cypress grows in marshlands, and in the north there are rolling hills of oak forest, with pine groves in the mountains to the west. Maryland's culture shifts with its geography: it's Appalachian on the west, more like the Northeast in the middle, while the part we're driving through is indistinguishable from the South we've been traversing since Georgia. No wonder the state calls itself "America in Miniature." The only thing it lacks is lakes.

"Did you know there isn't a single lake in Maryland?"

"Glaciers never made it this far south," Wayne says, and I look at him in wonder. His friend the novelist Matt Cohen once said that if Wayne's brain had a yard sale, it would take up a lot of sidewalk. Several blocks, I would think.

The part of Maryland we see through the windshield is fishing and farm country. Small towns dot the landscape: Eden, Greensboro, Locust Grove. The bulk of Maryland's population is clustered in Baltimore, the capital, and around Washington, D.C., which absorbs a chunk of the state. Intent on avoiding cities as long as we can, we head north up through Delaware, known as the First State, since it was the first, in 1787, to ratify the Constitution of the new United States of America.

We're crossing state lines every few hours now: North Carolina, Virginia, Maryland, Delaware. No two of them, it seems, can agree on how fast we should be travelling. On our way to El Paso it was eighty. In Arizona, New Mexico, and deer-infested Utah, it was seventy-five. Through the southern states it was seventy, and now, it seems, the powers that be have deemed speeds above sixty-five miles an hour suicidal. When we move to a two-lane highway, the legal speed drops again, to fifty-five.

"I wish they'd make up their minds," Wayne says, glancing at the rear-view mirror. Delaware is on a level plain, the lowest mean elevation of any state in the nation. There seems no good reason not to breeze along.

Before we know it, we're in Wilmington, slipping onto the I-95 and into Pennsylvania. No state signs here on the interstate, no cameos of William Penn, no prettily painted panels with *Enjoy Your Visit* or *Welcome!* or even the simple and direct *State Line*. Even the sign painters know it is hopeless to try to distinguish one blur of this throughway from another. We're in another megalopolis, the mirror image of the one we drove through at the beginning of this journey.

We skirt close to the Mason-Dixon Line, the border between Maryland and Pennsylvania that was defined as the line of latitude fifteen miles south of the southernmost house in Philadelphia, but it's unclear when, exactly, we cross from the Rebel South into the Yankee North. The view outside the window is relentlessly urban, but on the map, I spot a note of elegance: the shapely arc of the Delaware border with Pennsylvania, drawn at a twelve-mile radius from the cupola on the courthouse in New Castle. It is the only circular state boundary in the United States. In fact, I can't think of anything else like it on any map I've ever seen. It's nothing we'd be able to see as we drive, but

Delawarians must surely be aware of this curve, like a rose window at the top of their state.

All this time we have resisted what Steinbeck called "these ribbons of concrete and tar" that slash through the landscape, stopping for nothing, but we're road-weary, we're overstuffed with impressions. The damned throughways are almost soothing now.

It is dark by the time we take the exit for Princeton and pick up Route 1, the most easterly in the country. We stop for gas, and the attendant is terse, not unfriendly exactly, but not open either, held back in that northeastern way, waiting for us to speak first. Not like Bay Bridge Betty, not like Mary in Jefferson, and not at all like the man in Jackson who led us to the parade. In moments, we will be with our friends, with Canadians, but already I feel an ache for those places where strangers speak to us without reserve, where a man we've known for five minutes spreads his arms wide and grins, "Well, then, we're all of us connected."

★   ★   ★

*W*ALKING with us up Witherspoon Street, in downtown Princeton, our friend Lauren is recounting history. The street is history. The very air in Princeton is historical.

"The street is named for John Witherspoon," she says, "one of three Princetonians who signed the Declaration of Independence. The other two were Richard Stockton and Joseph Hewes."

Here in the East, I can't help feeling that history has weight, that the streets teem with the ghosts of the distant dead. New England has become Old America. There was history in the West, of course, but most of it was geological: four-thousand-year-old trees, four-billion-year-old canyons, ancient volcanoes, ageless deserts, timeless rivers. The land was old; the people were new. Here in Princeton, history seems to have galloped at a furious pace; the land recedes into the background, a backdrop to the human parade.

"On your way into Princeton, you came along Stockton Street, named for Richard Stockton," Lauren continues. "Hewes moved to Wilmington, I think."

Here is the parsonage where Paul Robeson was born. Here is Witherspoon Street Presbyterian Church, where Robeson attended the Witherspoon School for Colored Children, which was started in 1858 by Betsey Stockton, one of Robert Stockton's freed slaves. Here is Lahiere's, the restaurant where Albert Einstein often ate lunch. We can see his favourite table through the window. Einstein lived in Princeton from 1933, when he came to work at the Institute for Advanced Study, until his death in 1955, by which time the institute was being run by J. Robert Oppenheimer.

Lahiere's was owned by Joseph and Mary Louise Christen, who were from Zurich. For Einstein, eating there must have felt as though he were reliving his happiest years, which were spent in Zurich. Time collapsing and expanding, memories merging with contemporary events, faces dissolving and reappearing with altered features. No wonder he came to believe that there were aspects of reality that quantum mechanics, based as it was on mathematical probability rather than observation, couldn't explain. Life was improbable, and yet there it was.

Lauren and her husband Ron are expat Canadians, she from Montreal and Ron from Quebec City. Ron is the executive vice-president of customer management with Zurich Insurance, and Lauren is a novelist. They like the United States and have been welcomed into the Princeton community. Lauren is involved in a number of volunteer organizations and is the writer-in-residence at Trinity Church, where she teaches creative writing.

We walk past Princeton Cemetery, which occupies a huge portion of the town at the corner of Witherspoon and Wiggins. Merilyn, of course, has a brochure.

"President Grover Cleveland is buried here," she says.

"And Paul Robeson's parents," Lauren adds.

"Oh," Merilyn exclaims, "and Sara Agnes Pryor—founder of the Daughters of the American Revolution. And here's one for you, Wayne: John O'Hara, the novelist."

"*BUtterfield 8*," I say. "But you two are the novelists."

"He wrote his own epitaph. Haven't you always wanted to do that?"

"What did he say about himself?"

"'Better than anyone else, he told the truth about his time. He was a professional, he wrote honestly and well.'"

"I should start working on mine," I say. "I'm Canadian, so I can't say 'better than anyone else.' How about, 'As well as he could, under the circumstances, and given his limitations, he told what he knew of the truth about his time'?"

"You're too modest," says Merilyn. "And it's way too long."

This exchange brings us to Nassau Street, Princeton's main drag. On one side is the university; along the other, where we are walking, is a series of shops, including a bookstore.

"Why don't you two go on," I say to Lauren and Merilyn. "I'll just pop in here and meet you after lunch."

Micawber's is having a going-out-of-business sale. I feel like a vulture at a roadkill, sidling up to its half-price tables, but a bargain is a bargain. I gorge.

"Why are you closing?" I ask the young woman at the cash as she starts going through the pile.

"The university bookstore is expanding to two floors," she says. "We can't compete."

"You needn't worry," I say, thinking of the university bookstore in Athens. "The first floor will be all sweatshirts, coffee mugs, and backpacks. You'll need a tracking device to find the books."

"You're sweet," she says, smiling. "Do you need help carrying these to your car?"

"No, thanks. I've got my walker parked outside."

I stagger with my load up to a restaurant called the Alchemist & Barrister and find a table in a quiet corner. After ordering a plate of Irish stew and a half-litre of Côtes-du-Rhône, I take out my books. One of them is a biography of George Washington. By some fluke, I open it at a page describing Washington's expertise at breeding hunting dogs, one of which he called "the Virginian hound." He also bred bluetick coonhounds from a set of five English foxhounds given to him by the French general Lafayette in 1770. Washington was an avid fox hunting man; while serving in Congress in Philadelphia, he regularly crossed and recrossed the Delaware River to ride with the Gloucester Foxhunting Club. His favourite hounds had names like Sweet Lips, Venus, and Truelove. His less-favoured dogs were called Taster, Tippler, and Drunkard.

"Let's Face the Music and Dance" is playing softly on a speaker above my head, followed by "Come Fly with Me," and for once I don't bridle at the intrusion. I'm nearly alone in my section of the restaurant. Two tables away, a young man wearing a beret and dark glasses is sitting with three women, one about his age and two much younger. He smiles at me and says, "Sinatra," and I smile back. As a young crooner during the war, my father is said to have looked uncannily like Frank Sinatra; whenever a Sinatra song came on the radio, his eyes would crinkle and he would slip into a deep, happy reverie.

The four at the other table must have driven in from somewhere north of here, because I hear the older woman say something about black ice. Not wife and daughters, I think; maybe a professor and his seminar. "Where's everyone else?" he asks, looking over at me again. I take out my notebook and go back to George Washington.

Washington crossed the Delaware three times in five days during the winter of 1776–77, not to go fox hunting but to attack the British position at Trenton, New Jersey. After a surprising victory on Christmas Day, he retreated to Pennsylvania, then crossed back on December 29, when he heard that British troops under Lord Cornwallis were marching from Princeton to retake Trenton.

A few days before, Thomas Paine had published "The Crisis," the first in a series of patriotic pamphlets that provided the philosophical basis for American independence. "These are the times that try men's souls," it began. Paine exhorted all American men to volunteer and push the red-coated "devils" back to England. "Britain... has declared, that she has a right (not only to tax) but 'to bind us in all cases whatsoever,' and if being bound in that manner is not slavery, then is there not such a thing as slavery upon earth." Who, he asked, would willingly be a slave?

Americans heeded the call. On January 2, when Washington slipped his troops past Cornwallis and moved on to Princeton, he had 5,200 men under his command. The British had left only about 2,000 foot soldiers in Princeton.

Washington's general, Hugh Mercer, leading a brigade to destroy a bridge over Princeton's Stony Brook, ran into the British troops on their way to join Cornwallis. In their shared confusion, both American and British soldiers ran for high ground on the same side of the brook: the Americans got there first, and the British charged them, firing their muskets. Washington, hearing gunfire, leaped onto his white charger and galloped up the road. Mercer had been killed, stabbed to death by seven bayonets, and the Americans were fleeing from the charge. Washington waved his hat to the retreating men, shouting that they must stand their ground. He galloped past them to within thirty feet of the pursuing British soldiers and halted. The stunned British fired a volley at him, but when the smoke cleared he was still in his saddle, untouched. Inspired by Washington's bravery, the Americans rallied and fired at the British. Two American field pieces fired grapeshot into the British lines. The British returned fire. All this time, Washington remained on his horse, directly in the line of fire between the two opposing armies. Not a single bullet hit him.

The British soldiers gaped. Then, realizing they were greatly outnumbered, they abandoned their position and fled toward Princeton.

To do so, they had to charge directly through the American lines. When the British had broken through, Washington, the old fox hunter, still on his horse, led his men in pursuit of the redcoats, crying, "It's a fine fox chase, my boys!"

Nothing is more improbable than that George Washington survived volley after volley of enemy fire, point blank, a stone's throw from the British line. Had he been hit, Princeton would have fallen to the British and the American Revolutionary War would have been all but over. In other words, the very existence of the United States as an independent nation is an astounding improbability. If Albert Einstein wanted to mull over the problem of probability theory's inadequacy in explaining the mechanical function of the universe, he could hardly have come to a better place than Princeton.

The song above my head is now "From This Moment On." When I look up from my notebook, the man in the beret is looking vaguely in my direction. I smile at him and say, "Bobby Darin," but he doesn't smile back. He starts gathering papers, and the three women begin putting on their coats. As they brush past my table, I hear the man say something about "surveillance."

My God, I wonder, do they think I'm with Homeland Security?

"Doubtful," Lauren says when I tell her about the incident. "Princeton is full of eccentric people who sit in restaurants writing in their notebooks. No one would think for a minute you were spying on them."

Of course she's right; this is a university town. Then it must be me who is paranoid. This realization hits me with the force of a major revelation. Has my fear and distrust of America been the result of my own paranoia all along? The implications of this possibility loom so large that I have to take a glass of wine out onto Lauren and Ron's back deck and think about it for a while. They have a large yard, with benches and trees and an artificial pond that isn't running now because it's January. Could it be that my nervousness at crossing the border was unfounded? No one has turned me in to Homeland Security for having uncharitable thoughts about George Bush. This isn't Stalinist Russia. Everyone we've met has been friendly and helpful. And yet I feel this grand unease at being here—not here in Princeton, but here in America. I quite like being in Princeton. I liked being in Seattle, and Fairhaven, and Eureka. I really liked being in Santa Fe, and I didn't even mind being in Selma. And all those places were America. Why do I feel uneasy about being in places that I like?

My mind wanders back to Kafka's *Amerika.* It is a picaresque novel, which requires that its hero, Karl Rossmann, be entirely innocent, without volition, swept along by the vagaries of events. Every chapter in the novel is a change in Rossmann's fortunes; he rises and falls and rises, from disgraced son to wealthy nephew to penniless vagabond. America in *Amerika* is a nightmare on a vast scale. On a highway, he sees trucks laden with food bound for New York and hears "the cries of the carefree animals going to the abattoirs." Rossmann's uncle is at first a senator, then later is revealed to own "a sort of commissionary and forwarding business of a kind Karl thought probably didn't exist in Europe." In the end, we see Karl on his way "to the great Theatre of Oklahoma."

Kafka had never been to America. His dystopic view of the nation, like mine before this trip, was based on supposition and hearsay: he couldn't dislike the real America, so he disliked the *idea* of America. He was a great admirer of Charles Dickens (and in fact thought of *Amerika* as his Dickensian novel). He had read Dickens's *American Notes,* compiled during the British novelist's tour of North America in 1842. Dickens had found Americans to be "frank, brave, cordial, hospitable, and affectionate. Cultivation and refinement seem but to enhance their warmth of heart and ardent enthusiasm." But he also regretted "one great blemish in the popular mind of America," which he referred to as "Universal Distrust." This blemish overshadowed the idea of America in Dickens's mind. "Any man who attains a high office among you," he writes, "from the President downwards, may date his downfall from that moment; for any printed lie that any notorious villain pens, although it militate directly against the character and conduct of a life, appeals to your distrust, and is believed."

Have I, too, fallen into the same trap as Kafka, basing my assumptions of America on other writers' experiences? Dickens chided that "it would be well . . . if [Americans] loved the Real less, and the Ideal somewhat more." But perhaps I should stop thinking about the idea of America, and begin liking the Real somewhat more. Perhaps I've been so blinded by the sizzle that I couldn't see the steak.

★   ★   ★

*M*y computer is butting up against Wayne's. We're sitting opposite each other at Lauren's kitchen table, transcribing our notes from the past few days. Wayne types so fast that his screen hops toward mine, tap-tapping it companionably. We've never worked like this, in the same room, at the same desk. I like it.

Between us on the table lies the *Washington Post* we picked up when we stopped for lunch in Delaware. I open it with trepidation.

It is the tail end of January 2007, but already the headlines scream election. In the United States, there is only one election that seems to matter: the choosing of the president. (I wish Canadians knew with such certainty when they'd get the chance to oust a leader.) Bush has served his two terms and cannot serve a third. With the exception of that Texan in the bar of the Camino Real, no one we've met or overheard as we travelled across the country is inclined to regret that limitation. The beauty of the United States is: twice up to the plate and you're out.

Wayne and I are not political people. Neither of us has ever joined a party. But we always vote. We care about who makes the decisions (even though our candidate of choice rarely wins an election). It's been a long time since we've felt Canada has had a real leader and a long time, too, since the United States has had one to admire. But there's a voice I've been hearing, even in our media-starved state. A young Democrat whose background is a lot like Wayne's: the mixed-blood son of a black father and a white mother. And he's a writer. We like that. His books are good, not ghostwritten, like the works of so many politicians, and not written solely with votes in mind. His words come from the heart, stirred with a passion that hasn't been heard in America since Kennedy and King. *The Audacity of Hope: Thoughts on Reclaiming the American Dream* came out this fall, but I first heard him talk about hope in a speech he gave to the Democratic National Convention before the last presidential vote:

> I'm not talking about blind optimism here—the almost willful ignorance that thinks unemployment will go away if we just don't talk about it, or the health care crisis will solve itself if we just ignore it. No, I'm talking about something more substantial. It's the hope of slaves sitting around a fire singing freedom songs; the hope of immigrants setting out for distant shores; the hope of a young naval lieutenant bravely patrolling the Mekong Delta; the hope of a millworker's son who dares to defy the odds; the hope of a skinny kid with a funny name who believes that America has a place for him, too. Hope in the face of difficulty. Hope in the face of uncertainty. The audacity of hope.

He is an American: he holds to the usual imperialist line that began with Lewis and Clark and found its mantra in Manifest Destiny, the idea that America has not only the right but the obligation to spread its brand of democracy throughout the world, whether the world wants it or not. But when this man speaks, I hear something else. He uses words like "we" and "us." He extols Americans to work together. To help each other out. "For alongside our famous individualism," he says, "there's another ingredient in the American saga: a belief that we are connected as one people."

I hold up the headline for Wayne to see: "Obama Jumps into Presidential Fray."

"Who's Obama?" he says.

"Looks like he just might be the first black president of the United States."

Wayne looks dubious. I expect him to say something like, "Not a chance; he'll be shot first." But he doesn't.

"America," he says, "would be another country."

14 / THE EXIT CAFE

*M*y watch says seven, but it feels much earlier, the sun not yet discernible in the snow-blue sky. Lauren offers eggs and toast and coffee, but it's our last day as travellers in America: we'll have breakfast on the road.

We take the 206 up to the interstate and head north. The temperature has plummeted. The shorts and T-shirts people were wearing here over Christmas have finally gone into storage; children waiting for their school buses are all mittened and scarved and puffy-coated. Rock cuts cascade with flash-frozen waterfalls. A skiff of snow skitters across the highway.

"Looks like Utah," Wayne says, and I scan the ditches for deer.

Over the past week, waves of freezing rain have washed up from Texas into New England, dousing the lights and depositing a crystal shell of ice up to four inches thick. Eighty-five people have died. Oklahoma and Missouri have been declared disaster areas. After the rain has come the cold and the weather bombs: local storms that released explosions of snow over the Northeast, thirty-two inches in twelve hours in Quebec.

"More snow in the forecast," says the radio announcer. For the first time since Seattle, Washington, we're close enough to the border to pick up the CBC. "Major lake-effect snow is expected in the Great Lakes region over the next several days, with heavy local accumulations south of the lake, in some areas up to three hundred centimetres."

"That's almost ten feet!"

"We'll have to tunnel into the house," Wayne says.

"What's going on? I feel like Typhoon Mary. Everywhere we go, storms erupt."

"Get used to it, the climate's changing."

Change, when you're on the road, comes to seem like a way of life.

It's fully light but not much warmer by the time we stop for breakfast. We choose a small diner close to the interstate. The Exit Cafe. Two huge American flags are draped over the doorway; smaller flags wave at every table. We've travelled in the Northeast before, through New England villages clustered around quaint squares, into the hills where the British who became the first Americans settled. We always notice the flags. Flag-waving is not a Canadian thing. Here, they unfurl not only from government buildings but from every grocery store and video outlet, on the houses, too, every one of which seems to have a flagpole on the lawn or jutting out by the door. I always thought this flag flying was widely American, but we've seen little of it elsewhere in the country. It seems defensive to me now, the tic of a former colonial. Defiant, too: the reflex of a country perpetually under attack, which it hasn't been, at least not until recent years.

"What can I get for you?" the waitress says, automatically upending our coffee cups and starting to pour. I put my hand over the rim.

"Decaf, please."

"Oh, sure. Sorry. I'll put on a pot."

She speaks like we do. With a certain sadness, I realize that we are truly out of that part of America where language is distinct. Even in 1961, Steinbeck noticed that regional inflections were disappearing.

"Forty years of radio and twenty years of television must have this impact," he reasoned. "Communications must destroy localness by a slow inevitable process." Make that eighty-five years of radio, sixty-five years of television. Not much has survived the onslaught.

In the late 1890s, when Rudyard Kipling married an American and moved to Vermont (where he wrote *The Jungle Book*), he bridled at the accent he encountered. American English was "the language of thieves," he wrote. American publishers were distributing pirated editions of his books, just as Google is doing with ours. "Oliver Wendell Holmes says that the Yankee schoolmarm, the cider, and the salt codfish of the Eastern State are responsible for what he calls a nasal accent. I know better. They stole books from across the water without paying for 'em and the snort of delight was fixed in their nostrils forever by a just Providence. That is why they talk a foreign tongue today."

The time is long gone when a person's birthplace is apparent the moment he opens his mouth, not just in the way he forms his consonants and vowels, but in his choice of words, the idioms and phrases that once marked geography and nation as surely as the flag he saluted. A few years ago, Wayne wrote a book called *Chasing the Chinook*, essays that explore uniquely Canadian words such as "pogey" and "caboose" and "tuque." It scarcely made a ripple because, really, who cares in this Internet age about the provenance of words? People are writing more than ever, but is it in their own voice, their own words? I think not. We're all swirling toward a linguistic melting pot—one that's uniformly understandable but as bland as a room at the Days Inn or a meal at McDonald's. Local accent, local idiom, local rhythms and cadence, the deep rich poetry of individual expression: I fear it is going the way of the wild buffalo. Language can't be held back any more than life itself, of course, but that doesn't mean I won't mourn the passing of the particular, whether it's a swaggering Texas redneck or a tough pecan-picking Louisiana matriarch.

I quell the urge to answer the waitress in a borrowed Scottish brogue, and in tones indistinguishable from hers, I order my usual: hash brown potatoes and a single poached egg, medium. I have eaten this same breakfast all across the United States. As an antidote to my gloomy thoughts on the disappearance of distinctness, I recall how varied the response has been to my simple request. The eggs are sometimes golden, the colour of marguerites, and sometimes pale as cream. The potatoes may be grated, peeled or not, with onion or not, salted or not, peppered almost always, deep-fried or fried on a grill, with butter sometimes, or oil, many kinds of oil, or chopped up, deep-fried in tiny cubes or thin patties, occasionally parboiled, but usually fresh, and almost always straight from the fryer. Come to think of it, there has been little true local flavour to these variations, no hot peppers or okra, just the whimsy of countless cooks from Seattle through Sacramento and Needles and Taos to Jackson, Athens, Wilmington, and now a cafe I can't quite place, in northern Pennsylvania or maybe southern New York State.

The potatoes arrive in a mound, golden. They are leftover boiled potatoes, fried in a pan, with butter, I can taste it. The shreds of onion are translucent, the edges browned. The crisp exterior of the potato resists the fork, just enough, then the tines sink through the soft, moist flesh. Oh joy!

"Is everything okay here?" the waitress says. She looks a little worried. "Sorry, we didn't have any hash browns. The cook made you country home fries—I hope that's okay."

Country home fries. You get what you ask for, and I've been asking for the wrong thing all along.

★　★　★

"WHAT was important," writes Ryszard Kapuściński, "was not the destination, the goal, the end, but the almost mystical and transcendent act of crossing the border." We are on the I-81, just south of the Canadian frontier, and I'm beginning to feel like Kapuściński. For the last little while we've been following Merilyn's yellow highlighter through Onondaga, Cortland, and Oswego Counties, all of which were incorporated in 1792 under the name Mexico. Now it applies only to a small town squeezed between the interstate and Lake Ontario, close to an even smaller hamlet called Texas. It seems we're destined to relive the entire trip in our last thirty minutes in America.

"Want to go to Mexico?" I ask Merilyn.

"No, thanks," she says cozily. "Let's just get home."

As we near the border, I wait for my chest to tighten and my bowels to loosen, but so far I feel good. At least we're not crossing at Cornwall, where a few years ago we had some difficulty with a few undeclared bottles of wine. The swaggering youth at customs and immigration who pulled us over held us there for an hour, telling us he could confiscate our car if he wanted to, and then he let us go. Since then I've decided to declare everything, down to the last chocolate bar, the merest sliver of soap. I've kept every receipt we've been given, and last night I took them all out, added them up, and stapled them together. They're safely in the glove box with our passports. We're well under the allowable limit. We could even stop at the duty-free and pick up a few more items.

"Want to get some perfume?" I ask. "Or a scarf?"

Merilyn looks at me in alarm. Normally I try to talk her out of buying anything at these places. "Declare everything, have nothing" has been my motto. But now I think no border guard will believe we've been in the States for nearly two months and have nothing but a few books and two bottles of Virginia wine to show for it. In any case, I'm not worried. Really. I'm not wearing two pairs of pants. I checked.

"All right," Merilyn says. "And you can get some Scotch."

When I put the Scotch in the trunk, I see the cardboard carton holding Merilyn's novel resting on top of a bag of books, and I take off the lid and read the first page—guiltily, since she still hasn't told me I can read it. It's good. I read the next page, standing bent over with my head in the trunk. It's good, too.

"What are you doing back there?" Merilyn calls.

"Just organizing a bit," I say, closing the carton. When I'm back in the car I turn to her. "You know, when we get home, the first thing I'd like to do is sit down by the fire with a glass of this Scotch and read your novel. Would that be all right, do you think?"

To my consternation, Merilyn's eyes tear up. "Of course it would be all right, you goose. I've been dying for you to ask."

"Really?" I say, nonplussed. "I've been waiting for *you* to ask me to read it."

We sit in the parking lot for a while, patting each other's hands. Then I start the car and we drive the last two miles to the border.

⋆ ⋆ ⋆

*M*Y heart leaps at Wayne's suggestion, not because I want him to read the novel, which of course I do, but because it thrills me, it opens me up, to know that what I am, what I do, is of interest to him.

It's what we want from our friends, from our neighbours, too: a conversation that flows both ways. As we near the line that keeps Canada distinct from the United States, it occurs to me that the two countries have not been very good friends. Sure, we help each other out in times of crisis, but mostly, we're the kind of neighbours who look the other way rather than walk across the lawn for a chat.

"I've been thinking about all the people we've met, and you know what?"

"What?"

"I can't remember anyone who asked us about Canada. They asked where we'd been in their country, how we liked it, and where we were going. They were full of suggestions about things we should see in the United States, but not one person asked anything about *our* country. Isn't that strange?"

"Maybe Diana Athill had it right. In *Stet,* she says that Americans just aren't interested in Canada. We're not on their radar."

"But wouldn't you think that when they're discussing how to improve their health care system, people might be curious about what it's like to have universal health care? We told those snowplow drivers and that store clerk we were used to Canadian snow: wouldn't it be natural to ask where we were from, how much snow we get?"

"Americans don't seem all that interested in anything but themselves."

I scowl. In general, I hate generalizations, but this one seems true. We've met wonderful, kind, generous people on our travels in America, as we do everywhere. In many ways, people are all the same, no matter what flag flies overhead. But the landscape, the history, and the culture people are raised within can't help but affect their values, the way they think. Not all Canadians are self-effacing and community-minded, but as a culture we generally hold that the group is at least as important as the individual. If every person within a society is not looked after, then society itself fails, and the individuals will, too. Similarly, not all Americans are self-interested bullies, but as a culture, they have a history of aggression, of being blind or hostile to the values and beliefs of others. Maybe it's because they lack curiosity about what lies beyond their borders. For all the interest Americans have in Canada, we might as well be that vast blankness marked on ancient maps as *Terra Incognita.* They don't seem to care if there be dragons there. They assume there aren't. And maybe they're right: it's just mild-mannered Canada.

I look over my shoulder at the retreating nation of America and think: It's the U.S., but it's not us.

"How can you be friends with somebody who doesn't ever ask how you are, or who you are?" I say, more to myself than to Wayne.

"Men do that all the time."

It's true. Men aren't curious in the same way women are. What does it mean to be curious? When we stop for lunch, I find a place with

Wi-Fi and spend some time looking up the word, though I'm fairly certain I already know what it means. Curiosity, as defined by the British sources, is the desire to know and learn. That's exactly how I understand it—an honourable trait, one that leads to enlightenment. But when I check the modern American dictionary sites, I find something completely different. Curiosity, to Americans, "implies a desire to know what is not properly one's concern." The same example is cited more than once: "curious about a neighbor's habits."

Aha! So we've been speaking a different language all along. Those snowplow drivers and car mechanics and waitresses and fellow travellers were all being polite. *We* were being rude and pushy. They didn't ask us about ourselves because to do so would be to poke their nose in somebody else's business. Their lack of curiosity was a show of respect.

I have misunderstood their silence. Thoreau was right. Such misinterpretations are the tragedy of human intercourse, whether played out between a husband and wife in an Echo or between two countries that have shared a border for more than a hundred years.

* * *

*W*HAT do I think of when I think of America? The question, proposed by Ian Jack in *Granta*, seems an impossible one, for when I think of America I can no longer think of any one thing. I think everything of America. America is everything at once. No sooner do you have a conversation with a friendly waitress in a restaurant than you see a pickup truck in the parking lot with "Freedom Isn't Free!" on the tailgate, and you wonder which of the laughing, boisterous good old boys at the next table owns the truck. Or you think the country you are driving through looks just like Canada, until you see a billboard proclaiming, in ten-foot letters, *Firearms for Sale: No ID Required!* And you are reminded that you are in a country whose Declaration of Independence claims that "all men are created equal" and whose constitution contained a clause allowing its citizens to own slaves.

Partly, I still think what I thought before we made this trip, because those thoughts were based on the image America projects to the outside world: its overweening sense of its own rightness, its casual assumption that it can buy or sell whatever it wants, its ability to proceed as though everything were on the table, its refusal to learn from its own history.

I cannot forgive America for what it forced my great-grandfather to do. Or for what it has done to its rivers and forests and mountains and deserts, which seems to me to be almost on a par. Oh, but every country has done that, I might say; Canada has done that, and that is true, but that does not mean we should forgive. We should be implacable in our refusal to forgive, no matter how sweet the inducements to do so. But we cannot go back, and we cannot be unmoved, and so we must move on.

Am I still anti-American? No, and I suspect I never really was. It is not anti-American to wish America had been better than it was, or to want it to be better than it is. Perhaps because I am Canadian I have a sense of the value of an official opposition; Americans love their country nonetheless for hating what the government of the day does to it. America has an unofficial opposition in its writers, many of whom have come to mind during the course of these travels. They, too, have wondered at the sensitivity and strength of America's culture, and celebrated the honesty and humour of its people, and ground their teeth at the perfidy and ineptitude of its corporate and political leaders. Foreign writers have come and chided or mocked; American writers have stayed and wrestled and burned. As a Canadian, I feel somewhere between, chiding and burning, admiring and, essentially, being irrelevant.

The green light comes on, and I drive up to the customs kiosk.

"Passports, please," the officer says. Unlike the American official in Washington State, this Canadian representative of the government doesn't leave the shelter of her kiosk. It's snowing. Not hard—a gentle, Christmassy kind of snow.

"How long have you been in the States?" she says. She is a petite woman, with nicely permed hair and reading glasses. She looks more like a librarian than a border guard. She's not wearing a gun.

"About two months," I say.

"What's the value of the goods you're bringing back?"

I tell her. I have the sheaf of receipts in my hand, but she doesn't seem to want them.

"Any alcohol or tobacco?"

"Two bottles of wine," I tell her, "and I just bought some scotch at the duty-free."

She hands me back one of the passports.

"Would you mind telling me what that white powder is on your passport, sir?" she says, looking stern.

"White powder?" I say, holding the document open in the feeble, yellow light coming through the windshield from a lamp above the kiosk. Sure enough, there is a whitish film on the leaves. I know what she's thinking. "I have no idea. Really."

"Let me see that," Merilyn says, taking the passport from my trembling hands. She inspects it closely. She sniffs it. Then, to my amazement, she swipes her finger through the powder and licks it.

"I didn't mean for you to taste it, ma'am," the customs officer says sharply.

"Hmm," Merilyn says. I stare at her in horror and admiration. We are going to be arrested, but we will be arrested together. "It's coffee whitener. We've been keeping the passports in the glove compartment."

"Coffee whitener," says the officer, breaking into a smile. "That's what I thought, too." She hands me Merilyn's passport. "Welcome home."

ACKNOWLEDGEMENTS

*I*T took two countries to write this book: one to raise us and one to welcome us as travellers. To all those who shared their lives and stories for a moment or more, we extend our thanks. Particular appreciation to Russell Thompson, Mike Fischer, and Ron and Lauren Davis for their hospitality.

We would also like to thank Stella Harvey and the Vicious Circle for bringing us to Whistler, British Columbia, as writers-in-residence, thus giving us the time and a place in which to complete the manuscript. And thank you to Chris Pollock and Karen Landman for directions.

As always, our gratitude to our agent, Bella Pomer, for her constant faith and tireless efforts on our behalf, to Rob Sanders for being such a generous and willing publisher of Canadian writers, to Nancy Flight for her editorial acumen, and to Lara Smith for her eagle eye.

We gratefully acknowledge the support of the Canada Council for the Arts, which provided a grant for the writing of this book.